Essays and Studies 2024

Series Editor: Ceri Sullivan

The English Association

The English Association is a membership body for individuals and organisations passionate about the English language and its literatures. Our membership includes teachers, students, authors, and readers and is made up of people and institutions from around the world.

Our aim is to further the knowledge, understanding, and enjoyment of English studies and to foster good practice in their teaching and learning at all levels, by

- encouraging the study of English language and literature in the community at large
- working toward a fuller recognition of English as core to education
- fostering discussion about methods of teaching English at all levels
- supporting conferences, lectures, and publications
- responding to national consultations and policy decisions about the subject

More information about the Association is on our website: http://bit.ly/join-the-EA

Publications

The Year's Work in English Studies – published annually, *The Year's Work in English Studies* is a qualitative narrative bibliographical review of scholarly work that year about the English language or literatures in English, from Old English to contemporary criticism.

The Year's Work in Critical and Cultural Theory – a companion volume in the field of critical and cultural theory, recording significant debates in a broad field of research in the humanities and social sciences.

Essays and Studies – published since 1910, *Essays and Studies* is an annual collection of essays on topical issues in English, edited by a different distinguished academic each year. The volumes cover a range of subjects and authors, from medieval to modern.

English – published quarterly, *English* is a forum for people who think hard and passionately about literature and who want to communicate those thoughts to a wide audience. It includes scholarly essays and reviews on all periods of literary history and new work by contemporary poets.

English 4 to 11 – published three times a year, this magazine contains material produced by and for the classroom leader. It is a reader-friendly magazine, backed by sound pedagogy, offering ideas for developing classroom practice.
The Use of English – published three times per year, this journal's articles and reviews are designed to encourage teachers to further their own interest and expertise in the subject.
Newsletter – produced three times per year, the *Newsletter* contains topical articles, news items, and interviews about English studies and updates about The English Association's activities.

Benefits of Membership

Unity and voice – members join others with a wealth of experience, knowledge, and passion for English to foster the discussion of teaching methods and respond to national issues.
Resources – members can access high quality resources on the Association's website, and in its volumes, journals, magazines, and newsletters.
Networking – members can network with colleagues and leading practitioners, including joining national special interest groups and their local Regional Group. Members are also given reduced rates for the Association's conferences and other events.

Essays and Studies 2024

Literature and Institutions of Welfare

Edited by
Jess Cotton

for the English Association

D. S. BREWER

ESSAYS AND STUDIES
IS VOLUME SEVENTY-SEVEN IN THE NEW SERIES
OF ESSAYS AND STUDIES COLLECTED ON BEHALF OF
THE ENGLISH ASSOCIATION
ISSN 0071-1357

First published 2024
D. S. Brewer, Cambridge

D. S. Brewer is an imprint of Boydell & Brewer Ltd
PO Box 9, Woodbridge, Suffolk IP12 3DF, UK
and of Boydell & Brewer Inc.
668 Mt Hope Avenue, Rochester, NY 14620-2731, USA
website: www.boydellandbrewer.com

ISBN 978-1-84384-731-1

A CIP catalogue record for this book is available
from the British Library

Contents

Illustrations

The editor, contributors and publisher are grateful to all the institutions and persons listed for permission to reproduce the materials in which they hold copyright. Every effort has been made to trace the copyright holders; apologies are offered for any omission, and the publisher will be pleased to add any necessary acknowledgement in subsequent editions.

Notes on Contributors

Sarah Bernstein is a Senior Lecturer in English and Creative Writing at the University of Strathclyde. Her critical work has appeared in *Modern Fiction Studies* and *Contemporary Women's Writing*, among other publications. She is the author of two novels and a collection of poetry.

Josie Billington is Professor in English Literature at the University of Liverpool, where she co-leads the Arts, Mental Health and Wellbeing theme of the Centre for Health, Arts, Society and Environment (CHASE) and co-directs the MA in Health, Cultures and Societies. She has edited and published extensively on Victorian fiction and poetry and led multiple inter-disciplinary studies on the value of literary reading in relation to depression, dementia, chronic pain, prisoner health and community mental health. Her publications in this field include *Is Literature Healthy* (Oxford University Press, 2016) and *Reading and Mental Health* (Palgrave, 2019).

Beci Carver is a Lecturer at the University of Exeter. Her first book, *Granular Modernism*, was published by Oxford University Press in 2014, and her forthcoming book, *Modernism's Whims*, is due to appear with Oxford University Press in 2025. She has published articles and book chapters on a wide range of subjects, including tennis, kimonos, slot machines, gifts, banks, guts, crushes and cameras.

Helen Charman is a Fellow and College Teaching Officer in English at Clare College, University of Cambridge. Her first book, *Mother State: A Political History of Motherhood*, was published by Allen Lane in 2024.

Lara Choksey is Lecturer in Colonial and Postcolonial Literatures in the Department of English at University College London, where she is also Associate Faculty in the Sarah Parker Remond Centre for the Study of Racism and Racialisation. She has published articles and chapters in *The Sociological Review*, *Journal of Literature and Science*, *Medical Humanities*, *Journal of Historical Geography* and *The Palgrave Handbook of Twentieth and Twenty-First Century Literature and Science*, and she edited Gayatri

Chakravorty Spivak's *Readings* (Seagull, 2014). Her book, *Narrative in the Age of the Genome* (Bloomsbury, 2021), considers measures of the human in genomic narratives.

Jess Cotton is a Leverhulme Early Career Fellow at the University of Cambridge, where she is currently working on a literary and psychoanalytic history of loneliness. Her work has been published in *ELH*, *Textual Practice*, *American Literary History* and *New Formations*, and her book *John Ashbery* was recently published by Reaktion Books/University of Chicago Press.

Gareth Farmer is a Senior Lecturer in English literature at the University of Bedfordshire. He researches and writes on modern and contemporary experimental literature, poetry, poetics and critical theory. His most recent work is on the intersections between radical literary practices and Critical Disability Studies and he is currently developing a book-length project on 'Autistic Poetics'.

Matthew Holman is Lecturer in Literature and Fine Arts at the University of Hertfordshire. He holds a Ph.D. in American cultural history from University College London, and is the recipient of fellowships at Yale University, the John F. Kennedy Institute for North American Studies, The Courtauld Institute of Art and the Paul Mellon Centre for Studies in British Art. His research has been published in *Critical Quarterly*, *Women's Studies* and *The Oxford Art Journal*, and his first book, *Frank O'Hara: Curator of Modern Life*, is forthcoming with Bloomsbury.

Neil Vickers is Professor of English Literature and the Health Humanities at King's College London. He is also the co-director of the Centre for the Humanities and Health there. He was a founder member of the New Imago Group and is an academic member of the British Psychoanalytic Council. His book (with Derek Bolton) *Being Ill: On Sickness, Care, and Abandonment* will be published by Reaktion Books in September 2024. He is currently working on a history of the medical humanities.

Acknowledgements

The editor would first like to thank the contributors of the volume for their time, knowledge and creativity in thinking about the value of literature and the institutions of welfare. She is grateful to the Editor of the Series, Ceri Sullivan, for her work commissioning and editing the collection through its various stages. Finally, she wishes to express appreciation to the staff of The English Association and Boydell and Brewer for their assistance in the production of this volume.

Introduction

JESS COTTON

In his 1942 report 'Social Insurance and Allied Services', which was to become known as the Beveridge Report, William Beveridge proposed a number of substantive reforms to the system of social welfare in Britain. These were directed towards the abolishment of the 'Five Great Evils' – Want, Disease, Ignorance, Squalor and Idleness – that had plagued pre-war Britain, something which he saw as essential to furthering social progress.[1] The act of imagining an emergent welfare state was, in this way, embedded in the work of postwar reconstruction. The Report, which sold 630,000 copies, set the blueprint for a postwar system of social security.[2] At the heart of Beveridge's plan was a comprehensive programme of social insurance, and he directed the state to establish a national minimum below which no one's living standards could fall. A wave of publications on the reconstruction of Britain followed: in the popular press, pamphlets and government reports, the ruins of the Home Front were seen as an opportunity to imagine a brave new world. Literature in the early and mid-twentieth century, Benjamin Kohlmann writes, 'took on the task of imagining the kinds of life that would be possible under the auspices of the emerging welfare state – this involved an anticipatory vision of new kinds of active citizenship and a shared orientation towards the common good'.[3] The welfare state should be seen, in this regard, Kelly Rich contends, as an 'institutional formation at the center of mid-century culture, providing a language for its reformulations of belonging, personhood, and rights'.[4] Because the welfare state is heavily invested

[1]   William Beveridge, *Social Insurance and Allied Services* (London, 1942).
[2]   Valerie Holman, *Print for Victory: Book Publishing in England, 1939–1945* (London, 2008), p. 194.
[3]   Benjamin Kohlmann, *British Literature and the Life of Institutions: Speculative States* (Oxford, 2021), p. 5.
[4]   Kelly Rich, *The Promise of Welfare in the Postwar British and Anglophone Novel* (Oxford, 2023), p. 5.

in narratives of upward mobility, literature about welfare is also invariably about the experiences – but also the limits – of social mobility.

This volume traces lines of connection between literature and welfare state imaginaries. It is interested in the representational possibilities, the social arrangements and political claims that welfare makes possible. Contributors examine how literature communicates the value and character of the welfare state from the 1930s to the present in a British, Irish and US context. They demonstrate how welfare and reconstruction operate as much in fictive and poetic as in sociological discourses. The promises and failures of the welfare state are seen, in this way, as intimately connected to the communities which are imagined in interwar and postwar literature. The chapters presented here move – like the literature they examine – between a disenchantment with the institutions of welfare and an urgent need to articulate welfare's vision of social repair. Literature on the welfare state returns to Beveridge's founding vision, to reanimate the possibilities of welfare and to consider the social that made it democratic. The narratives of the welfare state that we have inherited today are embedded both with the conception of postwar history and with the sense of possibility that was occasioned through the welfare state policies of the 1940s: social insurance, the National Health Service, universal secondary education, the abolition of the Poor Law and fiscal redistribution. While, as welfare state historian Jose Harris writes, many of these policies have been 'portrayed as the fruits of compromise, pragmatism and technical adjustment [...] occupying the muddled middle ground between socialism, corporatism and free-market capitalism', they are nonetheless acknowledged as vital forces that are essential to maintaining the social fabric.[5]

The word 'welfare' was first used in the fourteenth century 'to indicate happiness or prosperity'. In the early twentieth century it acquired an 'extended sense [...] of organized care and provision [...] Thus [...] welfare policy (1905); welfare centres (1917). The welfare state [...] was first named in 1939'.[6] In the wartime and postwar period, the stigma which had historically been attached to welfare lessened, and the welfare state became the expression of national unity and social progress. But, Harris notes,

> the world of social welfare in the early 1940s was of course in no sense a clean slate. It was filled with a wide variety of partly complementary and partly conflicting policies and institutions. [...] Deeply embedded in and reinforcing

[5]   Jose Harris, 'Political Ideas and the Debate on State Welfare, 1940–45', *War and Social Change: British Society in the Second World War*, ed. Harold L. Smith (Manchester, 1986), pp. 233–63 (pp. 233–4).
[6]   Raymond Williams, *Keywords* (London, 1988), p. 264.

all these arrangements was the existence of the family, whose provision of a wide range of 'welfare' functions was tacitly assumed by social theorists and policy-makers of all political complexions.[7]

The welfare state is commonly seen as synonymous with an age of social consensus: the so-called 'golden age of welfare'.[8] But this image of commonality conceals the persistence of class, racial and gendered division, which was often exacerbated by welfare state policy. In exchange for welfare state belonging, citizens were often asked to conform to specific national projects, most notably the demand for women, and working-class women in particular, to leave the workforce after marriage. As such, welfarist modes of belonging created an illusory sense of social solidarity and at the same time encouraged the predominantly false expectation, as Ann Oakley writes, 'that things got – and had got – better and better all the time'.[9]

While many citizens rode on these waves of a new mood of institutional egalitarianism, one underwritten by the postwar drive and valorisation of education, the pervasive sense of welfare's global promise of repair left it 'peculiarly vulnerable to changes in political and economic climates, and to attacks from more rigorous and dogmatic intellectual rivals'.[10] Literary and historical accounts of the welfare state habitually acknowledge the political and emotional ambivalence that surrounds welfare imaginaries in Carolyn Steedman's classic autobiographical study, *A Landscape for a Good Woman* (1986).[11] A feminist historian, Steedman is both highly alert to the limits of social reform in a state that is rooted in the principles of liberal philanthropy and of the vulnerability of the welfare state to ideological attack. She narrates the welfare state from the perspective of her own life history. In the study she articulates how it fails to provide her mother, a working-class woman, with a structure of feeling that she could believe in; at the same time, she acknowledges that material provision by the state also bears a crucial symbolic weight in her own life, making her believe in her right to exist and to flourish. Such a first-person account of welfare works, then, against the coherence of welfarist fictions of class mobility.

---

[7]   Harris, 'Political Ideas and the Debate on State Welfare, 1940–45', p. 235.
[8]   Harris, 'Political Ideas and the Debate on State Welfare, 1940–45', p. 238.
[9]   Ann Oakley, 'Introduction', *The Politics of the Welfare State*, ed. Ann Oakley and Susan Williams (London, 1994), pp. 1–17 (p. 3).
[10]   Harris, 'Political Ideas and the Debate on State Welfare, 1940–45', p. 257.
[11]   Carolyn Steedman, *Landscape for a Good Woman* (London, 1986).

Reading literature alongside welfare allows us to see how the welfare state generated its own social fictions. Moreover, it allows us to think about postwar English literature and English studies as fields which are intimately connected to the values of welfare. English was seen in the postwar settlement as a subject that could transform society through the promotion of democratic values and an appreciation of the power of literature and language. A string of publications, such as David Daiches's *Literature and Society* (1938), encouraged the promotion of links between culture, education and society, underpinned by the idea that access to literature was a public good.[12] Such a public commitment to literature, Asha Rogers writes, led to a transformation of the relationship between literature and the state, and drove a new interest in 'who was writing, who was reading, and what they might need'.[13] In postwar classrooms, too, English as a discipline was animated by the social relevance of literature which, Alexander Hutton argues, produced 'literary critics for a welfare state era'. In return, new ideas about literature's social role had a significant impact on how it was used after a student's education ended. 'Precisely because a degree in English Literature allowed its possessor to enter a range of vocations rather than being confined to a particular [one], English had the potential to transform the way people thought and felt about and governed one another'.[14]

What has been the legacy of the writing of the welfare state, for thinking about the production of literature, the value of teaching English and the climate of feeling in which welfare prospers? This volume is interested in the welfare state as a 'conglomeration of legislation and services', in the affective register of welfare, and in the kinds of subjectivity and senses of belonging (or unbelonging) that it generated.[15] It is animated by the idea, expressed by the historian James Vernon, that

> we need better history, not just better ethics, to recuperate and reimagine the politics of welfare; recognizing the limit points of welfarist modes of belonging is not to disallow the provision of welfare – although it helps us explain its vulnerability to neoliberal critique – rather, it is to call for a critical reflection upon its historical forms so that they can be renewed in the present.[16]

---

[12] David Daiches, *Literature and Society* (London, 1938).

[13] Asha Rogers, *State Sponsored Literature: Britain and Cultural Diversity after 1945* (Oxford, 2020), pp. 2–3.

[14] Alexander Hutton, 'An English School for the Welfare State: Literature, Politics and the University, 1932–1965', *English: Journal of the English Association*, 65 (2016), pp. 3–34 (p. 3).

[15] Elizabeth Wilson, *Women and the Welfare State* (London, 2002), p. 7.

[16] James Vernon, 'Hunger, the Social, and States of Welfare in Modern Imperial

The chapters presented here examine the literary texts and traditions invested in the imagining of welfare, an imagining that is, in the words of Raymond Williams, central to generating a belief in the possibility of change and in the cultural and educative value of literature. In *The Long Revolution* (1968), he writes of how 'human learning in a genuinely open way' is 'the most valuable real resource we have and therefore as something which we should have to produce a special argument to limit rather than a special argument to extend'.[17] The question for the late 1960s is whether 'we replace' the 'privileges and barriers, of an inherited kind' with 'the free play of the market', or by 'a public education designed to express and create the values of an educated democracy and a common culture'.[18] From the vantage point of the present, this volume decries how the market has won.

What might it mean to consider literary education as a form of welfare that should be accessible to all? It is a vision that, far from utopian, was at the centre of the postwar consensus. 'Part of what is at stake here', Vicky Lebeau writes, 'is the mysterious labour of helping others to live, think, and create', a labour that is becoming increasingly hard to sustain in the face of repeated attacks by the conservative government and the right-wing press who are keen to remind the young that an English degree, in particular, and a humanities degree in general, will offer few remunerative rewards.[19] Contributors are alert to the way that, whilst welfare is a vital enabling force – a vehicle for upward mobility and a sense of the common good – it is nonetheless, as Bruce Robbins observes, an 'imperfect historical form'.[20] Welfare should be understood, Robbins writes, 'as a set of imperfect institutions, produced in part by management from above and in part by pressure from below, which also enters into the unfinished project of "social citizenship."' To reflect on the representation and the historical formation of the welfare state is also, then, to consider the possibilities and limits of social citizenship and its entanglement with the class, racial and gendered politics in the postwar period.

Contributors to this volume bring the value of literature into dialogue with the value of welfare to reveal the relationship between narratives of social mobility, welfare and cultural access. They move between the representation of the welfare state in literature and the role of literature under the

Britain', *Occasion: Interdisciplinary Studies in the Humanities*, 2 (2010), p. 7.

[17] Raymond Williams, *The Long Revolution* (London, 1975), p. 168

[18] Williams, *The Long Revolution*, p. 176.

[19] Vicky Lebeau, 'Feeling Poor: D. W. Winnicott and Daniel Blake', *New Formations: A Journal of Culture / Theory / Politics* 96-7 (2019), pp. 160–75 (p. 161).

[20] Bruce Robbins, *Upward Mobility and the Common Good: Toward a Literary History of the Welfare State* (Princeton, 2007), p. 9.

welfare state to think about the ways in which welfarist ideology has underpinned the teaching, reading and production of literature from the 1930s to
the present. Contributors consider the genres and forms in which welfare
is represented, the publishing contexts that produce certain narratives and
visions of welfare, and the value of studying English literature. The rationale
for the volume is to broaden our understanding of how literature relates to
the social aspirations and the institutions of welfare, and to show how they
bear on contemporary political thinking, invested as it is in the rollback of
the welfare state and of the humanities.

In her chapter 'Reading and Reality', Josie Billington draws on a psychoanalytic vocabulary to show how literary education has a socially transformative and therapeutic power. Billington reads literary realism as a genre that
is closely related historically and ideologically to the ambitions of welfare.
Drawing on her own experience in shared reading groups with the British
charity The Reader, her essay considers the kinds of reality that literary
reading gives access to, and its remedial value. Through an engagement with
D. W. Winnicott's and Wilfred Bion's psychoanalytic ideas, Billington
shows how shared reading creates a context in which literature can provide a
way of understanding the work of shared emotion. Such a context, generated
in a voluntary setting, is also a reminder of the two-way relation between the
welfare state and other voluntary organisations. Billington draws on several
case studies to show how people in these groups relate to characters and to
the representation of emotive and traumatic narratives, which allows them to
understand their own history and trauma with a greater complexity.

Turning from experiments in communal reading in contemporary Britain
to the United States in the New Deal era, Matthew Holman considers forms
of art that have been generated through state sponsorship. He focuses on
work that was produced by the theatrical production of the Federal Theatre
Project (FTP), which ran from 1936 to 1939 as part of the Works Progress
Administration's efforts to provide work for the unemployed during the
Great Depression. One of the divisions of the FTP was the Living Newspaper
Unit. Based in New York City, it created plays with scenes that dramatised
newspaper articles. In collaboration with the American Newspaper Guild, it
transformed current events – particularly of economic deprivation – from
the page to the stage. As Holman writes, it was the first time the federal government had subsidised the arts, and this short-lived experiment provided a
radical example of theatrical production as an extension of the welfare state.

If Billington reads realism as the genre that is most compatible with welfarist ideology, in her chapter on Christine Brooke-Rose's 1964 novel *Out*,
Sarah Bernstein considers how the avant-garde novel cultivates experimental
forms of attention that might point us to more experimental ways of think-

ing about care and welfare provision. Brooke-Rose's experimental tradition might, Bernstein argues, be a way of addressing the representational impasse of the postwar novel and the welfare state alike. 'In refusing the reader the usual consolations of narrative, character and plot', Bernstein writes, 'the novel asks for a different kind of reading, a different way of looking at the text and, by extension, at the world'. This experimental way of looking in the novel, Bernstein contends, resists both the politics of empathy and the forms of social control that were constitutive of the Beveridge-era welfare state, as well as the more privatised forms of welfare that would follow it as the postwar consensus unravelled. The novel, which is set in a dystopian future where mental health care has been replaced by algorithms and the unemployed are given dole pills, foreshadows much of the mechanical kinds of attention that would emerge from the marketisation of the welfare state in the 1980s. The work thus provides a provocative view of welfarist ideology, even in the supposedly 'golden age' of welfare.

There is still a tendency, Rodney Love reflects, to 'believe that the "classic" welfare state was a golden age of political consensus, economic growth, rising living standards and, consequently, social justice'.[21] But at the moment of its founding, writers questioned the coherence of its project of social transformation. Far from driving an idealised communality, the welfare state produced liberatory and aspirational feeling but also exclusionary and disciplinary structures and fraught emotions. Writers in the immediate postwar period – including Doris Lessing and Muriel Spark – ironicised the fantasy of the postwar project of reconstruction through characters like Nicholas Farringdon in *The Girls of Slender Means* (1963), who misreads the communality of a woman's boarding house as a 'microcosmic ideal'. Such an idealisation is exposed as a nostalgic fantasy for a 'beautiful heedless poverty of a golden age'.[22] In her interpretation of Doris Lessing's sociological imagination and the fantasy of the good neighbour, Jess Cotton considers the representation of literary realism and the sociological studies that underpinned welfarist imaginaries. Reading Lessing's novels *The Diary of a Good Neighbour* (1983) and *In Pursuit of the English* (1960) alongside Michael Young and Peter Willmott's 1957 study *Family and Kinship in East London*, she shows how sociological realism sustains certain pre-war fictions about British community and working-class lives. The chapter traces a through-line between Lessing's ironic sociological realism in her earlier novel and a literary hoax

---

[21] Rodney Lowe, 'Lessons from the Past: The Rise and Fall of the Classic Welfare State in Britain, 1945–76', *The Politics of the Welfare State*, ed. Ann Oakley and Susan Williams (London, 1994), pp. 37–53 (p. 37).
[22] Muriel Spark, *The Girls of Slender Means* (New York, 1998), p. 65.

she perpetrated, which allows us to see simultaneously the values of welfare and the disciplinary aspects of the welfare state.

During the so-called 'golden age' of welfare, a new kind of British poetry emerged that was closely associated with the values of welfare. In his chapter on Anna Mendelssohn, Sean Bonney and Fran Lock, Gareth Farmer considers a more radical poetics of welfare. Farmer makes the case that radical poetic form draws attention to the conditions of our common life that have been undermined by welfarist ideology. Finding connections between these poets' work, Farmer examines their contrasting responses to neoliberalism's attacks on welfare, and shows how a radical poetics provides a language for a complicated form of care that refuses the discourses of welfare. Farmer's contention is that this poetics points us to a more inclusive and critical British poetry and welfare state, alike.

Over the past three decades, the welfare state has been the site of feminist critique, particularly in relation to the family politics that it promoted, which have often been seen as incompatible with some of the more radical politics of the women's movement. In her article on Virago Press, Helen Charman examines how the publishing house's republication of older texts on the welfare state promoted a nostalgia for the 'golden age' of welfare, even while more contemporary publications, including Carolyn Steedman's *Landscape for a Good Woman*, troubled that nostalgia, foregrounding a more ambivalent relation to welfare. Steedman's study, Charman shows, works through case studies, myth, folk tales and fairy tales to consider the way that welfare is animated within the postwar imagination and how it conceals within it more traumatic, uneven and ongoing narratives of class transition.

The history of the welfare state is revealed in its complexity, Charman suggests, as a history-from-below. This mode of social history emerged on the New Left to examine the experience and history-making power of working people who had been overlooked in 'top-down' historical narratives. Histories-from-below might be the place we go, then, to recover a more radical vision of welfare. An historical approach to welfare reads past the national fantasy of the welfare state to consider its complex social and cultural entanglements; it allows us to see how the forms of care that the welfare state safeguarded were also frequently forms of social control. Such an approach might include the experience of race as well as class. Lara Choksey's chapter argues that the welfare state was frequently a racist institution that foreclosed more radical forms of social belonging. In her reading of Beryl Gilroy's *Black Teacher* (1976) and Caryl Phillips's *The Final Passage* (1985), two texts that were written either side of the Brixton Uprising of 1981, Choksey foregrounds a story of the welfare state from the perspective of Caribbean immigration from the Windrush in 1948 to the 1980s. She shows how Gilroy and Phillips draw attention away 'from the national provision of welfare – and the fiction of the immigrant who does or does not make the most of opportunities handed to them by a benevolent state – towards the subcultural affordances' and grassroots rearrangements, which provide more robust, if provisional, forms of welfare that might enable us to imagine a decolonised welfare state.

The legacies of the thinking around welfare, as it relates to English teaching, Beci Carver observes, have not always been straightforward. Carver's chapter examines the relationship between Raymond Williams's emergent ideas of literature as a social good and the legacies of the University of Cambridge's tragedy paper and T. S. Eliot's ideas of culture. English literature teaching, influence and socialist thought are entangled with the emergent welfare state and the legacy of more conservative ideals. The question of education as a form of welfare is likewise taken up by Neil Vickers. His autoethnographic account of the 1980s positions a literary education in relation to shifting ideas about the canon and the unstable politics of that decade in Ireland. Vickers contrasts this vision of education and literature as a transitional space which opens up new ways of being with the contemporary landscape of English literary teaching at university.

To read and teach English literature today is to be emmeshed with the affective currents, social affordances and ambivalent identifications of the welfare state. Narratives of welfare are all around us – particularly in the press – but when reading welfare in the classroom we are given space to examine those narratives with a greater degree of scrutiny and historical perspective. We are, to take up Steedman's autoethnographic approach, children of the welfare state, though we are in the awkward position of teaching English to those who are no longer afforded the transformative space that English-as-welfare once promised. How, then, to keep this model of welfare and English alive, without romanticizing the politics of welfare? By returning to the narratives that emerge within the nexus of the welfare state, we might continue to push for literary spaces and a landscape of higher education that is committed not simply to prepping students for an increasingly precarious labour market, but is rather directed towards a cultivation, in spite of the inhospitable climate, of a model of literary engagement: one which is recognised as a common good and as a form of social transformation directed towards the ongoing project of creating and recreating worlds.

1

Reading and Reality

JOSIE BILLINGTON

The title of this paper invokes three staples of literary form and psychoanalytic thought as touchstones for exploring literary reading as a therapeutic power. The first is literary realism, the mode of literature which is most loyal to 'real life', and which, arguably, is the genre most closely related historically and ideologically to the ideals and ambitions of the welfare state. The second, apparently at the other extreme, is Wilfred Bion's notion of the 'really real' or 'ultimate reality', a concept derived from philosophy, and applied to the experience of psychic truth within the psychoanalytic encounter.[1] The third is D. W. Winnicott's identification, in *Playing and Reality*, of 'an intermediate area of experience' – neither personal psychic reality nor the actual world in which the individual lives, but a space to which inner reality and external life both contribute.[2] Using very specific instances of reading moments, and analytical tools developed over many years of studying shared reading groups, this essay considers to what kinds of reality literary reading can give access, and why such access might have remedial value. At the core of what follows is the experience of people living with depression and chronic pain who are beneficiaries of the United Kingdom charity The Reader, a 'welfare' organisation of national and international reach.

Literary Realism

The history of literary realism is intimately intertwined, both chronologically and ideologically, with the origins and ideals of social welfare. In the first place, the Victorian novel, and the realist revolution in literature which it engendered, cannot be separated at any level from the social convulsions in which realism emerged. Technological developments in binding and printing, which increased the efficiency of the book market and brought book

---

[1] W. R. Bion, *Transformations: Change from Learning to Growth* (London, 1963), pp. 147–9.
[2] D. W. Winnicott, *Playing and Reality* (London, 1971), p. 2.

prices down, together with an increasingly literate populace (especially after the Education Act of 1870), meant that economic and social conditions were ripe for the production of large quantities of novels in the Victorian age. The market was driven as much politically and culturally as it was socio-economically. A new middle-class readership, expanded, emboldened and newly powerful after the 1832 Reform Act extended the franchise, wanted to read not about the exploits of a moribund aristocracy or warrior triumphs on the battlefield, but about people like themselves. One of the reasons for the unprecedented popularity of the novel in the nineteenth century was that it was democratic, treating the individual of whatever rank as inherently significant, giving ordinary life and ordinary men and women a place of regard in literature. Yet the novel did more than merely reflect the tastes and new ascendancy of the middle classes. Rather, a whole generation of readers and writers seemed to seize upon a form of literature that was large and loose enough to contain the amplitude, energy and amorphousness of their contemporary experience. It was the informality and inclusiveness of Victorian fiction, its incorporation of the tumultuous world outside and its giving shape to the growing shapelessness of life, which accounts in large part for its success.

An influential body of twentieth-century literary theory concluded from these determinants that Victorian realism was fundamentally a bourgeois genre, shoring up the ideological and cultural bent of the dominant class.[3] The circumstances of its production meant that the novel could hardly avoid assuming that role to a certain degree. But no genre did more to *resist* the ills of the very revolution which had given it life. All the great pioneering novelists of the Victorian period – the Brontës, Charles Dickens, George Eliot, Elizabeth Gaskell – had been born in the second decade of the nineteenth century and had thus lived through the turbulent upheavals and dramatic changes which the industrial revolution, and the shift from a rural to an urban mode of living, had brought about. In this displacement began the poverty, disease and divisive social formations which the welfare state would seek to address. These writers were all also literary inheritors of William Wordsworth, whose famous Preface to *Lyrical Ballads* was a virtual blueprint for the realist novel.[4] The pioneers of a fiction of ordinary life likewise shared an admiration for, and affinity with, the artistic and social principles of John

[3]   See Catherine Belsey, *Critical Practice* (London, 2002); C. MacCabe, 'The End of a Meta-Language: From George Eliot to *Dubliners*', *George Eliot*, ed. K. M. Newton (London, 1991), pp. 156–68.

[4]   William Wordsworth, 'Preface to *Lyrical Ballads* (1800 and 1802)', *William Wordsworth*, ed. S. Gill (Oxford, 2010), pp. 58–82 (pp. 58–9).

Ruskin. 'The truth of infinite value that he teaches is *realism*', wrote George Eliot; and she declared that art which was committed to depicting 'definite substantial reality', was the 'nearest thing to life'.[5] Analogously, in Ruskin's vision, the artist is a worker like any other. 'Whatever bit of a wise man's work is honestly and benevolently done, that bit is his book or his piece of art'.[6] And, as in Ruskin's searing vision of modern industrial life, the worker was becoming 'unhumanised' – all energy and spirit given to make a 'cog' of himself until 'the whole human being be lost at last, a heap of sawdust' – so the Victorian realist novelist sought to rescue the value of ordinary human life from whatever circumstances were conspiring to make it.[7] In Elizabeth Gaskell's case this meant making industrial life and class conflict subjects of the novel for the first time, and taking a working man, a trade-unionist, for her hero. Her purpose, as she put it in the preface to *Mary Barton*, was 'to give some utterance to the agony' which convulsed the urban poor amid the appalling living conditions of mid-nineteenth century Manchester, and thereby humanise the understanding and perceptions of her middle-class audience.[8] For Dickens, who, like Gaskell, played a huge role in publicising the problems created by industrialisation, the key and unashamed task was that of reaching directly and influentially into the emotional lives of his readers: to 'be in all homes and all nooks and corners [...] At the window, by the fire, in the street, in the house, from infancy to old age, everyone's inseparable companion'.[9] Dickens sought, says Juliet John, to 'realise community through imagination'. His frequent public readings (where it was as if 'the pulse of a crowded house beat like the pulse of one man') were a literal accomplishment of his ambition to have his reader feel along with him and in 'communion' with each other, so bringing a divided nation together through his books.[10] For George Eliot, offering 'a faithful and humble' representation of human life meant an 'extension of our sympathies' – 'surpris[ing]' even the trivial and selfish into that attention to what is apart from themselves',

[5]   George Eliot, 'Review of John Ruskin, *Modern Painters* III', *George Eliot: Selected Essays, Poems and Other Writings*, ed. A. S. Byatt (London, 1990), pp. 367–78 (p. 368); 'The Natural History of German Life', *George Eliot: Selected Essays, Poems and Other Writings*, pp. 107–39 (p. 110).

[6]   John Ruskin, 'Sesame and Lilies', *The Works of John Ruskin*, ed. E. T. Cook and A. Wedderburn, 39 vols. (London, 1903–1912), 18, p. 61.

[7]   Ruskin, 'The Stones of Venice II', *The Works of John Ruskin*, 10, p. 192.

[8]   Elizabeth Gaskell, *Mary Barton*, ed. Shirley Foster (Oxford, 2006), p. 3.

[9]   Charles Dickens, letter to John Forster, 7 October 1849, *The Letters of Charles Dickens*, ed. Madeline House and Graham Storey, 12 vols. (Oxford, 1965–2002), 5, pp. 622–3.

[10]   Juliet John, *Dickens and Mass Culture* (Oxford, 2010), p. 150.

thereby 'amplifying experience and extending contact with our fellow men beyond the bounds of our personal lot'.[11] Realism's loyalties were always double ones: serving the common life represented *inside* the novel by finding what was extraordinary and overlooked within its humble, plain and habitual contours; and serving the community of readers (and non-readers) *outside* the novel whose often hidden lives, needs and sufferings those very fictional characters sought faithfully to stand for and value.

No wonder this was the literary genre of choice when The Reader charity first began its outreach work. The charity, which was founded by extra-mural higher educational teachers, aims to take fiction and poetry out of a university context, into communities with multiple socio-economic and educational-cultural deprivations.[12] The first Shared Reading group took place in 2002 in Birkenhead Library, then and now one of the most disad-vantaged areas of the United Kingdom. The men and women who attended those early Shared Reading groups were people who had lived through the severest socio-economic downturn in the post-war history of Liverpool and its surrounding regions. Unemployment (twice the national average in the 1980s), civil unrest, political conflict, widespread poverty, drug abuse and low-quality housing had been exacerbated by the Thatcherite government's (1979–90) systematic dismantling of the social security system. What had been a fundamental principle and inviolable right of the welfare state was subject to 'death by a thousand cuts'. This was true especially of child and unemployment benefits in what proved to be 'a brutal decade for the poor' in Britain as a whole, and one with long-lasting consequences for Liverpool in particular.[13] A Joseph Rowntree study found that in 2000, 41.2 percent of inner-city Liverpudlians were classed as living in poverty; the figure was as high as 50–70 percent in parts of Birkenhead, the originating home of Shared Reading.[14] From that initial single reading group there followed liter-ally hundreds across Merseyside and beyond, running in doctor's surgeries, prisons, care homes, psychiatric units, mental health drop-in, asylum and drug rehabilitation centres, reaching people with mental and chronic health problems, the elderly and their carers, recovering drug or alcohol abusers,

---

[11]   Eliot, 'Review of John Ruskin', p. 368; 'Natural History of German Life', p. 110.
[12]   For a fuller history of the origin and evolution of The Reader, see Jane Davis, 'The Reading Revolution', *Stop What You're Doing and Read This!* (London, 2011), pp. 115–36.
[13]   Paul Pierson, *Dismantling the Welfare State?: Reagan, Thatcher and the Politics of Retrenchment* (Cambridge, 1994), p. 100.
[14]   Daniel Dorling et al., *Poverty and Wealth Across Britain: 1968–2005* (Bristol, 2007).

refugees, looked-after children, offenders and ex-offenders. How did this happen in severely disadvantaged communities where the reading of books was neither common, nor its value self-evident?

The Reader's unique model of reading group is significant in this regard. The works are not read in advance, but read aloud, word by word, page by page, within the group, initially by trained Reader Leaders and subsequently by group members as they choose or volunteer. This, from the first, was a radically inclusive model, reaching people of all ages who would not otherwise be reading, whether through difficulties with literacy, neurological disorders or impaired vision, or because reading serious literature had never seemed a resource to which they might turn. Stories and poetry came alive for people, often for the first time, through a combination, on the one hand, of their being read aloud, performatively, within the room and, on the other hand, through the emphasis on shared humane attention to the feelings and thoughts transmitted by the literary works in place of any narrow focus on improving literacy (too often literature's function in educational contexts) or influencing wellbeing (the aim of bibliotherapy). Both of these good effects happened, but would not have done so, our extensive research strongly suggests, had they been the primary goal. 'Not only is this not therapy – precisely by not being therapy it has a therapeutic effect'.[15]

The read-aloud model connects, in fact, with a socio-cultural tradition of family and community reading that became embedded and widespread in Victorian England.[16] Indeed, Clare Ellis, a Victorian scholar and long-time practitioner with The Reader, has made the connection directly between what happens in Shared Reading groups and Victorian reading practices. 'At its heart is the revival of a cultural movement that might be considered as essentially Victorian in character – the endeavour to bring people together through the arts and, more specifically, to bring people together as one community by reading literature aloud'.[17] As part of this 'revival', The Reader holds annual Penny Readings (reinstating a popular working-class tradition which began in the mid-nineteenth century) in St George's Hall in Liverpool, where Dickens himself delivered one of his public readings. Ellis goes on to point out that the form and mode of production of Victorian

---

[15] Philip Davis and Josie Billington, 'The Very Grief a Cure of the Disease', *Changing English*, 23.4 (2016), pp. 396–408 (p. 406).
[16] See Jonathan Rose, *The Intellectual Life of the British Working Classes* (New Haven, 2010); Matthew Bradley and Juliet John, eds., *Reading and the Victorians* (Farnham, 2015).
[17] Clare Ellis, 'The Sharing of Stories in Company with Mr Charles Dickens', *Reading and the Victorians*, ed. Bradley and John, pp. 143–57 (p. 143).

novels is particularly suited to the practice of Shared Reading. As many, those of Dickens included, were written for publication in weekly instalments for popular periodicals, 'each chapter [is] able to stand alone as a definitive episode within the overarching narrative journey'.[18] This means that a novel can often take weeks or months to complete in Shared Reading, which is itself a contemporary version of the contract of continuity which existed between the Victorian novelist and reader.[19]

Ellis reports on a research study we undertook together, almost ten years after The Reader was founded, on the benefits of Shared Reading for people living with depression.[20] This proved to be the first study in what was to become a body of work around Shared Reading and mental health, some of which I will refer to in what follows. The study took place in Bootle, an area which, as Ellis explains, has one of the highest indexes of multiple deprivation across the UK. Those who were living there had 'reduced levels of life expectancy', and, relative to the national average, were 'almost four times more likely to have below average mental well-being'.[21] The study took place in a mental health drop-in centre with people diagnosed with depression, most of whom had few or no educational qualifications (none had received higher education), and many of whom were unemployed, vulnerably housed and lonely. Towards the end of the twelve-month study, at the group-members' request, the group read Charles Dickens's *Great Expectations*. We audio-recorded and transcribed the reading group sessions for analysis by our multidisciplinary team drawn from Linguistics, Medicine, Sociology and Literature.[22] Where Ellis concentrates on the group's response to the first iconic scene and chapter of the book (Pip's encounter with the convict Magwitch), the session described below took place a few weeks into the group's reading of the novel, when the focus is on Pip's first visit, from his home at the blacksmith's forge, to Miss Havisham's where he meets with Estella. The two are playing cards:

'He calls the knaves, Jacks, this boy!' said Estella, with disdain, before our first game was out. 'And what coarse hands he has. And what thick boots!'

[18]   Ellis, 'The Sharing of Stories', p. 144.
[19]   Jennifer Hayward, *Consuming Pleasures: Active Audiences and Serial Fictions from Dickens to Soap Opera* (Lexington, 1997), pp. 1–52.
[20]   Chris Dowrick, Josie Billington, Jude Robinson, Andrew Hamer and Clare Williams [Ellis], 'Get into Reading as an Intervention for Common Mental Health Problems', *Medical Humanities*, 38.1 (2012), pp. 15–20.
[21]   Ellis, 'The Sharing of Stories', p. 145.
[22]   The project was approved by NHS Research Ethics. All quoted material from the study uses pseudonyms.

I had never thought of being ashamed of my hands before; but I began to consider them a very indifferent pair. Her contempt was so strong, that it became infectious and I caught it.

She won the game, and I dealt. I misdealt, as was only natural when I knew she was lying in wait for me to do wrong; and she denounced me for a stupid, clumsy labouring-boy.[23]

What follows is the group's immediate response to this scene and passage:

Amy: That's terrible. She – Estella – makes it about class very clearly doesn't she? He calls the knaves jacks, what coarse hands, and what thick boots. They're all the sign that he's a working boy, aren't they?

Ivan: It is very strong. How you could pick up vibes so quickly from somebody else and then suddenly you feel very, very small. She has absolutely – *reduced* him.

Cathy: It's so upsetting the way he is forced to look again at his hands, 'I never thought of being ashamed of my hands before'. It feels so *personal* – it feels as if he's forced to take his class sort of inside him. 'It became infectious and I caught it.'

Group Leader: Yes, as if it was breathing in germs, like TB or you know some terrible airborne disease.

Amy: I wondered, reading that, how long that feeling will stay with him, whether he will get over it or whether it would stick.

Ray: I think that word 'infectious' means that it will stick. It's not going to go straight away.

Ivan: He is going to go round for quite a while thinking 'where shall I put them?'.

Linda: Yes, feeling dirty.

Jed: And the one thing a blacksmith's apprentice will have to be is dirty.

Amy: Big, dirty –

---

[23] Charles Dickens, *Great Expectations*, ed. Charlotte Mitchell (London, 1996), pp. 60–1.

Jed: Working hands.

Group Leader: Workman's hands, yes!

Cathy: So, when he is in the blacksmith's, he is not having these negative feelings about himself, but in another setting, he is seeing himself in a completely different way.[24]

I sometimes show this and other such extracts to MA students on a module 'Reading Victorians', looking at such matters as who read in the period, what they read and how they read. The principal intention is to try to recreate something of those first readers' responses to the novel by showing how Dickens' words, in the north of England in the twenty-first century – for readers, as we've seen, who are at once inheritors of, and whose lives in many ways parallel, the conditions depicted in Dickens' work – can still be a powerful presence and 'companion'. Students are struck by the immediacy of the emotional reaction to Pip's humiliation ('That's terrible'; 'It's so upsetting'; 'very, very small ... *reduced* him'), and by the way the group members seem almost viscerally to feel Pip's class shame, as he feels it 'forced inside him' or almost physically 'sticking' to him, even as he can barely recognise his body as his own anymore ('seeing himself in a completely different way'), or finds there only a terrible, sudden and alienating 'sign' of his coarseness ('where shall I put them?'). Students have remarked that these reactions helped them to realise that Dickens shows how the age-old narrative of the fall from innocence to experience is infected by this brutalising contact with institutionalised class relations which are now the a priori conditions in which a child grows into the world and adulthood. The students describe the group's response, warmly, as one of empathy.

The language of empathy intersects with an influential body of current work in the psychology of reading, which holds that the value of reading literary fiction is its power to expand the mind and enlarge our range of feelings in respect of understanding and caring about other lives and selves.[25] Realist novels (the model of narrative fiction which this body of work self-evidently has in mind and uses in its studies) offer simulated models of experience

---

[24]   The extract comes from an unpublished transcript used in staff training by The Reader, which emerged from the Shared Reading and Depression study. See Dowrick et al., 'Get into Reading'; Josie Billington et al., 'An Investigation into the Therapeutic Benefits of Reading in Relation to Depression and Well-Being' (Liverpool, 2011). <Therapeutic_benefits_of_reading_final_report_March_2011.pdf>.
[25]   Raymond Marr et al., 'Exploring the Link between Reading Fiction and Empathy', *Communications*, 34.4 (2009), pp. 407–28.

which imaginatively exercise our cognitive, emotional and ethical capaci-ties.[26] Indeed, as I point out to the students, these extensive and esteemed research studies have demonstrated empirically that realist fiction can indeed achieve the ambition which the nineteenth-century realist novelists sought for it: 'The only effect I ardently long to produce by my writings,' wrote George Eliot, 'is that those who read them should be able to *feel* the pain of those who differ from themselves in everything but the *broad* fact of being struggling, erring creatures'.[27]

I admire this sentiment and I often make use of the contemporary work in reading psychology which vindicates it. I do not doubt, either, that empathy, thus conceived, can reap many personal, as well as wider societal, benefits; that it can enable people, especially those who are isolated or alone, to become, as Rhiannon Corcoran and Keith Oatley put it, 'more socially adaptable and able to make the most of opportunities and to successfully navigate the challenges of our social world in cooperative ways'.[28] But my questions as we conducted the Shared Reading and Depression study were these. First, if the value of literature is primarily that of 'educating' feeling and thought in relation to others, can this in itself explain the impact of Shared Reading on, specifically, depression? Our study, it needs to be noted, found a statistically significant reduction in depressive symptoms in those attending the reading group. Second, there is a strong sense in the extract above that not only might these readers bring their own raw feelings to this response as much as 'learning' an understanding of others, but that this expe-rience is not vicarious merely (seeing or feeling from another's point of view, putting yourself in their shoes) but an experience that directly *hurts*: 'It feels so *personal* – he's forced to take his class sort of inside him'. Could this be what psychologists meant when they wrote of fictional reading as a 'cognitive workout'? I didn't think so.

Reading, reality and 0

Let us look at this question again from a different place, with a different group, and a different literary text, yet one which offers close comparison

---

[26]   Keith Oatley, 'Why Fiction May be Twice as True as Fact: Fiction as Cognitive and Emotional Simulation', *Review of General Psychology*, 3 (1999), pp. 101–17.
[27]   George Eliot, *The George Eliot Letters*, ed. G. S. Haight, 9 vols. (New Haven, 1954–78), 3, p. 111.
[28]   Rhiannon Corcoran and Keith Oatley, 'Reading Minds: Fiction and Its Relation to the Mental Worlds of Self and Others', *Reading and Mental Health*, ed. Josie Billington (Cham, 2019), pp. 331–43 (p. 335).

with the examples witnessed above. The group is meeting in a pain clinic at a Liverpool inner city hospital, as part of a further research study developed with the pain consultants who run the clinic.[29] The group members all have a diagnosis of severe chronic pain, a condition which is officially defined by its duration: that is, pain that lasts for more than three months after tissue healing has occurred. 'The pain may have been triggered by tissue damage in the first place. It may not have been. But either way, chronic pain sufferers are experiencing something that is totally "inappropriate" – they're getting pain which is not [physiologically] justified'.[30] Chronic pain and depression are closely related and often co-morbid. 'Pain is depressing, and depression causes and intensifies pain. People with chronic pain have three times the average risk of developing psychiatric symptoms – usually mood or anxiety disorders – and depressed patients have three times the average risk of developing chronic pain'.[31] Home, friendships, work lives, financial security are all affected, and aggravate psycho-physical-emotional symptoms. Chronic pain is one of the most common health conditions in the Western hemisphere, reaching epidemic proportions in recent decades. A Public Health England Survey published in 2017 found that approximately one third of the population reported chronic pain symptoms, a figure which rose to forty percent in the most deprived areas.[32] The 'vast majority' of the patients attending the pain clinic which hosted our study, as the consultants with whom we collaborated explained, 'are living on benefits, and they've had a constant assault on their living standards for many years'.[33] In this session the group read Doris Lessing's short story 'A Sunrise on the Veld', which describes a teenage boy's rising before dawn, leaving his home-farm behind for the chilly wild to go hunt. 'I am fifteen! Fifteen! [...] There is nothing I can't become, nothing I can't do [...] I contain the world. I can make of it what I want.' Then, out of the depth of the morning silence comes the sound of pain, a frightened scream. He comes upon a small buck, trapped between two trees, 'black ragged tufts of fur standing up irregularly all over it, with patches of raw flesh beneath':

[29]   Josie Billington et al., 'A Comparative Study of Cognitive Behavioural Therapy and Shared Reading for Chronic Pain', *Medical Humanities*, 43.3 (2017), pp. 155–65. The project was approved by NHS Research Ethics. All quoted material from the study uses pseudonyms.

[30]   Billington et al., 'Reading and Chronic Pain', p. 142.

[31]   Billington et al., 'Reading and Chronic Pain', p. 146.

[32]   Public Health England, 'Chronic Pain in Adults', 2017. <https://assets.publishing. service.gov.uk/media/5fc8c6b78fa8f547585ed7f3/Chronic_Pain_Report.pdf>.

[33]   Andrew Jones and James Ledson, 'Reading in a Clinical Context', *Reading and Mental Health*, ed. Billington, pp. 433–41 (p. 435).

All the time the creature screamed, in small gasping screams, and leaped drunkenly from side to side, as if it were blind [...] Around him the grass was whispering and alive [...] black with ants, great energetic ants that took no notice of him, but hurried and scurried towards the fighting shape [...] the writhing blackness that jerked convulsively with the jerking nerves [...] The buck could no longer feel; its fighting was a mechanical protest of the nerves [...] He gripped the gun between his knees and felt in his own limbs the myriad swarming pain of the twitching animal that could no longer feel [...] His clothes were soaked with the sweat of that other creature's pain.[34]

During the reading aloud of this passage, one group member, Alison, instinctively covered her eyes. Sonya shuddered and turned away. It is one of the very few texts the group read which involved physical pain. Group members rarely spoke directly about their pain, in fact. Perhaps the force of the response can be explained by *realism* having almost the quality of *literalism* here. The response of the whole group was demonstrably visceral. 'He gets the pain while the buck can't,' said Sam. 'You're taking on the pain and the feelings of that animal [pressing his fist against his chest, grimacing]. You can *feel* the pain. It's sickening'.[35] Sam was visibly revulsed by the boy's pain. The boy, for his part, is, equivalently, feeling the pain in his own flesh, 'limbs' and 'sweat' on the animal's behalf. The pain which both character and reader feel actually 'belongs' to the buck. But it is a pain which the buck itself can 'no longer feel'. Here is the paradox. The pain, strictly, is *not there*. Nor is it ever actually 'real'. It is a fictional *invention* of the writer in the first place; it is *imagined* by the boy in the story, and by Sam, the reader, outside of it. Nonetheless pain is a wholly real experience at this moment. It is palpably felt, and 'taken on', by Sam and his fellow-readers. What is happening? Not empathy merely, that is for sure.

In *Dreaming by the Book,* Elaine Scarry offers a compelling theoretical account of the kind of literary reading phenomenon witnessed above, whereby mere verbal notation can be transformed into a primary emotional event that is painfully personal and close:

---

[34] Doris Lessing, 'A Sunrise on the Veld', *This Was the Old Chief's Country* (London, 2003), 26–34 (pp. 31–2).
[35] Cited in Josie Billington, *Is Literature Healthy?* (Oxford, 2016), p. 122, from an unpublished transcript emerging from the reading and chronic pain study. See Billington et al., 'A Comparative Study of Cognitive Behavioural Therapy and Shared Reading for Chronic Pain' (2017); Josie Billington et al., 'A Comparative Study of Cognitive Behavioural Therapy and Shared Reading for Chronic Pain' (Liverpool, 2016). <https://www.liverpool.ac.uk/media/livacuk/iphs/PDFComparing,Shared,Reading,and,CBT,for,Chronic,Pain.pdf.>.

Unlike painting, music, sculpture, theatre and film, [the verbal arts] are almost devoid of *actual* sensory content. There is nothing mysterious about the fact that a painting approximates or exceeds the vivacity of the visible world, since it is itself a piece of the visible world [...] saturates our eyes with sensory experience. The same is true of music (why should it not share the vividness of the audible world when it is itself audible?), of sculpture (which inhabits, and thus participates in, the vividness of the tactile and visible realms), and of theatre and film (brimming with auditory and visual commitments). But verbal art, especially narrative, is almost bereft of any sensual content. Its visual features [...] consist of monotonous small black marks [...] It has *no* acoustical features. Its tactile features are limited to the weight of its pages.[36]

'By what miracle', then, Scarry asks, 'is a writer able to incite us to bring forth mental images that resemble in their quality [our own] perceptual acts'.[37] Literary narrative, she posits, offers 'instructions for the production of actual sensory content'. The formulation Scarry uses is meant deliberately to 'shift the site of mimesis from the object to the mental act':

We habitually say of images in novels that they 'represent' or 'are mimetic of' the real world. But the mimesis is perhaps less in them than in our seeing of them. In imagining Catherine [Earnshaw's] face, we perform a mimesis of actually seeing a face, in imagining the sweep of the wind across the moors, we perform a mimesis of actually hearing the wind. Imagining is an act of perceptual mimesis.[38]

By analogy, when the readers see and experience Pip's degradation at Miss Havisham's, or the hunter-boy's response to creaturely suffering, they are cued by the words of the text to perform their own feat of imaginative realism, helped in Shared Reading, of course, by the fact that the authorial 'instructions' *are* mediated sensorily, through the vocal-emotional sound of a human voice reading. 'It seems amazing that what in perception comes to be imitated is not only the sensory outcome (the way something looks or sounds or feels beneath the hands) but the actual structure or production that gave rise to the perception, that is the material conditions that made it look, sound and feel the way it did'.[39] In partial explanation of this happening Scarry refers the reader to neuroscientific research showing that 'in making mental images we

36   Elaine Scarry, *Dreaming by the Book* (New York, 2001), p. 5.
37   Scarry, *Dreaming by the Book*, p. 7.
38   Scarry, *Dreaming by the Book*, p. 6.
39   Scarry, *Dreaming by the Book,* p. 9.

draw on the very neural mechanisms that we use in perceiving'.[40] A decade or so later, Vittorio Gallese (one of the neuroscientists who discovered mirror neurons) and Hannah Wojciehowski cite Scarry's work in defining a concept which verifies her intuition, that of 'embodied simulation'.[41] The term refers to how 'the activity of reading fictional narratives activates the same neural circuits that we use in everyday life – [brain] circuits that underpin all of our own actions, emotional and sensory experiences':

> When we navigate the parallel world of fictional narrative, we basically rely on the same brain-body resources shaped by our relation to mundane reality [...] the tears we weep when we are moved by a fictional narrative clearly are not 'quasi-tears'. Similarly, the strong feelings of anguish and compassion for characters we experience when reading their fictional misgivings and misadventures are not 'quasi-emotions', as they aren't less real than those we experience when engaged with real others; they can, in fact, sometimes be much stronger.

What constitutes empathy or imagination in reading fiction is actually the 'reuse of [our] neural sensorimotor' determined by the 'preexisting biological norms and constraints, which make it possible'.[42]

What is intuitively valuable about these complementary and compatible theories is the primacy and centrality given to the reader's experience. Scarry emphasises the mind. 'The material on which a writer works is not as with other artists, paint or wood or stone or canvas or paper or strings or reeds [...] but something alive'. The writer composes instructions for 'the live tissue of [the minds] that will mentally recompose the pictures as they read [...] the quick of the human mind – that is already itself in motion'.[43] Gallese and Wojciehowski emphasise the body. The brain-body resources that underpin our real-life experiences

> provide the functional scaffold and the building blocks that our engagement with fictional characters rearranges by means of different forms of framing

---

[40]   Scarry, *Dreaming by the Book,* pp. 255–6.
[41]   Vittorio Gallese and Hannah Wojciehowski, 'How Stories Make Us Feel: Toward An Embodied Narratology', *California Italian Studies*, 2.1 (2011) [unpaginated].
[42]   Vittorio Gallese and Hannah Wojciehowski, 'Embodied Simulation and Emotional Engagement with Fictional Characters', *The Routledge Companion to Literature and Emotion*, ed. P. Hogan et al. (London, 2022), pp. 61–73 (pp. 62–3).
[43]   Scarry, *Dreaming by the Book*, p. 241.

[...] These cues, which fiction creatively reconfigures, are the expression of social practices that readers recognize because they are part of readers' lives.

At the same time, embodied simulation does not consist of 'stereotyped and undifferentiated' responses. It is context-dependent and idiosyncratically linked to individuals' personal, historical, social and biological identities.[44] What accounts for the personally-felt 'pain' which is suffered in the reading encounters we have witnessed, then, is the fact that the living biological tissue of the reader is engaged, including everything (social, bio-physical, emotional, psychological) that has shaped the living sensate being. This, as Gallese and Wojciehowski point out, is why reading mobilises our capacities for empathic co-feeling with others so powerfully, because that co-feeling registers within our own bodies.[45] Still, there is nothing so far to explain why viscerally experiencing the class shame or physical pain of a fictional creation as if it were your own, and doing so in part *because* it *is* or closely resembles your own, should have therapeutic value. Our chronic pain study, like our study of reading and depression, showed clear benefit to participants, alleviating psycho-emotional and even physical symptoms. What psychological benefits do these 'real' emotions, experienced inside a realist fictional text, actually accomplish?

I have had recourse myself, in seeking to understand this phenomenon, to the geometrical language, if I may so call it, of the psychoanalyst Wilfred Bion. 0 is the sign Bion uses to signify the really real, the reality of anything whatever, Immanuel Kant's thing-in-itself. Locating and articulating the really real truth of the individual psyche, is, for Bion, the aim of psychoanalysis. While, however, psychotherapy goes in search of 0, crucially, 0 can neither be known nor thought: it must be, and can only be, *experienced*. Conversely, the point of thus experiencing 0 is to transform its emotional reality into a thought about inchoate emotional experience which makes that experience usable for growth. This is the psychoanalytic task. The reciprocal rules then are these: no growth without thought (where thought is commensurate with emotional experience and psychic truth); no commensurate (and therefore serviceable) thought without contact with 0 (the deep reality of emotional experience). 0, which cannot itself be thought, is nonetheless the necessary occasion and crucible of thought.[46]

---

[44]   Gallese and Wojciehowski, 'Embodied Simulation and Emotional Engagement', pp. 62–3.
[45]   Gallese and Wojciehowski, 'Embodied Simulation and Emotional Engagement', pp. 62–3.
[46]   See Bion, *Transformations,* pp. 147–9; and *Attention and Interpretation*

While classic theories of realism, which emphasise the genre's honouring of 'everyday practical reality', and post-modern characterisations of its cultural role, as a consoling 'fantasy' in the service of capitalist hegemony, render this literary tradition inimical to engagement with ultimate reality, I have argued on several occasions elsewhere that the latter might be regarded, on the contrary, as part of realism's stock-in-trade.[47] It is for this reason that the two passages of realist prose fiction discussed above readily offer examples of the reciprocal dynamic Bion posits between deeply experiencing the really real and the need (and difficulty) of knowing or thinking it. Here, together, are the immediate outcomes for the protagonists of the events quoted earlier:

I was so humiliated, hurt, spurned, offended, angry, sorry – I cannot hit on the right name for the smart – God knows what its name was – that tears started to my eyes. [...] I looked about me for a place to hide my face in, and got behind one of the gates in the brewery-lane, and leaned my sleeve against the wall there, and leaned my forehead on it and cried. As I cried, I kicked the wall and took a hard twist at my hair; so bitter were my feelings, and so sharp was the smart without a name, that needed counteraction.[48]

He was feeling with his whole body: this is what happens, this is how things work [...] *Nothing could alter it.* The knowledge of fatality, of what has to be, had gripped him for the first time in his life; [...] it had entered his flesh and his bones and grown in to the furthest corners of his brain and would never leave him [...] Suffering, sick, and angry [...] he found that the tears were streaming down his face [...] For a moment he would not face it. He was a small boy again, kicking sulkily at the skeleton, hanging his head, refusing to accept the responsibility [...] Really, he was tired. He walked heavily, not looking where he put his feet. When he came within sight of his home he stopped, knitting his brows. There was something he had to think out. The death of that small animal was a thing that concerned him, and he was by no means finished with it. It lay at the back of his mind uncomfortably. Soon, the very next morning, he would get clear of everybody and go to the bush to think about it.[49]

(London, 1970), p. 26.

47   Erich Auerbach, *Mimesis: The Representation of Reality in Western Literature* (Princeton, 2003), p. 554; Jean-François Lyotard, 'Answering the Question: What is Postmodernism?', trans. R. Drurand, *The Postmodern Condition*, trans. G. Bennington and B. Massumi (Manchester, 1999), pp. 71–82. See Josie Billington and Philip Davis, 'Realism's Concealed Realities', *Synthesis:An Anglophone Journal of Comparative Literary Studies*, 3 (2011), pp. 18–29; Billington, *Is Literature Healthy?*
48   Dickens, *Great Expectations*, pp. 62–3.
49   Lessing, 'A Sunrise on the Veld', pp. 32–4.

What we witness in these passages is the emergence of proto-thoughts, as Bion describes them: these are the undigested emotional matter that seeks articulation, and whose first expression is often the most primitive in biological and evolutionary terms: 'The tears started to my eyes.' 'He found that the tears were streaming down his face.' If thoughts do not adequately transform the emotional trauma, then these instinctive reactions ('Suffering, sick, and angry') – whether evasive ('I looked about me for a place to hide my face in'), or physically and violently expressive in relation to self and the outer world ('I kicked the wall and took a hard twist at my hair', '[I] kicked sulkily at the skeleton') – become repetitive and injurious patterns of behaviour in place of thought. That this might be a critical moment of such formation in these adolescent (or near-adolescent) boys' lives was not lost on the readers in the Shared Reading groups.

[The Bootle group]:

> *Ivan:* He knows the feeling doesn't he, but he doesn't know what to call it.

> *Amy:* 'So sharp was the smart without a name that needed counteraction.' He feels physically hit, injured, so sore. But if he can't give it a name, he can't fight back at it.

> *Ray:* It's becoming who he is. The bitterness he feels is against himself.[50]

[The pain clinic group]:

> *Sonya:* It's shocking to him. It's a new part of his life that he's not experienced before. He's come to a realisation that maybe he's not in control of everything. I think he's gone out of that window at four in the morning and come back a man.

> *Sam:* But I suppose, being fifteen, you're neither one or the other. It says, 'For a moment he would not face it. He was a small boy, kicking sulkily at the skeleton'. He's so tired on the way home. Before he was 'I am not tired, I am the master of sleep', now he's exhausted. Because he's gone through so much in that short period.

---

[50]   See footnote 24.

Alison: But he's gonna go out tomorrow and think about it again. He's going to have to go back and look at all his thoughts.[51]

Central to these passages and responses is Bion's recognition that emotional experience *requires* a thought to think, hold and contain it. This is a psychic necessity, if the damaging experience itself is not to overwhelm one and 'become' who one is. Thought is the 'needed counteraction'.

For the readers themselves as they imaginatively encounter the protagonists' emotional trauma, the literary work makes the experience so primary, so 'really real', as it acts on their 'living' mental, emotional and physical 'tissue', that it, too, demands thought. Here are two instances, one from each Shared Reading group. First, Linda, on *Great Expectations*. As Clare Ellis explains, Linda, in her 50s, is a survivor of domestic violence both as a child and as an adult, has learning disabilities and suffers from depression and anxiety. She lives alone (her daughter is currently in care) and feels very isolated. Before coming to the group, she had never read novels or poetry. She spoke very little during the sessions but listened, consistently and carefully. At the end of the first session, she told Clare: 'I think it's a bit scary. [Laughs nervously] It's frightening – you know, I'm scared'. In a later follow-up interview, Linda said of her first encounter with *Great Expectations*: 'my body went umph and I cringed my teeth. That bit about Pip at first was hard ... I thought he was very – well he reminded me slightly of myself'. Asked how this felt for her, Linda said: 'It does help because you can see it – I can see it – in something else. But it's painful as well because Pip has been through pretty harsh and rough things'.[52] Later Linda spoke of how she often felt her own story had been overlooked and how she would like to write it down if she was able to spell properly. Of the reading group, she said: 'Sometimes before the group I feel restless and anxious – like I can't settle – but then when I go into the group I can start to relax ... The reading group gets it out in the open. Whatever is hidden up and out – if you've got feelings put down they've got to come up and out otherwise your head would explode'.[53]

Now, Sam, on 'A Sunrise on the Veld' (using an amalgam of Sam's words in the session and later at interview): the story recalled several 'upsetting' experiences which Sam (now a father in his forties) had had as a younger man working on farmland in Australia. 'It takes me right back – "the fresh acid smell in his nostrils". I've smelt that. It's your body reacting to what you're

51   See footnote 35.
52   Ellis, 'The Sharing of Stories', p. 153.
53   Billington et al., 'An Investigation into the Therapeutic Benefits of Reading in Relation to Depression and Well-Being', p. 72.

seeing, what you're sensing.' Sam had witnessed the killing of a pig, shot in the head with a rifle:

> The pig looked up – as if wondering 'what was that' – and then started munching on the ground again. It was as if what was happening didn't concern the pig at all. It took five shots before the pig was dead. It was the way the pig looked up. Not realising. Not suffering. It doesn't understand that you're killing it, because it doesn't understand it's alive and it can die. And that played on my mind. It was horrible [forehead painfully furrowed]. I don't think I've come to terms with that really. All these years later, it still haunts me.[54]

This urgent, gut memory of an experience which, like the boy's, was 'by no means finished with', that did not end with the death of the animal which itself had no need to come to terms with it, was not only summoned by the story's transmission of the young boy's 'rage, misery and protest' at 'how things work'. The two lives, fictional and real, seemed barely separable as Sam spoke: 'He says "I can't stop it. I can't stop it. There is nothing I can do". Even though those creatures are so small, he still can't do anything. He's become very small in the scenery now, kind of shrunk into the grass, where he contained everything before. He seemed huge and the world was in him, and now ... You feel helpless.'[55] Sam is here beginning to do the thinking, on the boy's behalf and on his own, that the emotional experience insistently called for. Literary realism's representation of experience is not just itself an occasion for thought. Rather, it makes real personal emotion, hitherto buried or regretted or evaded for being too painfully intractable, an experience that *can* be thought. It gives emotional experience *form*, visibility ('I can see it', said Linda). It has present *reality* at every level of being.

Third Space

What I have described above might be understood in terms of the therapeutic relationship which Martha Nussbaum posits between book and reader, based on psychoanalyst D. W. Winnicott's developmental theories. Literary works, Nussbaum argues, operate as 'transitional objects' – the infant's treasured toy or cloth which substitutes for the absent care-giver – insofar as it is through them that we are able to 'explore aspects of our own vulnerability in

---

[54]   See footnote 35.
[55]   See footnote 35.

a safe and pleasing setting'.[56] For Winnicott, the transitional object is the first version of illusion or play in which the infant engages. It is play's (and literary narrative's) role in 'reality-testing' – examining 'me-' in relation to 'not-me-' experience – which Nussbaum seems to have most in mind. Realist narrative might be regarded, as the foregoing examples suggest, as a rigorous emotional and cognitive test in this respect. Both are closely related to a Winnicottian concept that is, perhaps, more compellingly analogous to *Shared* Reading specifically: that of transitional or '*potential* space' which renders the object neither internal nor external.

The transitional object, says Winnicott, 'start[s] each human being off with what will always be important to them, i.e. a neutral area of experience which will not be challenged'. This intermediate area, between internal reality and external life, between what is subjectively conceived and objectively perceived 'is necessary for the initiation of the child's relationship with the world'. It is assumed that 'the task of reality-acceptance is never completed, that no human being is free from the strain of relating inner and outer reality'; that 'of every individual who has reached to the stage of being a unit with a limiting membrane and an outside and an inside' there is this 'third part of the life of a human being' with 'direct continuity' with the earliest transitional phenomena:

> The object is a symbol of the union of the baby and the mother [...] It is at the place in space and time where and when the mother is in transition from being (in the baby's mind) merged in with the infant and alternatively being experienced as an object to be perceived rather than conceived of. The use of an object symbolises the union of two now separate things, baby and mother, *at the point in time and space of the initiation of their separateness.*

This intermediate experience not only constitutes the greater part of the infant's experience: '[I]t is in this potential space between the subjective object and the object objectively perceived' – the point in time and space where we first overcame the separation of loneliness – that the baby 'from the beginning ... has maximally intense experience'. 'It is not instinctual satisfaction that makes a baby begin to be, to feel that life is real, to find life worth living [...] [It is] a well-established capacity in the individual for total experience [...] in the area of transitional phenomena'. The essential precondition in the achievement of 'the separation that is not a separation but a form of union' is the infant's absolute confidence in the love of the mother. 'Where there is such trust and reliability, there is potential space, one that

[56]   Martha Nussbaum, *Upheavals of Thought: Intelligence of the Emotions* (Cambridge, 2001), p. 238.

can become an infinite area of separation which the baby, child, adolescent, adult may fill with playing [...] with all that eventually adds up to a cultural life'. That is to say, 'throughout life' the intermediate space 'is retained in the intense experiencing which belongs to the arts and religion and to imaginative living'.[57] Play expands into creative living and into all cultural experience.

The importance of this theory to the phenomenon of Shared Reading and its therapeutic potential seems two-fold. First, and perhaps most obviously, Shared Reading opens to its participants, often for the first time, the cultural heritage which, so Winnicott theorises, both springs from the first and most intense of human experiences – coming into individual being, life, reality – and fulfils the human needs first intuited in that space. 'Bringing books to life' has long been The Reader's mission, and is (indirectly) closely aligned with Winnicott's model of cultural value as meeting urgent, primal needs. The project's founder, Jane Davis, says, '[o]ver the last 100 years or so, the loss of the religious as a reputable discourse in common life has led to a poverty of language, and thus to a poverty of contemplative thought and feeling about what we are, and what we need. We need some inner stuff, scaffolding to help us get around our inside space, something to help us map, explore and even settle those places where we are still primitive'. Otherwise, 'what are we to do with that unnamed place, space, sense?'[58]

Second, and relatedly, Shared Reading provides 'a third area of human living', one neither inside the individual nor outside in the world of external reality. The power of the literary work, as we have seen, especially when read aloud, catalyses an emotionally warm shared atmosphere which permeates the membrane separating inner and outer. 'The book draws us all into another world,' as Amy in the Bootle group said, creating a trustworthy 'neutral' area for those who often cannot find, or perhaps have never fully experienced, such protected space for themselves.[59] It is not difficult to appreciate how needful this might be for a person like Linda whose internal and external reality feels unsafe. The 'special feature' of this intermediate space, Winnicott writes, is that *it depends for its existence on living experiences* not on inherited tendencies'. Compared to the relative 'fixity' of the external environment, on the one hand, and psychic reality (insofar as it is maturely established as an organised personality), on the other, the third way of living possesses 'infinite variability' as an 'area for manoeuvre' because 'the third area *is a product of the experiences of the individual person in the environment that obtains*' [my

[57]   D. W. Winnicott, *Playing and Reality* (London, 1971), pp. 47, 11, 15, 3, 114, 116, 16.
[58]   Davis, 'The Reading Revolution', pp. 133–4.
[59]   Ellis, 'The Sharing of Stories', p. 155.

emphasis].[60] What this means, for example, is that in the environment of the reading group, Linda's all-too fixed (and albeit sadly untold) story can indeed, at some level, be re-written. Or, more simply, that third space can be personally recovered in some form. So, for instance, the description of the boy getting up before the dawn, full 'with the joy of living', in 'A Sunrise on the Veld', recalled to Sonya how she had once made room in her life for contemplation.[61] 'I used to love taking the dog first thing in the morning. I liked the feeling of being the first up. There's no real sense of time. Out and alive.'[62] Though Sonya was referring to a time before the onset of illness ('I *used* to love'), her tone was more exhilarated than regretful. No longer in first youth, and severely disabled, she is put in touch here, through the sudden and vital energy borrowed from the text, with a space or dimension of self where she feels most alive. This third area 'can be looked upon as sacred to the individual in that it is here that the individual experiences creative living'.[63]

Perhaps it is no historical accident that the theory of object relations which frames Winnicott's thinking, with its emphasis on the interpersonal and intersubjective, should have originated in Britain in the same period as the establishment of the welfare state. For it addresses the deeply personal and individual welfare that a system of large-scale collectivised responsibility for a national community must inevitably, at one level (as a necessary compromise in utility), leave out. Remarkably, Shared Reading instantiates the ideals of both visions of human relationship; it is at once democratic and personal, equal and individual, publicly shared and privately meaningful. Like the realist novel, on whose literary ambitions The Reader's mission consciously builds, Shared Reading comprises both levels of reality, the ordinary and 0, and keeps open the contact between them.

[60]   Winnicott, *Playing and Reality,* pp. 129, 127, 124, 125.
[61]   Lessing, 'A Sunrise on the Veld', p. 58.
[62]   Billington et al., 'A Comparative Study of Cognitive Behavioural Therapy and Shared Reading for Chronic Pain' (2016), pp. 60–1.
[63]   Winnicott, *Playing and Reality,* p. 121.

2

Instruments of Imagined Power: New York's Living Newspaper Unit and the Theatre of Welfare

MATTHEW HOLMAN

The Federal Theatre is a pioneer theatre because it is part of a tremendous rethinking, redreaming, and rebuilding of America. Being a part of a great nation-wide work project, our actors are one, not only with the musicians playing symphonies in Federal orchestras; with writers recreating the American scene; with artists compiling from the rich and almost forgotten past the Index of American Design; but they are also one with thousands of men building roads and bridges and sewers; one with doctors and nurses giving clinical aid to a million destitute men, women, and children ... Whatever it may or may not become, its deep and not-to-be-forgotten immediate significance for American life is that papa's got a job.

—Hallie Flanagan, 'The Drama of the Federal Theatre Project'.[1]

After Black Friday, or the Wall Street Crash, in October 1929, there were four million unemployed Americans within a year, rising three-fold to twelve million by 1932, or around ten percent of the population. Markers of poverty were found in most towns and cities, from the abandoned family-run shop on the high street, to the unmanned factory, to crowds snaking around the block hoping for bread and work, as well as the proliferation of 'Hoovervilles' – or homeless shantytowns – in empty car parks and under highways. With 'a clear mandate from the people', Franklin D. Roosevelt was elected to the White House after a pounding win over Edgar Hoover's Republicans, and with him a new liberal vision for the United States which signalled a decisive legislative shift to state intervention in the economy.[2] For many, there

[1]   Hallie Flanagan, 'The Drama of the Federal Theatre Project', *New Deal Thought*, ed. Howard Zinn (Indianapolis and Cambridge, 1966), pp. 172–9 (p. 178).
[2]   Franklin Delano Roosevelt, 'Text of the Inaugural Address: President for Vigorous Action', *The New York Times*, 5 March 1933.

was a kindling of hope. In his inaugural speech, Roosevelt demanded 'that Americans must forswear the conception of the acquisition of wealth which, through excessive profits, creates undue private power over private affairs and, to our misfortune, over public affairs as well.'[3] While Roosevelt recognised 'the greater ability of some to earn more than others', his commitment to relief and welfare programmes chimed with patriotic sensibilities of the constitutional right to the pursuit of happiness, and asserted that 'the ambition of the individual to obtain for him and his family a proper security, a reasonable leisure, and a decent living throughout life is an ambition to be preferred to the appetite for great wealth and great power.'[4]

In his first term, which commenced on 6 May 1935, Roosevelt established the Works Progress Administration (WPA), an employment relief programme principally designed to support jobseekers to carry out public works projects, from mural-making in libraries, schools, and hospitals, to the construction of new municipal buildings and roads. Led by Harry Hopkins, Roosevelt's steely chain-smoking lieutenant, an intellectual architect of New Deal liberalism and future envoy to Winston Churchill during the Second World War, the WPA established four art divisions as part of Federal Project Number One. The Federal Art Project, which is best known for its support of social realist painting and narrativised struggles of American labour in murals, as well as launching the early careers of the Abstract Expressionists, the Federal Music Project (which established thirty-four new orchestras across the country, and which underwrote foundational studies on cowboy, Creole, and 'Negro' music), the Federal Writers Project (which funded novelists, poets, journalists, teachers, and librarians, and which produced state-by-state guidebooks that captured the highways and folkways of America), and the Federal Theatre Project.[5]

---

3   Roosevelt, 'Text of the Inaugural Address'.
4   Roosevelt, 'Text of the Inaugural Address'.
5   There has been renewed popular interest in Federal One over the last decade, which has often sought to find parallels and areas of policy comparison between the New Deal response to the Great Depression and a cautious neoliberal state during the Great Recession and the post-Covid 19 inflationary crisis. See, for the Federal Music Project, Peter Gough, *Sounds of the New Deal: The Federal Music Project in the West (Music in American Life)* (Champaign IL, 2015); for the Federal Writers Project, Scott Borchert, *Republic of Detours: How the New Deal Paid Broke Writers to Rediscover America* (New York, 2021); for the Federal Dance Project, Elizabeth Cooper, 'Tamaris and the Federal Dance Theatre 1936–1939: Socially Relevant Dance Amidst the Policies and Politics of the New Deal Era', *Dance Research Journal*, 29.2 (1997), pp. 23–48. Two recent books have been particularly useful for my own research: Rania Karoula, *The Federal Theatre Project, 1935–1939: Engagement and Experimentation* (Edinburgh, 2021); and Jordana Cox, *Staged News: The Federal*

The Federal Theatre Project (FTP) was established in 1935, and was operative until 1939, when the twin wrecking balls – congressional conservative attacks and anti-communist persecutions led by the Dies Committee on one side, and the march to war on the other – brought down the programme for good. The Project was run by the Harvard-educated Hallie Flanagan, a close friend of Hopkins who, by the mid-1930s, had established a formidable reputation for radical leftist theatre productions, most famously her adaptation of *Can You Hear Their Voices?* by Whittaker Chambers (who was then a Soviet spy), at Vassar College's Experimental Theatre (one of the country's most advanced dramatic units) in 1931. The vexed question over whether the theatre was a worthy beneficiary of debt-based spending for the federal government during the Great Depression was defended, often forcefully, as Hopkins and Flanagan travelled the country by train to promote Federal One relief support of the arts in public, and fine-tune the details of the FTP in private.

As Flanagan recounted in *Arena,* when the pair stopped at Iowa State University, one of the assembled yelled 'Who's going to pay for all that?'. Hopkins, as Flanagan recalled, was as calm as ever: this was, after all, 'the question they had been waiting for'.[6] This was his moment to unfasten his tie, take it off and roll up his sleeves. In his Iowan drawl, the homecoming statesman leant forward and said: 'You are'. The American taxpayer would cover the bill because it would benefit all Americans:

> And who better? Who can better afford to pay for it? Look at this great university. Look at these fields, these forests, and rivers. This is America, the richest country in the world. We can afford to pay for anything we want. And we want a decent life for all the people in this country. And we are going to pay for it.[7]

Pay for it they did. The FTP employed more than thirteen thousand theatre professionals (around ninety percent of its $46 million budget), with the remaining ten percent funding space rentals and costume and scenery design. Publicity was also important and the posters promoting many of the FTP productions are some of the most lasting cultural contributions of the programme, such as the Constructivist rectangularity and bold colouring to advertise *Injunction Granted* (fig. 1), or the red-on-black silhouette for *One Third of a Nation* (fig. 2), which anticipated the mid-distanced vantage point Jacob Lawrence used in paintings like *Harlem Street Scene* (1942) and *This*

Theatre Project's Living Newspapers in New York (Journalism and Democracy) (Amherst MA, 2023).

6   Hallie Flanagan, *Arena* (New York, 1940), p. 28.

7   Flanagan, *Arena*, p. 28.

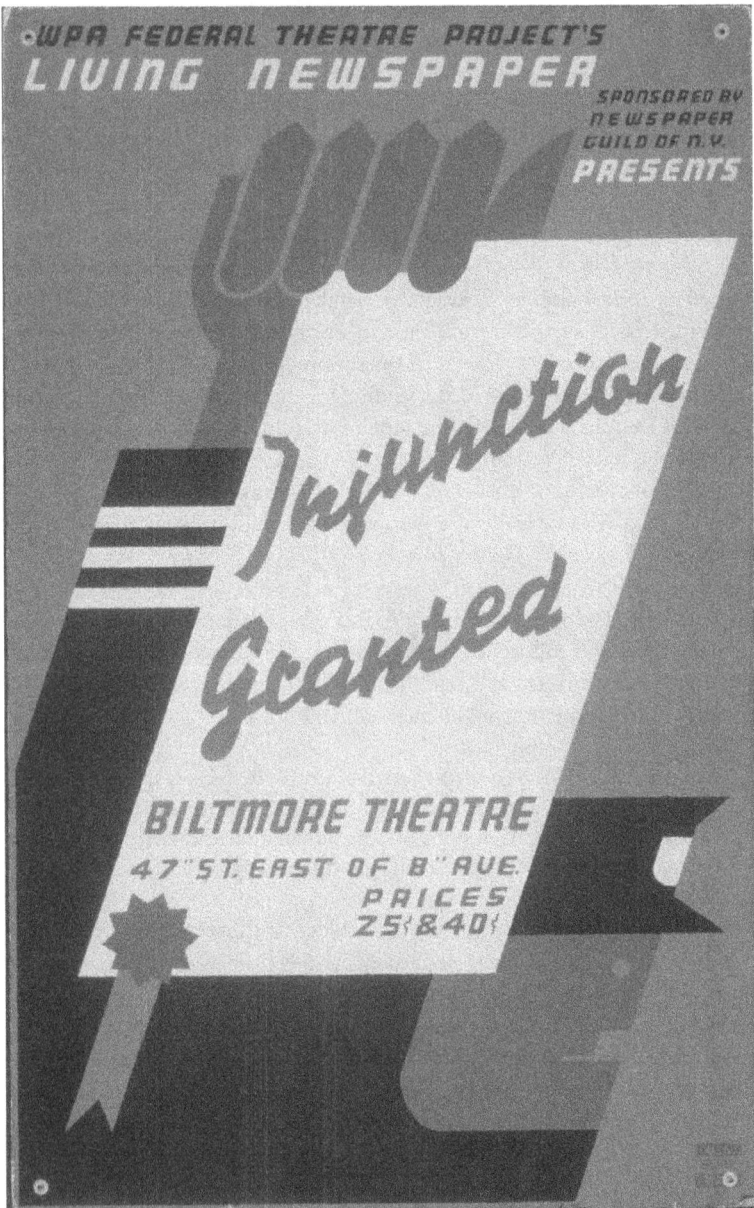

Figure 1. Silkscreen poster for Federal Theatre Project's *Living Newspaper* presentation of *Injunction Granted* at the Biltmore Theatre, 47th St. east of 8th Ave., New York, showing police officer holding up court order. Library of Congress Prints and Photographs Division Washington, D.C. LCCN: 98516142.

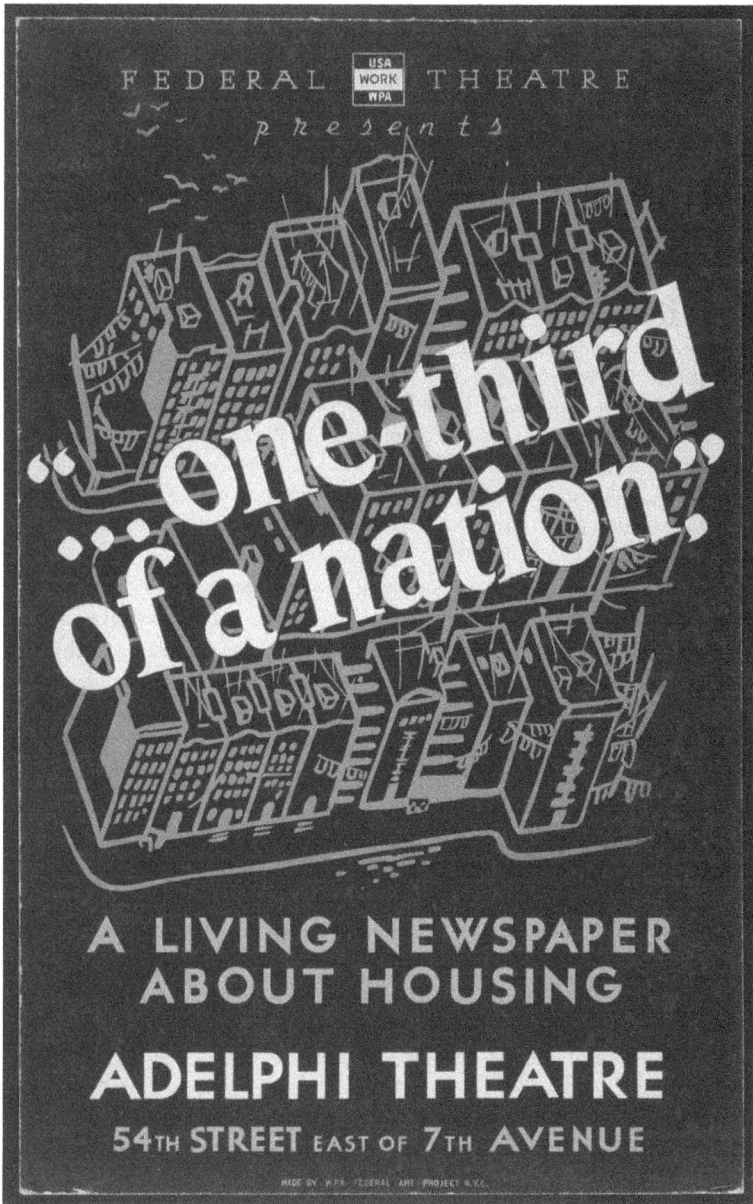

Figure 2. Poster for Federal Theatre Project presentation of *One-Third of a Nation* at the Adelphi Theatre, showing drawing of urban row houses. Library of Congress Prints and Photographs Division Washington, D.C. LCCN: 95509661.

is Harlem (1943). By July 1936, or within a year, the FTP was operating in thirty-one states and averaging national weekly audiences of half a million.

A National Theatre and a Federation of Theatres

Outwardly to her critics, Flanagan used the language of the American frontier and patriotism to defend its purpose:

> The Federal Theatre is a pioneer theatre because it is part of a tremendous rethinking, redreaming, and rebuilding of America. Being a part of a great nation-wide work project, our actors are one, not only with the musicians playing symphonies in Federal orchestras; with writers recreating the American scene; with artists compiling from the rich and almost forgotten past the Index of American Design; but they are also one with thousands of men building roads and bridges and sewers; one with doctors and nurses giving clinical aid to a million destitute men, women, and children.[8]

At the same time, Flanagan stressed that it was 'not a national theatre in the European sense of a group of artists chosen to represent the government' and expressly not 'a *national* theatre [...] rather a *federation* of theatres'.[9] This federation was a broad church, mixed high and low, esoteric and popular styles, reviving popular old forms of performance like vaudeville, while also adapting European avant-garde techniques, and reissuing dramatic classics and foreign-language dramas. The theatre critic Rosamund Gilder wrote that the

> salary scale is low, according to union minimums but few producing organizations in America pay salaries month in and month out, whether a play is in rehearsal or performance, whether it is a hit or a flop [...] Federal Theatre cannot and should not be evaluated on a bookkeeping basis because its reason for being is not theatre, but unemployment, not business or even art, but plain necessity.[10]

Flanagan was a staunch defender of the FTP against its tight-pocketed congressional critics, who sat on both sides of the aisle, and who questioned the value of state-sponsored theatre programmes outside of the commercial market whatever their content, but whose influence was amplified after a

---

8   Flanagan, 'The Drama of the Federal Theatre Project', p. 178.
9   Flanagan, *Arena,* p. 34.
10   Rosamond Gilder, 'The Federal Theatre: A Record', *Theatre Arts Monthly,* 20.6 (1936), pp. 430–8.

series of controversies that saw the FTP accused of Communist-sympathetic agit-prop. From the outset, Flanagan hoped to allay fears:

> It is not a relief project in which artificial jobs are dealt out to people of inferior talent, but rather a plan which begins by saying: in rethinking theatre activity in terms of the art and economics of 1935, we need theatre enterprises which will supplement our already existing splendid New York stage.[11]

Flanagan makes two important points. First, it was necessary to defend the FTP against the reactionary assumption that the programme – *the theatre,* with all the cosmopolitan elitism that implied – was the beneficiary of welfare *per se,* and certainly not the unctuous recipient of governmental assistance akin to those programmes funding better homes for the metropolitan 'worthy poor' or unemployed farmhands, but cultural professionals who now found themselves out of work because of the Great Depression. After all, in her praise of Hopkins's foresight in ringfencing funds for the WPA, Flanagan had said that 'unemployed theatre professionals and their fellow musicians, painters and writers could get as hungry as unemployed engineers'.[12] Second, by using the capitalist's vocabulary of speculative 'enterprises' and arguing that the FTP offered an equally popular alternative to the commercial Broadway performances, Flanagan made a case for an 'economics' of theatre that responded to the crisis of overaccumulation and underconsumption that precipitated the Great Depression.

If the Great Depression was caused by insufficient national demand, then the production of art in its widest sense offered a coherent economic strategy for New Deal policymakers. As Michael Szalay has explained, 'the New Deal [...] placed at the core of modern welfare the conviction that markets were not the most successful means of recording and even creating American publics.'[13] The FTP was forbidden by the WPA to compete with commercial projects. As such, the FTP did not seek to eradicate the market for culture organised by the major profit-driven theatres, but to create more audiences, more consumers, for American-made theatre, while holding out a life-raft for the unemployed to weather the crisis. But Flanagan was a theatre person through and through, a gifted performer who knew well that the best actors might read one line while the audience knew they meant another. Despite

---

[11] Hallie Flanagan, 'Federal Theatre Project', *Theatre Arts Monthly*, 19.11 (1935), pp. 865–70 (p. 865).
[12] Flanagan, 'The Drama of the Federal Theatre Project', p. 172.
[13] Michael Szalay, *New Deal Modernism: American Literature and the Invention of the Welfare State* (Durham NC, 2000), p. 6.

outwardly seeking to promote a federalist 'American' national theatre – indeed, one might argue, *create* an American theatre – Flanagan's vision was to represent disenfranchised constituencies first and foremost.

It is worth remembering that the FTP was the first time the United States government funded the arts in any comparable way to the British, German, and Russian theatre models, which had developed forms of their own and promoted them overseas as forms of cultural diplomacy. Dismissing Broadway as too complacent and middle-class, and mostly catering to escapist cultural demand during crisis, Flanagan sought out playwrights, productions and performances that could articulate not only the kinds of society that its (predominantly working-class and unionised) audience saw all around them, replayed in a kind of feedback loop of affirming experience, but what might be done to alleviate the crisis. As such, for Barry Witham, the 'Federal Theatre Project [...] was a unique and influential experiment in American theatre; not just for its outspoken politics, but because it reimagined the very way that theatre was produced in the United States [...] the first time in the history of the country theatre was subsidized by the federal government, a practice with widespread precedents in Europe and Asia, but one that was totally out of step with free enterprise business practice and a culture that had banned plays in its Second Continental Congress'.[14] Funded by the state for the first time, the FTP was able to do two things. First, in a manner not dissimilar to social realist painting, the FTP looked to represent the conditions that led to the need for a federalist theatre to be funded in the first place. Second, by not being tethered to for-profit incentives or the ideologies of individual patrons, the FTP was able to take more aesthetic risks – the kinds of avant-garde risks that were commonplace in Europe – which may, and did, lead dramatists away from a purely realist programme.

The Living Newspaper: Between *New York Daily News* and Avant-Garde Little Magazine

Under the auspices of the FTP, several smaller collectives and semi-autonomous production companies, or 'Units', were established in cities across the country, from New York City to Durham, North Carolina, Cleveland, Ohio to Los Angeles, each serving distinct, although often overlapping, target audience constituencies. Headed by both white (John Houseman, Orson Welles, in 1935) and Black (Edward Perry, Carlton Moss, H. F. V. Edward,

---

[14]   Barry B. Witham, *The Federal Theatre Project: A Case Study* (Cambridge, 2003), p. 1.

from 1936) directors in its New York branch, which was located at the Lafayette Theatre in Harlem, The Negro Unit produced popular plays like *Macbeth* (1935), which reimagined Shakespeare's tragedy in Haiti.[15] The Children's Theatre sought, as characterised by historian Leslie Elaine Frost, to 'socializ[e] and educat[e] children to appreciate the theatre as a site of civic engagement.'[16] Flanagan described the FTP as a truly national programme, one that benefited from the cultural pluralism of the United States. If 'the Federal Theatre had ever wanted to produce a cycle of plays epitomizing its own projects,' Flanagan wrote, 'New York would have been staged as a living newspaper, Los Angeles as a musical comedy, the South as a folk play, and Chicago as melodrama.'[17]

Established by Morris Watson in 1935, soon after the establishment of the FTP in August 1935, the Living Newspaper dramatised the most pressing social issues of the Great Depression, from the dilapidated slums that sprawled across the inner cities to local outbreaks of venereal disease, to audiences across the country. While many of the agit-prop ideas that underpinned the Living Newspaper in New York can be traced to the American workers' councils of the 1920s, as well as the Prolet-Bühne (a German workers' group founded in 1925), Artef (a Yiddish Workers' Theatre, established in 1926) and the Workers Laboratory Theatre (headquartered at 42 East 12th from 1928), the architects of the Unit borrowed both its name and its documentary focus from troupes in early Soviet Russia and Weimar Germany.[18] In these revolutionary environments, avant-garde dramatists recognised the need to combat illiteracy among the working class, as well as create a permissive culture for radical transformations of society using the emergent modern tools of mass media and spectacle, and so saw live theatre, as Sara Freeman and Robert Shimko have explained, as a 'liminal realm somewhere between an intimate coffeehouse discussion and the massively wide address of a television or radio broadcast'.[19]

[15] Scenes in several New York Living Newspaper Unit productions were set in courtrooms, including *Injunction Granted, One-Third of a Nation, Events of 1935*, and *Power*. George MacEntee's *The Case of Philip Lawrence* (1937) was a courtroom melodrama.

[16] Leslie Elaine Frost, *Dreaming America: Popular Front Ideals and Aesthetics in Children's Plays of the Federal Theatre Project* (Columbus OH, 2013), p. 4.

[17] Flanagan, *Arena*, p. 134. See Elizabeth A. Osborne, *Staging the People: Community and Identity in the Federal Theatre Project* (New York, 2011), pp. 1–14.

[18] See Douglas McDermott, 'The Living Newspaper as a Dramatic Form', *Modern Drama*, 8.1 (1965), pp. 82–94.

[19] Sara Freeman and Robert B. Shimko, 'Theatre, Performance, and the Public Sphere', *Public Theatres and Theatre Publics*, ed. Sara Shimko and Robert B. Freeman

Flanagan travelled to Europe under a prestigious Guggenheim fellowship for much of 1926, and it was on this journey that she began to formulate what would become the aesthetic strategy and ideological choices of the FTP and Living Newspaper. Flanagan visited London, where she felt the theatre was flat and bourgeois, was invited to lunch by the Abbey Players in Ireland, visited Henrik Ibsen's house in Oslo, and had tea with August Strindberg's widow, Harriet Bosse, in Uppsala. But it would be Flanagan's visit to Moscow that had the greatest impact on her. In her remarkably detailed account, Rania Karoula notes how Flanagan's visit, on the ninth anniversary of the October Revolution, exposed her to 'new ways of performing [which] included the living newspaper, mass spectacles re-enacting recent historical events (such as Vladimir Mayakovsky's re-enactment of the storming of the Winter Palace), theatrical trials and literary montage combining slogans, poetry, speeches and other texts', and so witnessed first-hand what the 'Zhivaya Gazeta', or living newspaper, might achieve.[20] While Flanagan saw plays performed at Constantin Stanislavski's Moscow Art Theatre, which was a laboratory for his naturalistic 'system' of embodying psychological depth, and would be repackaged as the 'method' by Stella Adler and Elia Kazan in New York, it was Stanislavski's best student, Vsevolod Meyerhold, and his ideas of 'bio-mechanics', which Flanagan saw as the future of the theatre. Meyerholdian 'biomechanics' transformed the relationship between the actor and the audience, by incorporating techniques like stripping the stage of a curtain to undermine the sequencing of scenes and realistic illusionism, or having the actors emerge from the audience to perform in the aisles, as well as jux-taposing elements from the new media technologies like projected film and newsreels, as well as optical, acoustic, and moving mechanical devices. The avant-garde troupe The Blue Blouse was also important and developed the notion of 'the living newspaper' as 'a presentation in "agit-form" of reality, a "montage of political facts"; it was adaptable to widely different conditions of performance; it was created by the working class [...] – brief, precise, and compelling; it was derived from "popular forms"; and it sought working-class audiences in their own locations.'[21]

But more than theatrical performances and new ideas for the stage, Flanagan saw an expanded sense of what public welfare meant in the Soviet municipality's attitude to architecture and civic planning. While Flanagan conceded that 'the living quarters are extremely congested, and the housing problem unsolved', she noted that 'there is an amazing amount of space

---

(Newcastle upon Tyne, 2012), pp. 1–19 (p. 6).

[20]   Karoula, *The Federal Theatre Project: 1935–1939*, p. 15.

[21]   Robert Leach, *Revolutionary Theatre* (London and New York, 1994), p. 169.

devoted to theatre, museums, libraries, scientific laboratories'; she delighted in the fact that every 'inch in Moscow is used, but rather for public than for private good.'[22] Flanagan's visit to Moscow therefore furnished her with two convictions that would form the ideological and aesthetic basis of the FTP and the Living Newspaper's social theatre: first, that engaging working-class audiences need not be reductive, but could develop popular forms of drama alongside more experimental and avant-garde techniques; second, that the 'public good' was mutually implicated between the theatre and welfare provision, and that the two were co-dependent.

In what follows, I will argue that the Living Newspaper Unit staged performances that depicted the United States judiciary as having failed the working class, most devastatingly during the years of the Great Depression. As explained and historicised by the Voice of the Living Newspaper, an intermediary between the players and the audience, these productions operated as a kind of deliberative democratic exercise to reflect on injustices ranging from the plight of indentured workers in the seventeenth-century colonial project to land accumulation in 1930s New York. The theatre was designed to promote values of democratic participation and collective organisation but was undermined over the extent of its independence from its New Deal paymasters.

Joseph Losey: The Fixer

Around the time that the Living Newspaper was established in 1935, its most important practitioner, Joseph Losey, had just returned from Moscow. Losey is best known for his collaborations with Bertolt Brecht, especially on the 1947 Hollywood and New York productions of *Galileo,* which led to Brecht's interrogation that October by the House Un-American Activities Committee and Losey's swift exile to London to make films with Harold Pinter. Before his life in London, Losey was the most important producer of plays for the Living Newspaper; he also greatly admired Meyerhold and appropriated Russian Living Newspaper ideas, after visiting the Soviet Union in 1935. The Living Newspaper productions were shaped by Brechtian 'epic' theatrical conventions, especially in their sublimation of the coherence of individual characters to situate their position within broader class struggle.[23]

22   Hallie Flanagan, *Shifting Scenes* (New York, 1928), p. 88. See also Lynn Mally, 'Hallie Flanagan and the Soviet Union: New Heaven, New Earth, New Theater', *Americans Experience Russia: Encountering the Enigma, 1917 to the Present,* ed. Choi Chatterjee and Beth Holmgren (London, 2012), pp. 31–49.
23   See James K. Lyon, *Bertolt Brecht in America* (Princeton NJ, 1980).

Nikolay Okhlopkov, Meyerhold's protégé, had created stage-sets that, for Losey, broke down 'the proscenium and present[ed] theatre in the round and the rectangle and the hexagonal as it has never been dreamed of before or since.'[24] Describing his Living Newspaper productions, Losey claimed that it was 'a real breaking down and rebuilding [...] this was Brechtian Theatre, but I didn't know it.'[25]

Losey directed the first Living Newspaper production, *Triple-A Plowed Under,* which ran from 14 March to 2 May 1936 at the Biltmore Theatre. Collectively written by a team of editorial staff and investigative journalists led by Arthur Arent, *Triple-A Plowed Under* focused on the Agricultural Adjustment Act of 1933 and the desperate experiences of Dust Bowl farmers. It was staged in twenty episodic tableaus that documented the long history of American agriculture: War and Inflation, The Price of Milk, Farmers Organize, Milk Strike, The Harvests Burn, Drought, The Sherwood Affair, The Supreme Court. Parts of the stage (which was raised at different levels) were picked up by spots, so the performance could run like a film with cuts from scene to scene. Virgil Thomson's musical score was performed by a large orchestra with only trombones and percussion. The audience witnessed how farmers were enlisted in the First World War and how their contribution was paid in the foreclosure of their mortgages, the deliberate scorching of crops to keep prices up during a sequence of inflationary crises, and the harrowing impact of the 1934 drought which decimated American agriculture. In what would become a concluding trope of the Living Newspaper, the farmers create co-operatives and are significantly assisted by Roosevelt's Agricultural Adjustment Act in 1933, a federal New Deal law designed to boost agricultural prices directed for the farmers themselves, by reducing surpluses and purchasing livestock for slaughter.

Of the Living Newspaper performances, Jordana Cox has written that they 'resist powerful journalistic norms or, more specifically, distinctions: between objectivity and bias, bearing witness and taking action, propaganda and democratic communication, public interest and exclusion.'[26] But after the production of *Triple-A Plowed Under,* how did the Living Newspaper's resistance to these distinctions relate to both the FTP's means of funding, the American state, and its subject matter: affordable housing, the suffering of Dust Bowl farmers, and labour law? New Deal policymakers were taking a calculated risk by supporting programmes like Federal One and, as the his-

---

[24]   Joseph Losey, 'The Individual Eye', *Encore: the Voice of Vital Theatre*, 8.1 (1961), pp. 5–15 (p. 11).
[25]   Losey, 'The Individual Eye', p. 11.
[26]   Cox, *Staged News*, p. 87.

torical record has borne out, especially the Living Newspaper Unit, which proved to be its most controversial section. But the Living Newspaper was controversial because it was accused of seeking to achieve two (mutually incompatible) outcomes. The first was that it staged agitational and participatory theatrical productions, inviting large numbers of unionised workers at vastly subsidised rates as its audience to bear witness to, and to be aggrieved by, the institutional machinery – from the accumulation of land by property speculators, to the plutocratic law courts, and a United States government that refused to implement proper housing reforms – which perpetuated the appalling material conditions of contemporary American society. Second, reactionary critics in the press, Southern Democrats, and culturally conservative Republican congressmen claimed that the Living Newspaper was a mouthpiece and a propaganda tool for extravagant New Deal policies, to which it owed its existence. The danger, then, is in retrospectively viewing the Living Newspaper as a platform to put forward the ideological argument for New Deal programmes, demonstrating the profound need for welfare provision against the right and warding off more militant insurgency against the left.

Another production, and another courtroom drama, *Events of 1935,* which collaged scenes from news events in that year, ran for only thirty-four performances and was the least successful of the Living Newspaper productions. That said, critics were attentive to the deliberative model of 'the American Public, represented by twelve men and women' who neither 'vote[] for or against the motion' which is 'passed by unanimous indifference'.[27] But later in the year, the Living Newspaper staged *Injunction Granted*, which was a rip-roaring hit. *Injunction Granted* was the third production by the Unit and the second by Losey, who once more sought to theatricalise 'the news' through various Brechtian dramaturgical strategies, while at the same time serving to dramatise 'welfare' as a distinctly American project. Losey believed *Injunction Granted* to be 'much more advanced theatre' than *Triple-A Plowed Under,* which he chastised as 'more successful because it was more conventional, and also because it didn't tax the audience at all [...] they didn't have to cope with Virgil Thomson's score, and with the mime either.'[28] The title 'injunction granted' refers to the temporary court orders that empowered employers to wantonly break strikes. Funded by the New Deal, the writers

[27] 'Events of 1935 Dramatized by WPA Actors', *New York Herald-Tribune,* 13 May 1936, transcribed clipping in Library of Congress Federal Theatre Program, Production Records, Container 1047.
[28] Joseph Losey, cited in David Caute, *Joseph Losey: A Revenge on Life* (London, 1994), p. 56.

took the money and ran, making an intensely anti-capitalist play. The final scene resolves that the solution to labour exploitation and suppression of wages was not to be found in Roosevelt's National Industrial Labor Relations Act, passed by Congress in 1935, but by militant labour organising.

While Arent has been often credited with writing the play, it was collectively written by some thirty-five research workers who were briefed on nearly four hundred assignments, as they frantically collated newspaper clippings on court injunctions and labour law history told through the press. As Colin Gardner put it: 'unemployed journalists became the research force for a documentary theatre dramatizing social problems and class conflict from a radical, anti-capitalist perspective.'[29] Arent managed to edit the unwieldly manuscript down, supported by sponsorship from the recently inaugurated Newspaper Guild of New York, the journalists' labour union. Hjalmar Hermanson's set design was inspired by Meyerholdian principles and featured a circular winding ramp that allowed for elevated vantage points for the actors at different moments, which created an atmosphere of closed-off circularity that mirrored the judicial no-man's land of the plot (fig. 3).

Injunction Granted, which performed to full houses for three months, opens in seventeenth-century England on the eve of the British colonial project in north America. The Herald, the intermediary between the theatrical action and the audience, is an updated and individuated Greek chorus. The Herald was performed as though it were a trusted newsboy, and grounds us in this historical moment:

> The British Crown has just acquired a vast colonial empire in the New World. Of this strange, untapped area, but three things are known; it is called America; its inhabitants are red men with high cheekbones; and volunteers must be found to work in the fields.[30]

Officials announced the material prosperity open to the most adventurous in the new world. Their less than subtle mission, though, is to round up indentured servants for the Dutch West India and Virginia Companies. 'There is bread and freedom in America', the officials promise: 'It is an earthly paradise.'[31]

---

[29]   Colin Gardner, 'The Losey-Moscow Connection: Experimental Soviet Theatre and the Living Newspaper', *New Theatre Quarterly*, 30.3 (2014), pp. 249–68 (p. 255).
[30]   The Editorial Staff of the Living Newspaper, *Injunction Granted,* publication no. 9-S, January 1938. Federal Theatre Project Records, George Mason University, Fairfax VA.
[31]   The Editorial Staff of the Living Newspaper, *Injunction Granted.*

Figure 3. Hjalmar Hermanson, '*Injunction Granted*: Sketch no. 1, Unidentified Scenery (Human Figures Silhouetted against Red, White, and Gray)', Library of Congress <https://www.loc.gov/item/musftpsets.200217896/>.

The play then moves historically through various disputes between labour and capital, including the Philadelphia Shoemaker strike of 1806 and the U.S. Steel strike of 1919. Given that the play was written by unionised workers for the Newspaper Guild, it may come as no surprise that in Scene 23, Arthur Hays Salzburger, proprietor of the *New York Times*, says: 'I think reporters have the right to organize [...] but I think it is a right they ought to forgo!'[32] Some critics snarked at the simplicity of these kinds of populist critiques of the newspaper industry. In Scene 25, William Randolph Hearst, proprietor of the *New York Journal* and former Republican Representative for New York's 11th district, is knocked out in a boxing match but is declared the winner by a rigged referee.[33] The critical reception was mixed. The *World Telegram* wrote that even 'if it had not proved its worth with its previous publications, the WPA Living Newspaper more than justified its existence and Uncle Sam's venture on Broadway when it offered *Injunction Granted!* [...] The first half has a vitality, an excitement and an interest seldom found

32 The Editorial Staff of the Living Newspaper, *Injunction Granted*.
33 The Editorial Staff of the Living Newspaper, *Injunction Granted*.

in the more commercial Broadway offerings.'[34] The left-leaning newspapers were ebullient in their praise, with Richard Watts Jr of the *Herald Tribune* celebrating a 'bitter and sardonic cartoon chronicle of the struggles of organized labour against reactionary opposition' and Alexander Taylor of *New Masses* wincing with hyperbole: *Injunction Granted* was in 'spitting distance of being the greatest show on earth.'[35] B. Compton in the *Daily Worker* wrote that each scene 'in itself, stands as a vital and often dynamic piece of drama [...] The technique developed by The Living Newspaper is probably the most valuable contribution of the entire Federal Theatre project to the American theatre.'[36]

In Scene 28, the final scene, entitled 'Labor-1936-Finale', *Injunction Granted* ends with a vociferously polemical address by a character playing the role of John Llewellyn Lewis, leader of organised labour and the driving force behind the Congress of Industrial Organizations (CIO), to an audience of various workers, many members of the Iron and Steel Institute, who have been put down once more by a legal framework to defend the interests of capital. The Judge decrees that any form of collective bargaining is unconstitutional, advocating only for the legality of private bargaining within the contractual framework. The workers respond, announcing the establishment of the CIO. The CIO was formed of twelve unions of the American Federation of Labor, and described by Charles Noble as a 'secession movement' and the 'long-sought organizational vehicle through which the interests of millions of industrial workers in public provision could finally be articulated.'[37] Lewis addressed the disgruntled workers who were looking for solutions after being denied time and time again by the courts on their right to organise:

> My voice is the voice of millions of men and women employed in America's industries, heretofore unorganized, economically exploited and inarticulate. These unions, comprising the Committee for Industrial Organization, adequately reflect the sentiment, hopes and aspiration of thirty million additional Americans who heretofore have been denied by industry and finance the privilege of collective organization. This statement issued by the Iron and Steel Institute is designed to be terrifying to the minds of those who

[34]   'Our Critics Say', *The Living Newspaper* 1.3, Federal Theatre Project Collection (Production Records, Playbills File, 1934-1939), Library of Congress, Washington D.C., <https://www.loc.gov/resource/musftpplaybills.200220862.0/?sp=3&st=image&r=-0.629,-0.018,2.257,1.527,0>.
[35]   'Our Critics Say', The Living Newspaper.
[36]   'Our Critics Say', The Living Newspaper.
[37]   Charles Noble, *Welfare as We Knew It: A Political History of the American Welfare State* (Oxford, 1997), p. 55.

fail to accept the theory that the financial interests behind the steel corporations shall be regarded as the overlords of industrial America. That statement mounts to a declaration of industrial and civil war. It contravenes the law. It pledges the vast resources of the industry against the right of its workers to engage in self-organization of modern collective bargaining. Organized labor in America accepts the challenge of the overlords of steel.[38]

The workers lift up their signs, and the curtain goes down. Audiences would have been familiar with the CIO from the papers. Factory workers in the automobile, rubber, textile, and steel industries were seizing factories across the country, often by force, as they sought official recognition from their employers and from the state union representation from the CIO. It made front page news throughout the year. Rubber workers forcibly took control of the Goodyear plant in Akron, Ohio, three times in four months in the winter of 1935–36. Ira Katznelson recounts how CIO members organised 'huge picket lines and arm[ed] themselves with clubs and sewed-off billiard cues to resist efforts by police to end the disturbance', as those 'involved in this "epic struggle" won a settlement for the new United Rubber Workers (URW) union on March 21', just four months before the opening of *Injunction Granted*.[39] But despite the 'widespread class-conflict rhetoric, even in Congress', as Linda Gordon put it, during that febrile spring and summer in 1936, 'no mass socialist orientation spread' and 'Depression insurgency was remarkably restrained and limited, relative to the severity of the situation'.[40] The ultimate failure of organised labour to form an urban-rural alliance that might have strengthened the hand of the CIO negotiators never materialised, no matter how much Losey transposed the momentum from the newspaper stories of brave, successful striking workers from the picket line onto the stage. But this did not stop Flanagan feeling the heat. Red-faced by scenes of Communist Party hawkers leafleting in the theatre, Flanagan wrote to Losey to revise the ending and delivered an ultimatum: 'Whatever my personal sympathies are I cannot, as a custodian of federal funds, have such funds used as a party tool.'[41] Faced with pressure from

[38] The Editorial Staff of the Living Newspaper, *Injunction Granted*.
[39] Ira Katznelson, *Fear Itself: The New Deal and the Origins of Our Time* (New York, 2013), p. 174.
[40] Linda Gordon, *Pitied but Not Entitled: Single Mothers and the History of Welfare 1890–1935* (Cambridge MA, 1998), p. 250.
[41] Hallie Flanagan, letter to Joseph Losey, reprinted in Stuart Cosgrove, 'Federal Theatre: The Living Newspaper, Strikes, Strategies, and Solidarity', *Nothing Else to Fear: New Perspectives on America in the Thirties*, ed. Stephen Baskerville and Ralph Willett (Manchester, 1985), pp. 236–58 (p. 249).

above, with even Hopkins querying support, Flanagan knew that Losey had crossed the line. The FTP could not align itself so explicitly with the CIO, even if that was what she, and many of her audience of millions, believed was a solution to the ongoing failures of labour to push the New Deal policymakers to the left. Despite Roosevelt's dramatic re-election that year, and anti-capitalist rhetoric in Congress, Flanagan changed approach.

A New New Deal

On the steps of the East Portico of the United States Capitol, and beset by relentless rain, Roosevelt delivered his second inaugural address to the nation in January 1937. In it, he pledged to fulfil the promise of the New Deal in his renewed term of office: 'We are beginning to wipe out the line that divides the practical from the ideal, and in so doing, we are fashioning an instrument of unimagined power'.[42] These ideals were matched by practical commitments. As he looked ahead to signing the Wagner-Steagall Housing and Social Security Acts into law, Roosevelt explained that while it was impossible to 'insure one hundred percent of the population against one hundred percent of the hazards and vicissitudes of life', he expressed the hope that these provisions of an infant welfare state would give 'some measure of protection to the average citizen'.[43] This was not insignificant, especially given that prior to the passage of the national security programme, only twenty-eight states ran old-age pension plans. Roosevelt had every reason to believe that he could match his rhetoric with policy victories in Congress. Polls the previous year had indicated that 77 percent of respondents wanted the government to decisively intervene in the economy and find jobs for everyone who wanted to work; 68 percent wanted the government to levy taxes to invest in public works jobs (such as the Works Progress Administration, what would become the primped pump of the Second New Deal); 74 percent wanted free medical provision for the poor.[44] This strong hand was bolstered by the most dramatic congressional achievement of any political party since 1800. Roosevelt carried forty-six states, four more than in 1933, to

---

[42]   President Franklin Delano Roosevelt, 'Second Inaugural Address', 20 January 1937, *The Avalon Project Documents in Law, History and Diplomacy*. <https://avalon. law.yale.edu/20th_century/froos2.asp>.
[43]   Roosevelt, 'Second Inaugural Address', 20 January 1937.
[44]   See Noble, *Welfare as We Knew It*, p. 75.

Republican candidate Alf Landon's two, winning seventy-six Senate seats and 331 of 435 House seats.[45]

The American welfare state in the New Deal period emerged because several conditions had been met. Despite arguing that his administration had brought 'private autocratic powers into their proper subordination to the public's government', fuelled by combative rhetoric that 'democratic' processes had 'challenged and beaten' those vested interests, his programmes could only be maintained with key capitalists' support.[46] By supporting Roosevelt, they were able to ensure reform suited their purposes by dampening mass discontent, militant labour organising, and directing attention away from a more funda- mental restructuring of the political economy. Nathan Straus, a journalist and then a member of the New York State legislature, was appointed by Roosevelt to head up the newly inaugurated United States Housing Authority in 1937. Straus delivered a speech on 18 November 1937 to the right-wing conference of the United States Chamber of Commerce, in which he appealed to their head and heart on the need for slum clearance. While, on the one hand, Straus asked the business leaders to imagine 'the hopeless plight of a mother trying perhaps to nurse a sick child in a room without light, without air, without running water, and without adequate heat', he assured them that the 'slums must go or the society that tolerates them will', thus risking 'our democratic form of government and our free institutions'.[47]

'I see one-third of a nation ill-housed, ill-clad, ill-nourished'.[48] These words, delivered in Roosevelt's second inaugural address, inspired the title and subject for a new Living Newspaper Unit production, another long history of American class but this time focusing on property accumulation on land, and the early corruption of the New York City Housing Authority (NYCHA), established in 1934 by Mayor Fiorello La Guardia, known for his fizzing energy and diminutive stature. The physical *The Living Newspaper* journal, dated 17 January 1938, ran with the headline 'Slum Housing Dramatized: President Suggested Title'. Also, in 1936, 'one third of a nation' gave its name to a painting, a gift to the Metropolitan Museum of Art from the New York City Works Progress Administration in 1943, by the Cairo-born artist, O. Louis Guglielmi (fig. 4). This surrealist landscape depicts the corner of a drab street, with hostile tenement buildings the colour of burnt copper, recently adorned with an iron floral wreath. This leitmotif of death and dying is fore-

---

[45]   See Noble, *Welfare as We Knew It*, p. 75.
[46]   Roosevelt, 'Second Inaugural Address', 20 January 1937.
[47]   Nathan Straus, 'End the Slums', *New Deal Thought*, ed. Zinn, pp. 158–66 (p. 160).
[48]   Roosevelt, 'Second Inaugural Address', 20 January 1937.

Figure 4. O. Louis Guglielmi, *One Third of a Nation*, 1939. Oil and tempera on masonite, 76.2 cm × 61 cm (30.0 in × 24 in). The Metropolitan Museum of Art, New York. Gift of New York City W. P. A., 1943.

grounded by oblong forms that resemble coffins on the deserted pavement below. The whole scene broods with an elegiac atmosphere.

Unusually for Guglielmi, the scene features no people. In other paintings, such as the sardonically titled *The American Dream* (1935), which sees a silver-hatted soldier humiliate a picketing worker by knocking him to the ground with an implement that resembles a medieval torture device, class violence and the alienation of man from his labour was invariably his subject. *One Third of a Nation* signalled a shift in thinking for the Living Newspaper, away from the discourse of 'civil war' between labour and capital that marked the end of *Injunction Granted*, and towards legislative solutions. The focus of the play is on the long history of property accumulation in New York City and how slum housing had proliferated across the five boroughs. The play begins with a tenement fire, which might have taken place on '397 Madison Street, New York [...] It might be 245 Halsey Street, Brooklyn, or Jackson Avenue and 10th Street, Long Island City'.[49]

Each of these addresses were sites of major tenement fires, as documented in the city's newspapers. *The New York Times'* front page report on 19 February 1924, the one that inspired the play's researcher-playwrights to refer to a fire on Madison Street, detailed a horrific series of avoidable catastrophes: an inferno engulfed a five-storey tenement building on the East Side, which started in the hallway and laid several charred baby carriages to waste, while thirteen were killed, including seven children, who were trapped by the flames or suffocated in their beds. In the published preface to the play, Arent writes:

> Housing, a major problem of modern existence, was filling the columns of our metropolitan newspapers. Legislation was being drafted in Washington, and in our own City and State, groups were working for appropriations, not only for slum clearance, but also for housing projects. The production of *One Third of a Nation* on January 17th, at a time when there was so much activity in the national housing field, indicates the vitality of the Federal Theater.[50]

The play was seen by two hundred thousand in its first run, before being staged with predominantly local casts and directors in Cincinnati, New Orleans, Seattle, Detroit, Portland, Philadelphia and San Francisco throughout 1936. *One-Third of a Nation* was the most successful Living Newspaper

---

[49] Arthur Arent, *One Third of a Nation*, publication no. 44-S, April 1938. Federal Theatre Project Records, George Mason University, Fairfax VA.

[50] Arent, *One Third of a Nation*.

production; it marked a shift towards hope in legislative solutions, as Stuart Cosgrove explains:

> The militant influence within the Unit waned and the form became more closely aligned with the politics of the New Deal. Whilst stressing the significance of this transition, it would be wrong to conclude that the Living Newspaper abandoned its progressive intentions [...] *One Third of a Nation*, whilst ideologically closer to New Deal reformism than *Injunction Granted*, still advocated substantial social change. The Living Newspaper was still a politically progressive form of drama but had now forsaken its revolutionary heritage in favour of the political expediency of social reformism.[51]

Cosgrove is right to note how the Living Newspaper became increasingly dimmed in its revolutionary verve and moved to more conciliatory positions that did not depart, or did not depart so forcefully, from the solutions proposed by the Second New Deal agenda. However, if *Injunction Granted* ended on an appeal to its working-class audience to join a union (and specifically the militant CIO) and to organise against the capitalists and the property developers, withstanding the fact that Lewis called for a 'civil war' to do so, then the force of change embodied by the Republican Mayor LaGuardia taking on one of the last statements in support of the Wagner-Steagall Act may seem like a damp squib. Equally, though, as LaGuardia argues for the 'provisions for 500 million dollars for rehousing the nation', he acknowledges that it is 'a step in the right direction, but only a step - a drop in the bucket!'[52] He then proposes 'a resolution appropriating funds to take care of interest charges and amortization of capital investments for the construction of low rent houses.'[53]

What is also true is that by 1937, on housing at least, significant conflict between organised labour and the New Deal establishment had thinned. Alexander von Hoffman credits the pioneering work of trade unionist Catherine Bauer, a leader at the American Federation of Labor, and one of the powerful 'public housers' who 'against great odds' pushed the 'passage of the landmark Wagner-Steagall Act of 1937 that permanently established public housing in the United States'.[54] Bauer wrote a resolution commit-

---

51   Cosgrove, 'Federal Theatre: The Living Newspaper, Strikes, Strategies, and Solidarity', p. 249.
52   Arent, *One Third of a Nation*. In a footnote, Arent and the Living Newspaper reports note that LaGuardia's line on 'a drop in the bucket!' was taken from an interview on 7 December 1937.
53   Arent, *One Third of a Nation*.
54   Alexander von Hoffman, 'The End of the Dream: The Political Struggle of

ting trade unions to continue the fight for a government programme on a national scale to provide large-scale community housing for poor and working-class households. Indeed, as Michael Denning writes, 'the heart of the Popular Front as a social movement lay among those who were non-Communist socialists and independent leftists, working with Communists and liberals, but marking out a culture that was neither a Party nor a liberal New Deal culture.'[55] By December 1935, thirty local labour housing committees had been set up; three months later, there were over seventy.[56] 'In city after city, the sound of the wrecker's hammer is heard, sites are being cleared, the excavators are at work, and the superstructures are going up', Nathan Straus exclaimed, '[By] next summer [...] five thousand families will be moving from the slums into new and decent homes'.[57]

On 30 June 1939, the FTP was shut down by Congress and its thousands of employees were once again out of work. Contrary to the hopes of many of the people who worked for Federal Program One, the FTP and correlative WPA initiatives in the arts were always viewed by policymakers as temporary, relief measures, but the government had become tired with the FTP's political posturing. Flanagan's 'attempt to create a pioneer theatre that would be part of rethinking, rebuilding and redreaming America, a vital force in democracy', as Karoula writes, 'was unceremoniously but, ironically, democratically disbanded.'[58] If the story of the Living Newspaper was an argument over ideas, both on and off the stage, over the solutions to the economic crisis of the thirties and the 'welfare problem', it is an irony that, at the very moment the Unit sought solutions from democratic socialism and the power of collective bargaining, the other hand of that solution silenced it. This was even the case in the last year of the FTP, when Flanagan was accused by the Dies Committee in July 1938 of being anti-American.[59] This indicated a general trend as huge swathes of the Marxist intelligentsia and cultural elite in New York were moving away from a belief in revolutionary and even democratic solutions, in part because of the Moscow Purges

---

America's Public Housers', *Journal of Planning History*, 4.3 (2005), pp. 195–292 (p. 195).
55   Michael Denning, *The Cultural Front: The Laboring of American Culture in the Twentieth Century* (London, 1996), p. 5.
56   See von Hoffman, 'The End of the Dream: The Political Struggle of America's Public Housers', p. 240.
57   Nathan Straus, 'Housing – A National Achievement', *Atlantic Monthly*, 163 (February 1939), pp. 204–10 (p. 210).
58   Karoula, *The Federal Theatre Project*, p. 5.
59   Flanagan, *Arena*, p. 343.

and show trials between 1936 and 1938. Meyerhold, for one, was arrested in June 1939: he was tortured, his wife was murdered, and he was executed on 2 February 1940.

But the Living Newspaper and the FTP had died with a furtive legacy. Flanagan argued that the greatest achievement of the FTP was its creation of an audience, who 'proved that the need for theatre is not an emergency' and that arenas for artistic production to be discussed and understood in general, and the communal space of shared audience experience and often participation, in particular, was 'a necessity because in order to make democracy work the people must increasingly participate; they can't participate unless they understand; and the theatre is one of the great mediums of understanding'.[60] In four years, the experiments in democracy articulated in the theatre were held back by the democratic institutions that underwrote it. But if nothing else, and to paraphrase Flanagan, if papa didn't have a job in 1935, he did have a job for four years at least. From the global Green New Deal campaign to the creation of a new Federal Writing Project under the Department of Labor in the aftermath of the Covid-19 pandemic in 2021, a succession of urgent economic crises has led to renewed interest (and wide-eyed nostalgia) in the creative possibilities of the New Deal and ambitious state provision for society. But even as the United States lurches from one economic crisis to another, comprehensive funding for the theatre has never felt more remote since the New Deal as it does today.

[60]   Flanagan, *Shifting Scenes of the Modern European Theatre*, p. 59.

3

Affective Publishing Histories: Virago, the Women's Movement and the Welfare State, 1975–1990

HELEN CHARMAN

In *Landscape for a Good Woman* (Virago, 1986), recalling her 'South London fifties childhood' from the vantage point of the mid-1980s, Carolyn Steedman reflects that she 'would be a very different person now if orange juice and milk and dinners at school hadn't told me, in a covert way, that I had a right to exist, was worth something'.[1] Steedman's autobiographical class analysis combines her recollections of her own 'South London fifties childhood' with a consideration of her mother's childhood in Burnley, Lancashire, in the 1920s. Reading these two histories together provides the framework for a text that tries to find a way to articulate stories that do not fit into the prevailing iconography of working-class lives: 'lives,' in Steedman's words, 'for which the central interpretative devices of the culture don't quite work'.[2] *Landscape*'s first chapter is called 'Stories', and case studies, myths, folk tales and fairy tales structure the book in its entirety. For Steedman, the project of telling the story of her life is the project of unearthing other lives, too: not only her mother's, but 'the marginal and secret stories' of other working-class girls and women.[3] This is made clear, too, by the context of its publication: Virago was a feminist publishing house set up by Carmen Callil, Ursula Owen and Harriet Spicer in 1973, and its list was centred around republishing 'forgotten' texts as well as commissioning new feminist work. This chapter, taking Steedman as its pattern, traces the history of the relationship between – both new and 'rediscovered' – Virago publications, feminism and the emerging, then endangered, welfare state.

Immediately after her assertion about milk, Steedman continues: 'Being a child when the state was practically engaged in making children healthy and literate was a support against my own circumstances'.[4] Healthy *and* literate: the

---

1   Carolyn Steedman, *Landscape for a Good Woman* (London, 1986), p. 122.
2   Steedman, *Landscape for a Good Woman*, p. 5.
3   Steedman, *Landscape for a Good Woman*, p. 5.
4   Steedman, *Landscape for a Good Woman*, p. 122.

juice, milk and dinners that fed Steedman are important not just as nourish-
ment but for the context in which they were provided. At school, belly full of
milk, you could learn to read the stories that helped you pave the way, eventually, to a method of telling your own.[5] The biggest division between Steedman's
childhood and her mother's is not the two hundred and fifty miles between
London and Lancashire but rather the realisation, at least in part, of the social
democratic vision of the 1942 Beveridge report. Born in 1947 at the peak of
the baby boom, Steedman is a member of what the historian Eve Worth has
recently termed 'the welfare state generation', or, to borrow a term from the
writer Sarah Campion, one of the first 'national babies'.[6] Her readers are left
with no doubt that her life was made possible by the postwar social democratic
contract, from primary school to higher education: in 2017, considering the
1963 Robbins Report which recommended the foundation of six new universities and an increase in the number of students able to enter higher education in
Britain, she writes of being moved to tears, reflecting on her own time at one
of these new universities (Sussex), by this 'government report compiled in the
spirit of social justice!', comparing its scope to the Beveridge report. 'I love the
state,' she continues, 'because it has loved me'.[7]

    If, in Steedman's account of her own life, state welfare is represented as
something revolutionary, almost miraculous, in the story she tells of her
mother things are not quite so straightforward. Born into the traditional
Labour-voting background of the 'old' working class, Steedman's mother
'rejected the politics of solidarity and communality, [and] always voted
Conservative, for the left could not embody her desire for things to be
really fair'. This fairness, explicitly gendered, expresses itself in possessions
and in the logic of a fairy tale ending: it is a desire 'for a full skirt that took
twenty yards of cloth, for a half-timbered cottage in the country, for the
prince who did not come', none of which the state could provide.[8] These
desires are easy to belittle, but Steedman offers a defence of 'people wanting
things' in the context of 'the structures of political thought which have
labelled this wanting as wrong', offering a corrective to traditional, mascu-

---

[5]   *Landscape* is full of recollections of Steedman's voracious childhood reading,
both in the classroom and in the local public library. See, for example, p. 46.
[6]   See Sarah Campion, *National Baby* (London, 1950); Eve Worth, *The Welfare
State Generation: Women, Agency and Class in Britain since 1945* (London, 2022);
Carolyn Steedman, 'Middle-Class Hair', *London Review of Books*, 39.20 (October
2017) < https://www.lrb.co.uk/the-paper/v39/n20/carolyn-steedman/middle-class-
hair>.
[7]   Steedman, 'Middle-Class Hair'.
[8]   Steedman, *Landscape*, p. 47.

line stories of working-class childhood, characterised by solidarity and the dignity of going without.[9]

Contemporary reviewers understood the work to be 'an absorbing critique of welfare socialism'.[10] Raymond Williams, writing in the *London Review of Books*, cautioned against Steedman's 'assertion that poor people justifiably want things they see others much like themselves enjoying', however 'robust and welcome', as one that chimed uncomfortably with the 'now rampant politics of the Right, which seeks to substitute such individually-shaped desires for the difficult practices of common and sharing provision'. Williams cautions against the 'dilution' of the principles of the 'immediate post-war world', in which, 'through the common action of the Labour movement, the poor got a health service and a generation of children got better care than ever before in history'.[11] From the vantage point of the mid-1980s, seven years into Margaret Thatcher's eleven-year-long premiership, Steedman's approach to the complexities of her mother's life and relationship to both her class and the state felt dangerously ambiguous: to suggest that her mother 'learned selfishness in the very landscape that is meant to have eradicated it' was to undermine the already wearied social democratic project itself.[12] Williams's reading, however, overlooks the feminist dimension of Steedman's argument. In *Landscape*, the problem of how to tell her mother's life is a problem of gender: her desires, feminised as they are (the desire for a New Look skirt, to marry a prince), are a marker of difference that relate specifically to her own understanding of her value as a woman in the marriage market. Steedman's mother's is very much a woman's story.

Landscape for a Good Woman was, in many respects, a typical Virago book: intertwined with its other titles, written by a member of the advisory board and, crucially, engaged with the recovery of women's history. Indeed, Steedman makes it clear in her acknowledgments that the book's existence is impossible to disentangle from the Virago project as a whole. 'The idea', she writes, 'was Carmen Callil's': Steedman had written the introduction to the press's reissue of Kathleen Woodward's 1928 book *Jipping Street* in 1983, after which Callil had seen 'that there was much more to say'. Thus, part of *Landscape* appeared in the Virago anthology of autobiography, *Truth, Dare or Promise: Girls Growing Up in the Fifties*, which was edited by Liz Heron and published in 1985. Virago's first publication, in 1975, was Mary

---

9   Steedman, *Landscape*, p. 23.
10   Hetty Startup, 'Review: [Untitled]', *Oral History*, 15.1 (1987), pp. 60–2 (p. 61).
11   Raymond Williams, 'Desire', *London Review of Books*, 8.7 (April 1986). <https://www.lrb.co.uk/the-paper/v08/n07/raymond-williams/desire>.
12   Steedman, *Landscape*, p. 109.

Chamberlain's *Fenwomen: A Portrait of Women in an English Village*, a pioneering work of oral history compiled of interviews with women living in Gislea, an isolated village in the Cambridgeshire fens. Chamberlain, like Steedman, was involved with Raphael Samuel's History Workshop and Virago was intertwined from the start with the new context in which social history, oral history and history from below were offering new approaches to the stories of women's lives. Its first decade of operation saw the establishment of the Feminist History Group and the Feminist Archive and one early plan for a nonfiction book was simply called 'A History of Women,' a co-publication with *Spare Rib,* who – or so the plan was – would serialise the book in the magazine.[13]

In *Landscape*, Steedman identifies Virago books like 1983's *Fathers: Reflections by Daughters* edited by Owen as texts which generated for her a 'painful and familiar sense of exclusion from these autobiographies of middle-class little-girlhood and womanhood': these were part of the gap in the literature she was seeking to fill.[14] In offering an alternative, feminised reading of working-class consciousness before the welfare state, Steedman is not so much diminishing what the state in its golden age would go onto provide, but offering a way of addressing an uncomfortable reality that, in the 1980s, was impossible to ignore: some working-class women saw their interests best represented by the Tory party. The year after *Landscape* was published, Virago released Beatrix Campbell's *The Iron Ladies: Why Do Women Vote Tory?*, in which Campbell, an erstwhile member of the Communist Party of Great Britain and a founding editor of the feminist magazine *Red Rag,* argued that the 'Tory woman' is a 'remarkably unstudied political animal': 'We take her for granted, and we don't take her seriously'. Of the feminist movement, Campbell writes that any 'indifference' toward the figure of the Tory woman 'may have been because we've had other things on our mind – we have been busy creating our own politics and recovering our own history'.[15] Campbell observes that Thatcherite gender politics reconfigured the complex historical relationship between women and work. As more women were encouraged to re-enter the workforce, they were not

---

[13] See D-M Withers, *Virago Reprints and Modern Classics: The Timely Business of Feminist Publishing* (Cambridge, 2021), p. 20; Sheila Rowbotham, whose *Hidden from History* pamphlet (London, 1973) was an influential text in this historical reclamation, had a historical feature in the first three issues of *Spare Rib*, originally intended to be a regular instalment.

[14] Steedman, *Landscape*, p. 17.

[15] Beatrix Campbell, *The Iron Ladies: Why Do Women Vote Tory?* (London, 1987), p. 1.

understood to have been 'proletarianised' but rather 'bourgeoisified': regardless of the actual status of women as labouring subjects, it was aspirational to be a career woman, not a shop steward. This 'recovery' of history was central to Virago: the press understood itself, in its reprints of 'forgotten' texts by women, to be involved in the active construction of a canon of rediscovery, contributing to the project of women's liberation in the present by identifying the conditions from which the contemporary feminised consciousness had been produced (even conservative ones).

Indeed, the politics of Virago itself were far from straightforwardly left-wing. Virago understood itself to straddle the divide between feminist organising and the market. Although it had its origins in the Women's Liberation Movement (WLM) – it was originally going to be called Spare Rib Editions, and the Spare Rib Collective remained on its advisory board – it soon settled into an uneasy relationship with it, not least because of Callil's emphasis on 'changing the world' (something she said in almost every interview about the press) by reaching men as much as women, and on making *money*.[16] Unlike the proliferation of feminist presses of the period (the Women's Press, Sheba Feminist Publishers, Black Woman Talk, Open Letters, Pandora Press, Silver Moon Books to name just a few), and the Do-It-Yourself mimeograph culture of the literature of the movement as a whole, Virago was unique in considering itself both a part of the WLM and a competitively commercial publishing house. Simone Murray describes this 'attempted unification' between capitalism and feminism as 'in retrospect, a radical position,' and this is what the self-mythologisation of its founders certainly sought to perpetuate, yet this was far from an easy or obvious path to tread. As Murray continues, the 'twin goals of political commitment and profit generation' tended to 'pull any such feminist publishing operation in mutually incompatible directions'.[17]

Callil, in particular, was eager to differentiate herself from the collective impulses of the women's movement. In a memoir written by Lennie Goodings, who joined the company in 1978, she quotes from her letter of

---

[16] Lennie Goodings, *A Bite of the Apple: A Life with Books, Writers, and Virago* (Oxford, 2020), pp. 5–6. See also Goodings, *A Bite of the Apple*, p. ix; Marina Warner, 'Diary: Carmen Callil's Causes', *London Review of Books*, 44.24 (December 2022). <https://www.lrb.co.uk/the-paper/v44/n24/marina-warner/diary>; Ella Creamer, '"People still do not want women to succeed or be equal. While that is true, you need Virago": 50 years of the Warrior Publisher', *The Guardian* (28 June 2023). <https://www.theguardian.com/books/2023/jun/28/people-still-do-not-want-women-to-succeed-or-be-equal-while-that-is-true-you-need-virago-50-years-of-the-warrior-publisher>.

[17] Simone Murray, *Mixed Media: Feminist Presses and Publishing Politics* (London, 2004), p. 2.

application in which she calls Virago a 'co-operative' with an 'alternative approach to publishing'. In reply, Callil writes, 'I was interested to read your letter, though I think you are under a bit of a misapprehension about our company. We are not a co-operative but a limited company and we operate in a normal business way'.[18] The organisation was hierarchical (Murray calls it 'Thatcherite'), with overwork, low pay and large workloads seen as normal. Goodings, who was working four days a week at the co-operative Writers and Readers at the time, recalls making a pros and cons list of leaving for Virago. She found the lack of hierarchy at Writers and Readers difficult to navigate in practice, but on the other hand, found that Virago's 'politics [were] hazy'.[19] Callil was definitely not a socialist, recalling in a 2008 interview that 'I had the sisters to contend with. Some of the early feminists were socialists. There were jolly socialists, and there were wretched socialists who didn't have any joy in life. I had to think of a way of not offending them' (perhaps unsurprisingly, given her combative tone, she did not succeed).[20] Talking to Goodings a decade or so later, she compares the atmosphere of 'those early days of feminism' to the convent school she attended in Australia: 'In the service of The Cause, we were monstrously hard on each other. All movements thrive on a sense of pouncing disapproval in the air'.[21]

Many of the texts which Virago republished focussed on working-class women's struggles before and immediately after the postwar settlement. This project of recovery can be read as an explicitly political one, closely allied to the gains made by the feminist movement since 1945, especially in relation to unearthing women's lost 'voices'. A sense of history, in fact, was central for many in the WLM: in *Sweet Freedom*, their 1982 account of Women's Liberation, Beatrix Campbell and Anna Coote wrote that earlier generations had 'lacked the means to transmit their politics to a new generation and so to consolidate their gains'.[22] This was particularly true in relation to the welfare

---

[18]   The problem of people expecting the company to be something it was not persisted: Goodings writes of the press's advisory group that some of them initially were under a misapprehension. and thought they were being brought in as though to a co-operative. *A Bite of the Apple*, p. 43.

[19]   See Murray, *Mixed Media*, p. 39; Goodings, *A Bite of the Apple*, p. 32.

[20]   Rachel Cooke, 'Taking Women Off the Shelf', *The Guardian* (6 April 2008). <https://www.theguardian.com/books/2008/apr/06/fiction.features1>.

[21]   Goodings, *A Bite of the Apple*, pp. 48–9.

[22]   Anna Coote and Beatrix Campbell, *Sweet Freedom: Struggle for Women's Liberation* (Oxford, 1987), p. 4. Of course, every generation does, to some extent, think their forebears failed. See Gail Lewis, 'Whose Movement Is It Anyway? Intergenerationality and the Problem of Political Alliance', *Radical Philosophy*, 2.14 (2023), pp. 64–74.

state: to know what to fight for, it was essential to understand what had already been lost, and what it had sought to remedy. Yet, it was also a shrewd financial decision: it was much cheaper for a new, independent company to reprint older texts, especially with the advent of photocomposition as the dominant method of typesetting, than to commission new ones.[23] In this sense, *Landscape for a Good Woman* is a text that articulates the complex relation between politics, nostalgia and desire in the women's movement more generally. In troubling the nostalgia invoked by some forms of feminist heritage, while refusing the contemporary radical feminist tendency to reject the state entirely as a patriarchal tool, Steedman depicts the affective complexities of welfare: how it felt to be, in Steedman's words, 'loved' by it, and how writers were endeavouring to understand such feelings in relation to the idea of feminist history being, in this particular moment, by necessity a form of history from below.

Feminist Nostalgia

To tease out the relationship between the positions taken on the state by mainstream feminist publishing and the divisions over the same issue within the movement more generally, it is necessary to consider the history of Virago itself. Ursula Owens recalls that, in her view at least, Virago's aim of 'reclaiming' both 'a feminism and a literature which had been lost or neglected' drew on 'new writing in social and cultural history [...] most significantly E.P. Thompson's *The Making of the English Working Class* and Raymond Williams's *Culture and Society*'.[24] Yet, amongst the New Left generally, there was a sense that women's history was to be treated the same way as the resurgent feminist interest in psychoanalysis: with suspicion at best and, at worst, ridicule.[25] At the 1969 Ruskin History Workshop, those who proposed that a meeting could be convened on 'Women's History' were greeted

---

[23] See Withers, *Virago Reprints*, p. 10. See also the Virago 1978 'Company Statement', British Library Add MS 89178/1/8, and Catherine Riley, *The Virago Story: Assessing the Impact of a Feminist Publishing Phenomenon* (Oxford, 2018).
[24] Goodings, *A Bite of the Apple*, p. 26. There was a significant overlap between Virago authors, members of the Virago advisory board and writers for the *History Workshop* journal. See also Steedman's moving obituary for Raphael Samuel, 'Raphael Samuel, 1934–1996', *Radical Philosophy*, 82 (1997), pp. 53–5.
[25] Juliet Mitchell (the lone woman on the editorial board of the *New Left Review* at its founding in 1960) was at the forefront of this dual-pronged dismissal. See Lynne Segal, 'Psychoanalysis and Politics: Juliet Mitchell, Then and Now', *Radical Philosophy*, 103 (2000), pp. 12–17.

by a 'gust of masculine laughter'.[26] The project of Virago, then, was essential to establishing not just the importance of women's history but its very existence. Hilary Mantel, speaking in 2008 about the significance Virago held for her, recalled 'a man sneering at me at a dinner party circa 1975: "Women have no tradition." Actually, they had, and here was some of it in print'.[27]

The Virago Modern Classics series, which republished 'forgotten' novels, was established in June 1978 with the publication of Antonia White's *Frost in May*. Before this, the Virago Reprint Library had been the earlier catch-all term for fiction, history and memoir.[28] In the January 1982 to March 1983 catalogue, a Non-Fiction Classics series was announced: this included both reissues and new works, including Steedman's *Landscape* and, at the beginning of the 1990s, Jacqueline Rose's *The Haunting of Sylvia Plath*.[29] As the newly formal disciplines of Women's Studies, Liberal Studies and Cultural Studies appeared in British universities, the idea that what counted as history was closely aligned to prevailing ideas of value became both more established and popular.[30] Speaking in 1986 at Women in Publishing, one of six conferences organised in the 1980s at the University of London Institute of Education, Callil declared that 'the biggest battle still to be fought by all feminist publishers is, I believe, the battle for school and university curricula', and the advisory group that guided the editorial board was made up of mostly 'academically inclined women'.[31] D.-M. Withers argues in their recent book *Virago Reprints and Modern Classics,* focusing on Virago's reprints from 1973 to 1989, that its historical publications were so successful because, 'as feminist texts, their political purpose was legible'. Moreover, the press's market-driven focus also enabled it to reach out beyond the thirty thousand people that the historian Margaretta Jolly estimates were connected to the WLM itself by the beginning of the 1980s.[32]

---

[26] Sally Alexander, *Becoming A Woman* (London, 1994), p. 99.

[27] Cooke, 'Taking Women Off the Shelf'.

[28] Many people, inspired by the project, wanted to assist in the creation of such an archive: 'The world,' Callil reminisced in the Guardian in 2008, 'came to my door. Bookshops would ring, and the public, and friends', Cooke, 'Taking Women Off the Shelf'; Withers, *Virago Reprints*, pp. 8, 32.

[29] 'Virago Press: New Books & Complete List, January 1982–March 1983', British Library 6 Add MS 89178/6/8.

[30] Elaine Showalter's *A Literature of their Own*, which had been published by Virago in April 1978 and was an inaugural text of feminist literary studies, was often used as a sourcebook for Virago republication, and sold very well.

[31] See Murray, *Mixed Media*, pp. 50, 224; see also Withers, *Virago Reprints*, p. 25.

[32] Withers, *Virago Reprints*, pp. 5, 36; Margaretta Jolly, *Sisterhood and After: An Oral History of the UK Women's Liberation Movement, 1968–Present* (Oxford,

The first book that Virago published as a fully independent press, rather than a subsidiary of Quartet, was *Life As We Have Known It* (1977), a collection of memories from members of the Women's Co-operative Guild, edited by Margaret Llewelyn Davies. Originally published by Hogarth Press, it boasted an introductory letter by Virginia Woolf, which perhaps contributed to it becoming a bestseller (another Co-operative Working Women's title, *Maternity: Letters from Working Women,* followed the year after). In Anna Davin's foreword to the Virago edition of *Life*, she writes that 'Personal testimony, like the memoirs here reprinted, has a particular importance for anyone who is interested in the history of ordinary people, and most of all for those who want to explore hidden areas like the experience of childhood and family and the lives of women'. Like the welfare state, which brought private experiences out into public spaces and therefore into public responsibility, these texts drew out what was hidden, which was mostly reproductive labour, both literal and social. Unlike the annals of traditional history, Davin continues, for which there is plenty of material —archives of 'government and law, of trade and transport, of every kind of institution'— these testimonies provide the perspective not of 'administration' but 'experience'.[33] Woolf's introductory letter to *Life* speaks of how 'this book is not a book'. It is, instead, an uncategorisable object, causing her to question the 'qualities' it has, the 'ideas' it suggests, and the 'old arguments and memories' it was capable of 'rousing' in her.[34]

Withers suggests that Virago 'fulfilled' what Sally Alexander called in 1992 the 'first wish of feminist history – to fill the gaps and silences of written history, to uncover new meanings for femininity and women, to propel sexuality to the forefront of the political mind'.[35] Alexander goes on to compare this 'first wish' to 'the intentions and scope of psychoanalysis': what they both share is an interest in 'the discovery of a subjective history through image, symbol and language'.[36] It is not so much a question of the filling itself, but what it gets filled with. For Withers, this manifested itself in a concretisation of the 1970s as a historical moment in which 'the "untimely" feminism of the past became aligned with feminist times opened up and probed in present'.[37] In the texts Virago was both publishing and republish-

---

2019), p. 96.

[33] Margaret Llewelyn Davies, ed., *Life As We Have Known It, by Co-Operative Working Women* (London, 1977), p. vii.

[34] Llewelyn Davies, *Life As We Have Known It*, p. xvii.

[35] Withers, *Virago Reprints*, p. 35.

[36] Sally Alexander, 'Feminist History', *Feminism and Psychoanalysis: A Critical Dictionary*, ed. Elizabeth Wright (Oxford, 1992), pp. 108–13 (p. 109).

[37] Withers, *Virago Reprints*, p. 7.

ing, the psychosocial life of women was contextualised within the historical structures that they were, to varying extents, produced by.

Yet the question of who precisely counted as a subject for republication was a source of contention within the broader feminist movement as a whole. In 1983, Callil sent a memo round to all staff that details the ratio of dead to living authors, and which ends 'of our 249 books in print by the end of 1983, 124 are dead, 125 alive!'[38] Clearly, critiques of the tactic of republication had struck a nerve: they were perhaps spurred on by the fact that the most successful book that Virago reissued was Vera Brittain's *Testament of Youth* in 1973, which was wildly successful, thanks in part to its dramatisation by Elaine Morgan as a BAFTA-winning BBC serial in 1979. Its reissue was perhaps Callil's most canny business decision: she capitalised on the heritage boom.[39] There was discontent at their prioritisation of publishing dead white writers over living writers of colour (there were no Caribbean or African American authors in the Modern Classics series until 1982, when Phyllis Shand Allfrey's *The Orchard House* and Paule Marshall's *Brown Girl, Brownstones* were introduced), and this led directly to the Women's Press, another feminist publishing house, running a publicity campaign declaring 'Live authors. Live issues'.[40]

When Virago did publish contemporary writing by living non-white writers, the press often failed to give the books the political space they deserved. In the fortieth anniversary edition of her hugely influential *Finding A Voice: Asian Women in Britain,* Amrit Wilson documents her difficulties in 1978 when she protested at the printing of certain sections of her book in a newspaper. Her threat of direct action was received, Wilson writes, with horror: 'She's running amok in the *Observer* office! Stop her'. The 'displeasure' that this event generated persisted: 'I realised that the warmth and support that they had shown me when I was writing the book had been conditional on my accepting their white middle-class version of feminism'.[41] Virago was, seemingly, more comfortable with work by (mostly white) living

---

[38]   'Memo from Carmen Callil to Ursula Owen, Lennie Goodings, Kate Griffin and Harriet Spicer, Regarding the Image of Virago Press, 13 April 1983', British Library Add MS 89178/1/71.

[39]   The Virago collective had originally intended Angela Carter's *The Sadeian Woman and the Ideology of Pornography* to be their first publication (later published in 1979). This, a book that claimed the Marquis de Sade as a 'moral pornographer' and a sexually liberating figure for women, would have been a markedly different tone to strike than *Fenwomen.*

[40]   Murray, *Mixed Media*, p. 45. See also Eileen Cadman, Gail Chester and Agnes Pivot, *Rolling Our Own: Women as Printers, Publishers and Distributors* (London, 1981), pp. 28–9.

[41]   Amrit Wilson, *Finding a Voice: Asian Women in Britain* (Quebec, 2023), p. xvii.

writers that focused on the past, rather than explicit manifestos for change like Wilson's. If the purpose of Virago was indeed to assert the importance of the experiences 'of ordinary people', then it was clearly more comfortable with some kinds of experience than others.

In these texts, as with *Landscape for a Good Woman*, an affective rather than explicitly proactive politics emerges through memoir, almost always recalling the welfare state in its earliest years, and contrasting strongly with the explicit anti-state attitude articulated in Marxist-feminist publications of the same period). The former approach is taken in *Truth, Dare or Promise: Girls Growing up in the 50s*, edited by Liz Heron and published in 1985. The book is made up of twelve chapters, each detailing memories of a 1950s childhood in, variously, Glasgow, the Grampians, Lanarkshire, Blackpool, Manchester, London, Kent, Derby, Surrey, Anglesey, Gloucester, Liverpool, Leeds and the Isle of Wight. The collection is full of ambivalence, mirroring the gap between, as Heron writes in the introduction, 'the spirit in which the good things of the Welfare State were given and our subjective experience of receiving them'.[42]

The inequalities inherent in state provision – including benefit allocations, the stratified educational system and racism both structural and interpersonal – may well have been the *de facto* reality of life in the 1950s, but the felt experience of it was both more positive and diffuse: 'the reality of our childhood experience', Heron writes:

> was that these good things were our birthright. We took them for granted, just as we took for granted our right to be in the world. Along with the orange juice and the cod-liver-oil, the malt supplement and the free school milk, we may also have absorbed a certain sense of our own worth and the sense of a future that would get better, as if history were on our side.[43]

This sentiment is echoed repeatedly throughout the collection. Harriett Gilbert, noting that her generation, 'pumped full of National Health orange juice, further education, [and] our parents' relative prosperity' was a 'Peter Pan generation', which refused to grow up and also refused to play by the old rules. This generational identity 'had all the cohesiveness of class. We even thought, with more or less conviction, that we might have abolished the latter altogether'.[44] The orange juice, milk and malt extract and the fact that this welfare state generation grew faster and taller than their parents

---

[42] Liz Heron, ed., *Truth, Dare or Promise: Girls Growing up in the 50s* (London, 1985), p. 5.
[43] Heron, *Truth, Dare or Promise*, p. 6.
[44] Heron, *Truth, Dare or Promise*, pp. 45–6.

are mentioned so many times in the book that this peculiar combination of flavours takes on a kind of definitional synaesthetic character. That is what the state tasted like: milk, malt and orange.

Each chapter of *Truth, Dare or Promise* ends with a section detailing where the author was in their lives at the time of writing, almost always detailing their political and professional commitments: the WLM comes up a lot, and so does *Spare Rib*, but also more eclectic organisations like the Welfare State Theatre Group or the magazine *City Limits*. For many, socialism, Marxism and anti-racist organising are as or more significant than feminism: Gail Lewis writes of her involvement with the Angela Davis Defence Campaign as a defining moment in the development of her own politics.[45] Denise Riley, in the final page of the entire book, problematises the neat mapping of 'adult beliefs' on childhood experiences alone. 'I could say, for instance', she writes, that

> My life was formed only by means of the public library which provided me with my only uncensored access to books. When I was fifteen or sixteen I found a confirmation of my interest in what it is to take on your own past in some of Sartre's work. I read *The Second Sex* and *A Room of One's Own* at the same age, and thought of myself as a feminist, though this had to remain a privately held conviction for several years more. In this spirit I joined the Abortion Law Reform Association while still at school; this was just before the passage of the 1967 Abortion Act. The political developments of 1968 and the first national conference of the Women's Liberation Movement spanned my time as a student and rapidly thereafter as a mother. As for many, the Vietnam demonstrations of 1967 were my first.

But, she immediately declares, echoing Steedman's concern with autobio-graphical forms, that 'this would only be a story, and would not ring true'.[46]

Within Riley's story there are many aspects that could stand for the book as a whole: the public library is the only place where the intrusions of reli-gious schooling and a controlling family life (Riley was the adopted daughter of strict Protestants, who nevertheless sent her to a Catholic school) are kept from the young woman's psychic life; the state offers a sanctuary of imper-sonality and of choice. The books Riley reads, too – historical texts written by two women iconic in the feminist bibliography of the 1980s, Woolf and de Beauvoir – affirm the impulse behind the Virago project: reading women's writing from the past could open up possibilities of political identification that could fortify you in the present. Yet such stories risk ignoring the reali-

---

[45] Heron, *Truth, Dare or Promise*, p. 236.
[46] Heron, *Truth, Dare or Promise*, p. 248.

ties of political life. Sheila Rowbotham, at the end of her own contribution, observes that, from the vantage point of 1985, 'the clarity of vision in those early years of women's liberation has gone. It seemed possible then to order the past through the focus of feminism. It is less one-dimensional for me now. Feminism is a given – but I want more than the political outline. I want a culture which you can tug and shape with complexity.'[47]

In and Against the State

In *Theatres of Memory*, Raphael Samuel pays close critical attention both to the mania for 'heritage' in postwar British culture and to the 'heritage-baiting' of its detractors, both on the left and within the field of academic history.[48] Rather than a symptom of national decay, a signal (as Robert Hewison wrote in 1987) that history was 'over', or a 'sore on the body politic', cheapening the past through mass-produced trinkets, television shows and museum 'experiences', it indicates an 'enlargement of the historical in everyday life'.[49] It is interesting that such a critique of heritage came at a time when feminists in Britain had begun to confidently stake a claim on the political nature of texts detailing women's experiences in the past. But it was also a time when the dismantling of the state was being done by a woman, Margaret Thatcher, who, as Marina Warner observed in 1986, manipulated figures straight from British history, ensuring the fantasy of 'women of discipline' could be found in her, as 'Nanny, matron, governess: characters from the youth of the landed classes, of the Edwardian nursery and the prep school dorm'.[50] In January 1983, Thatcher had given an interview to the London Weekend Television programme *Weekend World* in which, describing her plan for a more 'self-reliant' society in which 'people are more independent of the State' rather than expecting their 'standard of living to be guaranteed by the State', she expressed her desire for a return to 'Victorian Values', on which 'our country became great', a fantasy of 'independence and initiative' rather than 'compulsion by the State'.[51]

[47]   Heron, *Truth, Dare or Promise*, p. 211.
[48]   192 Raphael Samuel, *Theatres of Memory: Past and Present in Contemporary Culture* (London 1994), pp. 261–2, 152–3, 265.
[49]   Robert Hewison, *The Heritage Industry: Britain in a Climate of Decline* (London, 1987), p. 141.
[50]   Marina Warner, *Monuments and Maidens: The Allegory of the Female Form* (Berkeley CA, 1985), p. 52.
[51]   Brian Walden and Margaret Thatcher, 'Victorian Values' (TV Interview for London Weekend Television Weekend World), 16 January 1983. See also Helen Charman, *Mother State: A Political History of Motherhood* (London: Allen Lane, 2024), p. xxxii.

Welfare dependency was an obsessive concern of Thatcher's, most often remembered by a statement she made in a 1987 *Woman's Own* interview, usually paraphrased as 'there is no such thing as society,' in which she outlines exactly how little care the state should provide. In it, she explicitly identifies children as prime culprits: 'I think we have gone through a period when too many children and people have been given to understand "I have a problem, it is the Government's job to cope with it!"'[52] Thatcher, in other words, sought to destroy the equation in which state-provided milk, juice and dinners equalled a sense of nurture and love. In this context, then, we can see that a publishing house like Virago (which, in 1984, announced a new series, 'Virago Victorian Classics') was placed in a strange position. The fact that the election of the first female Prime Minister was a Conservative one, who so reified the image of the housewife and traditional feminine values, put mainstream feminists in a difficult position; in her reclamation of 'Victorian Values', heritage became easy to associate with conservatism of both the big and the small-c variety.[53] Their case was not helped by their choice of Britannia reading a Modern Classic as the symbol of the series, given this was another image that Thatcher had laid claim to: on the day of the 1983 General Election, the front page of *The Sun* featured a large mock-up of Thatcher as Britannia, replete with a trident, a Union Jack-emblazoned shield and a lion, headlined 'She is carrying the banner for ordinary people'.[54]

In such a context, it is easy to assume that the feminist position on the welfare state was generally a positive one. Indeed, the first four demands made by the WLM, decided at the 1969 Ruskin conference, were all asking for something from the state: equal pay, equal educational and job opportunities, free contraception, abortion on demand and free twenty-four-hour nurseries. Further demands added in 1974 (legal and financial independence for all women and the right to a self-defined sexuality) and in 1976 (freedom for all women from intimidation by the threat or use of violence or sexual coercion regardless of marital status, and an end to the laws, assumptions and institutions which perpetuate male dominance and aggression to women) were also engaged, to different extents, with state provision. Yet, for many radical feminists, the state could not be recuperated: not only was its provision of support structured by racism, ableism and homophobia, but it was an organ for reinforcing, as Catherine MacKinnon wrote in 1983, the 'systemic

---

[52]   Douglas Keay, 'Interview with Margaret Thatcher', *Woman's Own* (31 October 1987).

[53]   Withers, *Virago Reprints,* p. 85.

[54]   See Withers, *Virago Reprints,* p. 80, and Warner, *Monuments and Maidens,* p. 40.

and hegemonic' male perspective.[55] By the final National Conference of the WLM, held in Birmingham in 1978, the splintering within the movement between socialist, radical and revolutionary feminists, including lesbian separatists, culminated in a group of revolutionary feminists submitting a proposal to cancel all previous demands: it was 'ridiculous', they felt, to 'demand anything from a patriarchal state – from men – who are the enemy'.

For socialist feminists like Sheila Rowbotham, Juliet Mitchell, Jean McCrindle and Lynne Segal, the reform of the state was embedded with questions of social reproduction: how could the tension between women's productive and reproductive roles be lessened? These disagreements were complicated by the fact that the state, in the 1970s, could be understood as both a local and a national structure. The municipal control exercised by local councils meant that one thing could be going on at a national level and quite another at a local one, with left-wing governing bodies like the Greater London Council, in which Rowbotham and other socialist feminists actually entered local government, with the result that radical projects were countenanced and even publicly funded in some areas.[56] The political theorist Katrina Forrester, in her work on feminism and the state during British deindustrialisation, introduces, via a pamphlet produced by the London-Edinburgh Weekend Return Group, the concept of feminists advancing a tactic of working 'In and Against the State.' Acknowledging that 'resources we need involve us in relations we don't' could assist with the project of disentangling state support from state control: the goal was to try and redistribute such resources, without becoming ensnared in their traps.[57]

The problem the welfare state posed for feminism became fiercer and, perhaps also, more diffuse as the munificence of the state became the focus of an attack from the right. In the wake of the Conservative election victory in 1979, the future looked bleak. In *Beyond the Fragments: Feminism and the Making of Socialism*, Rowbotham, Segal and Hilary Wainwright attempted to summarise the history of the WLM and how it linked to other movements: what Wainwright describes, rather glibly, in her introduction as 'the women's movement, the trade union movement, the black movement etc'.[58]

---

[55]   Catherine MacKinnon, 'Marxism, Method, and the State: Toward Feminist Jurisprudence', *Signs*, 8.4 (1983), pp. 635–58 (pp. 635–6).
[56]   On socialist feminism, see Angela Weir and Elizabeth Wilson, 'The British Women's Movement', *New Left Review*, 148 (1984), pp. 74–103.
[57]   Katrina Forrester, '"In and against the state": Revolutionary Feminism During Deindustrialisation', Quentin Skinner Lecture, University of Cambridge (9 June 2023). <https://www.crassh.cam.ac.uk/events/38363/>.
[58]   Sheila Rowbotham, Lynne Segal and Hilary Wainwright, *Beyond the Fragments:*

A significant aspect of the book's argument was the suggestion that the reason so many people voted Tory and so few Labour, despite the decade of industrial and social organising that preceded the election, was that Labour had become totally integrated in the capitalist state. There were dissenting voices on the left, and within feminism particularly: in an article entitled 'Rest in Pieces', published in *Red Rag* in August 1980 by the Socialist Feminist Social Policy Group, the idea that the state is always an antagonist is described as unhelpful, a 'naïve simplification'. The state, they argue, does not act on women per se or women as a class, but on women in specific and diverse situations. The question they ask is: 'Should socialist feminist policy be directed against the state? Or are demands to be made on the state? And how does this relate to the question of men as the oppressors of women?'[59]

In one sense, the case for the welfare state was that it at least proved a preventative for some kinds of private violence, particularly those that occur within marriages, enforced by prevailing ideas about what domestic roles should look like. As Lynne Segal wrote in 2000:

> The continuing offensive against welfare provides perhaps the single most general threat to Western women's interests at present – at least for those many women who are not wealthy and who still take the major responsibility for caring work in the home. As feminists in the 1970s made so clear, and sought so hard to transform, women are most vulnerable to the very worst pathologies of dependency when they are most at the mercy of husbands or male partners, especially during and after pregnancy and childbirth.[60]

And yet, it proved difficult to separate these kinds of intimate abuses from their wider sociopolitical context: the reproductive body was a legislative and conceptual battlefield. Some feminists became vocally critical of the role played by psychoanalysts like John Bowlby, whose ideas about separation from the mother were often employed, according to *Spare Rib*, to 'attack women who go to work while their children are still babies', or to reinforce ideas about what a mother should be. In 1977 Elizabeth Wilson, who was also a member of the Communist Party of Great Britain and a Gay Liberation Front activist, published *Women and the Welfare State*, an expanded version of a *Red Rag* pamphlet. In it, she declares that 'Feminism and socialism meet in the arena of

---

Feminism and the Making of Socialism (London, 1979), p. 4. See also Charman, *Mother State*, pp. 93–95.

[59]   Socialist Feminist Social Policy Group, 'Rest in Pieces', *Red Rag*, 9 (August 1980), p. 34. See also Charman, *Mother State*, pp. 93–95.

[60]   Lynne Segal, 'Subject to Suspicion: Feminism and Antistatism in Britain', *Social Text*, 18.1 (2000), pp. 143–51 (p. 143).

the Welfare State, and the manipulations of the Welfare State offer a unique demonstration of how the State can prescribe what a woman's consciousness should be'. The Welfare State, in Wilson's terms, is a 'conglomeration of legislation and services' that can only be understood with the tools that feminism provides, particularly in its critique of the idealisation of motherhood:

> Only feminism has made it possible for us to see how the State defines femininity and that this definition is not marginal but is central to the purposes of welfarism. Woman is above all Mother, and with this vocation go all the virtues of femininity; submission, nurturance, positivity. The 'feminine' client of the social services waits patiently at clinics, social security offices and housing departments, to be ministered to sometimes by the paternal authority figure, doctor, or civil servant, sometimes by the nurturant yet firm model of femininity provided by the nurse or social worker; in either case she goes away to do as she has been told – to take the pills, to love the baby.[61]

'To take the pills, to love the baby' vividly identifies the woman's body as the site where the intrusion of the state was most feverishly imagined. In the context of the ongoing assaults on the 1967 abortion act, the idea of state intervention into reproduction was, for many feminists, a horrifying one. In 1979, Virago published the novel *Benefits* by Zoë Fairbairns, a vision of a dystopian future in which a far-right political party, the 'Family Party', reforms the welfare payment system in order to compel women to reproduce. Although it was written between 1976 and 1978 and so pre-dated Thatcher's punitive welfare reforms, it was widely read after its publication as an explicit critique of them. Thatcher was an irresistibly identifiable target: a stage version produced at the Albany Empire in 1980 featured Shelagh Stephenson playing Isabel Travers, the leader of the Family Party, in what essentially amounted to a Thatcher costume, including her famous handbag.

Fairbairns was active in the feminist movement. During the period she wrote *Benefits* she worked at the Women's Research and Resources Centre near Euston, an antecedent of the Feminist Library, 'cranking out newsletters on our huge, noisy Gestetner duplicator', documenting the controversies generated by the Wages for Housework campaign. The novel 'grew', in Fairbairns's words, 'out of fact': over the Labour government's 1976 U-turn over the introduction of child benefits. To fund the scheme, fathers would have to pay more income tax, resulting in 'a transfer of money from wallet to purse'.[62] The Trade

---

61   Elizabeth Wilson, *Women and the Welfare State* (London, 1977), pp. 7–8. See also Charman, *Mother State*, pp. 93–95.
62   Zoë Fairbairns, 'Introduction to the 2012 ebooks edition'. <http://www.zoefairbairns.co.uk/benefits.htm>.

Unions Council (TUC) was furious at this reduction in take-home pay, and the government backtracked in May that year. Feminist groups and prominent figures, including the Labour MP Barbara Castle, as well as Conservative and religious women's groups, protested at this capitulation; the government eventually reinstated the child benefit plan, but at a lower level. This had ongoing implications in the relationship between the TUC and the feminist movement more broadly, which persisted well into the 1980s, despite the alliances made between the TUC and the National Abortion Campaign in 1979.[63] Opening in 1976 with a description of these events, alongside the contemporaneous introduction of new restrictions on abortion rights, *Benefits* centres on Lynn, a journalist living in South London, as she becomes more involved with political organising in the Collindeane Tower, an abandoned block of council flats that has become home to a radical feminist community. Lynn's attraction to the women's commune is inspired by twinned reproductive injustices: 'The mammoth arrogance of a government closing off women's escape route from unwanted pregnancy while at the same time withholding the tiny improvement that they'd promised in mothers' financial position, made Lynn sweat with rage'.[64] This interpretation of welfare as a resource to be fought for, even one with redistributive power, does not, however, last long.

The novel continues through the 1980s and 1990s, charting the rise to power of the Family Party, who introduce a new payment for mothers, called simply 'Benefit'. Decrying a society which 'penalises' motherhood and traditional family roles, the Party introduce a financial incentive, controlled by the new Department for Family Welfare: 'All mothers, regardless of race, marital state or domestic competence would be eligible for the weekly payment so long as they stayed home and looked after children under 16'.[65] Benefit is a policy of broad brushstroke eugenics: the welfare payment is denied to mothers who do not perform their duties according to state dictates, to lesbians, feminists, those who try to find work outside the home and those who refuse to have sex with their husbands, or, worst of all, leave them. These women are sent to re-education centres, while

> any woman of child-bearing age seen on the streets without children in tow ran the risk of being stoned, spat on or refused admission to public buildings or transport. Some reported attacks by gangs of men who threatened a repetition

---

[63]   For a comprehensive account, see Stephen Brooke, *Sexual Politics: Sexuality, Family Planning, and the British Left from the 1880s to the Present Day* (Oxford, 2011).
[64]   Zoë Fairbairns, *Benefits* (London, 1979), p. 6.
[65]   Fairbairns, *Benefits*, pp. 55–6.

if the women did not go back to their children. The policemen wrote down the details carefully. Then they said, 'Are you sure you didn't ask for it?'[66]

Eventually, the plot incorporates the medical establishment in its eugenic turn. 'Undesirable' women are sterilised, and Lynn's own daughter, Janet, a member of the Young Family Party, resorts to a back-channel method to have her own 'contraceptive pellet' removed, since government Women's Centres will not perform the surgery (an attempt to eradicate the inherited genetic disorder cystic fibrosis). Feminist resistance builds around the squatted tower block, where a successful strike action is mobilised. 'The Women' refuse *en masse* to care for their children, leaving them with their fathers, making visible the daily labours of the household. But the real blow against the government comes through the state's medical over-reaching, rather than any successful organising. After contaminating all the reservoirs in the country with a contraceptive chemical, the Family Welfare department then administer the antidote in tablet form to women who meet their desirable maternal criteria. This policy backfires, resulting in a series of stillbirths and birth deformities that is uncomfortably reminiscent of the Thalidomide crisis.

Benefits is not a good novel, populated as it is with stock characters and plot points which draw heavily on ableist stereotypes, but it is a historically significant one. Fairbairns, immersed as she was in the WLM and very much an identifiably Virago kind of writer – her subsequent novels *Stand We At Last* (1983) and *Closing* (1992) were published by the company – was attempting to synthesise an understanding of the positive history of what the state could provide for women, such as child benefit, with a profound suspicion of the welfare system as a site of patriarchal social control. Toward the end of the novel, after the death of David Laing, the first Family Party Secretary of State for Welfare, his successor and former second-in-command Mr Peel reflects on Laing's failings, first among which is his 'squeamishness' at taking payments away from undeserving mothers:

> He was of the soft generation, of the post-war guilt-ridden child-obsessed baby boom. They rode a roller coaster of gratuities: free milk, free cod liver oil, free schools, free medicine, free grants to go to college ... it was Peel's view that the trauma of the seventies, the sudden realisation that the party was over and they couldn't get what they wanted by slapping on the label rights and howling, had blighted the generation for life, had rendered them incapable of understanding how life works.[67]

---

[66]   Fairbairns, *Benefits*, p. 140.
[67]   Fairbairns, *Benefits*, p. 168.

The milk and orange juice function in the novel as an unsettled symbol of ambivalence. Laing, an architect of a welfare policy that embodied contemporary feminism's worst fears, had been fed on the very state that had empowered so many of them in their own childhoods. The affective power of the postwar bounty, however, lingered on despite his attempts to disavow it throughout his villainous political career: at least at the level of his conscience, the memory of that universal maternal good remained, and acted explicitly to prohibit his punishment of mothers in particular.

* * *

Virago played a historic role in making texts written by and about women more accessible, and narrativizing the feeling of growing up with the promises of welfare. But their impulses toward posterity have been thwarted by the market. The Virago Modern Classics series now numbers over seven hundred titles, but, after the sale of the company to Little, Brown in 1996, many of the recovered and resurrected authors that began the series – now including some works by men – have once again fallen out of print.[68] Feminist conversations about the welfare state today take place in a landscape of scarcity even more austere than that of Thatcher's premiership: malt, milk and juice are distant memories, and famous footballers are more concerned about hungry schoolchildren than the Labour Party.[69] In 2023, a study was released suggesting British children raised under austerity are shorter than their European counterparts, an inversion of all that rapid growth documented in *Truth, Dare or Promise*.[70] Ultimately, Virago shied away from the revolutionary articulations that are required to transform society, to make or even attempt to make a feminist state. What it continues to offer us, nonetheless, is an affective record of the welfare state, its memorialisation, and its implicit endorsement of life: its 'love'.

[68] Cooke, 'Taking Women Off the Shelf'; see also Murray, *Mixed Media*, pp. 28–31.

[69] See Owen Jones, 'England's Footballers Speak for the New Generation Better Than Any Politician', *The Guardian* (14 July 2021). <https://www.theguardian.com/commentisfree/2021/jul/14/england-footballers-new-generation-britain-progressive-young>.

[70] Amelia Hill, 'Children Raised Under UK Austerity Shorter than European Peers, Study Finds', *The Guardian* (21 June 2023). <https://www.theguardian.com/business/2023/jun/21/children-raised-under-uk-austerity-shorter-than-european-peers-study>.

4

Consent or Dissent?
Poetry and the British Welfare State

GARETH FARMER

The history of the idea of culture is a record of our reactions, in thought and feeling, to the changed conditions of our common life.

—Raymond Williams, *Culture and Society, 1780–1950*[1]

This chapter examines poetry as a cultural site of contestation about the welfare state. In *Culture and Society, 1780–1950* (1958), Raymond Williams meticulously outlines how 'culture' became a nexus for class conflicts as well as a site for the expression of visions of society. Culture can demonstrate prevailing hopes for 'ways of life', as Williams puts it, which can oscillate between those imagining an individualist society, to those hoping for more robust structures of collectivism and solidarity.[2] But 'culture', to Williams, is rarely a fixed conduit for 'social and personal directive'; rather, it is a 'process, not a conclusion'.[3] Literature, as one expression of collective cultural thought and feeling, offers reactions to what Williams describes as 'general and major change in the conditions of our common life'. These reactions in relation to the welfare state, while apparently similar in calling for a more compassionate culture of welfare, are often realised with starkly different aesthetic choices. Some writers choose a direct lyric mode to bear witness to social and political inequalities. Other writers develop radical poetic forms to challenge cultural forms in general, drawing attention to the conditions of our common life that continue to impede solidarity. All the poetry examined in this chapter raises awareness of social inequity, particularly in relation to the welfare state, but the aesthetic strategies of the poems are very different. In what follows, I explore why this might be.

[1]   Raymond Williams, *Culture and Society, 1780–1950* (Harmondsworth, 1963), p. 285.
[2]   Williams, *Culture and Society, 1780–1950*, p. 306.
[3]   Williams, *Culture and Society, 1780–1950*, p. 285.

Britain emerged from the war years with a commitment to the social value of literature, and poetry in particular was seen to play an intimate role with the welfare state in its foregrounding of the social democratic powers of language. Both Williams and Richard Hoggart (in *The Uses of Literacy*, 1957) assessed the improved conditions of the British working classes since the Second World War, improvements to which mass publishing and a broader democratisation of media contributed in no small part.[4] Philip Larkin's 'mainstream' poetry provided the literary equivalent of welfare ideology, and its tone, style and poetic techniques offered a landscape by which to capture the state of the nation. Despite Larkin's tone of deep scepticism, his vision of England was rooted in the narrative of political progress and renewal outlined in Williams's and Hoggart's work, as well as an investment in the social: an idea that reading literature was continuous with other affordances like access to the National Health Service. In the 1970s, however, as the welfare state came under increasing pressure, another kind of poetry emerged that was more critical of the language of welfare and welfarist ideology. This welfare-resistant poetics is particularly discernible in the work of Anna Mendelssohn, a poet whose investment in anarchist politics resulted in the production of poetry that contests welfare ideology, and which pushes towards more revolutionary structures of care.

My examination of poetry in this chapter is broadly chronological. All the poets featured critique the welfare state from broadly leftist perspectives, but the resulting poetry is very different. That is to say, the starting points of drawing attention to precarity and inequality as well as to the bureaucratic institutions of welfare are the same, but the aesthetic choices of expressing these issues vary widely. In my analysis of these different poetries, I offer some suggestions as to why aesthetic decisions might illustrate broader political commitments. I will first discuss the poetry of Mendelssohn, particularly moments in which she attempts to grapple with social precarity and women's rights. I then turn to an examination of poetry in defence of the welfare state, broadly representative of 'mainstream' lyric poetry (that is, work written in tone and style in the legacies of Larkin and 'Movement' poetry, featuring declarative, lyric voices describing the state of the nation). The latter stages of the chapter return to the radical vision of welfare poetics represented by Mendelssohn, looking at the work of Sean Bonney and Frank Lock to think about its importance for the welfare state today. All these poets have personally experienced the violent realities of welfare's limits. They offer contrasting poetic responses to neoliberalism's attacks on welfare and show how

---

4   Richard Hoggart, *The Uses of Literacy* (London, 1957).

the more radical work provides a language for a more inclusive and critical approach to both poetry and the welfare state.

Mendelssohn, Bonney and Lock break with conventional language practices, producing alternatives to the social and cultural despair and stasis that Williams registered in the late 1970s, particularly in his work on tragic form.[5] In the words of Andrew Cooper and Julian Lousada, these poets pose an explicit challenge for 'our collective and individual capacities to sustain *knowledge* of the social, personal, and physical conditions of life that the welfare state was created to address'.[6] This chapter argues that radical poetries resist conventional language practices which reinforce the fixed social and political positions of 'dependency' and 'parasitism', consistently reinforced by current welfare institutions. Through their aesthetic, they resist stigma and despair.

'London 1971': Anna Mendelssohn and the Poetics of Refusal

One of the poets who explores the relationship between radical poetics and radical politics most explicitly during the 1970s, including the limits of the welfare state for guaranteeing safety, is the English poet Anna Mendelssohn. Mendelssohn, who sometimes published under the name Grace Lake, was born in Stockport in 1948, to a working-class Jewish family, the year the welfare state was founded. Her mother was an activist with the International Women for Peace Movement and her father was an International Brigades veteran, a former member of the Communist Party and a Labour Councillor. Mendelssohn, who was brought into radical poetry circles during her time at the University of Essex in the late 1960s, was involved in housing activism in the early 1970s and was also, famously, associated with the Angry Brigade, a libertarian Communist group in England that carried out a series of non-fatal bombings against such targets as the Miss World Pageant and the residence of Home Secretary Robert Carr. At the age of twenty-four, Mendelssohn was charged with credit card and cheque fraud and was also convicted of conspiracy to cause a series of explosions. On 6 December 1972 she was imprisoned, spending four years in jail.

In 1968 Anna Mendelssohn had been involved in the large-scale protests in London against the Vietnam war. As Sara Crangle writes, she 'appeared

---

[5] Raymond Williams, 'Afterword to *Modern Tragedy*', *Politics of Modernism: Against the New Conformists* (London, 2007), pp. 95–106.
[6] Andrew Cooper and Julian Lousada, *Borderline Welfare: Feeling and Fear in Modern Welfare* (London, 2005), p. 9.

with a group of students in the conclusion of Jean-Luc Godard's documentary on student unrest in England, British Sounds (1969)', where she is filmed arguing 'for properly controversial counter-lyrics to the Beatles's curiously resigned "Revolution"'.[7] This reaction against mainstream or popular protest, and call for 'counter-lyric' practice, is crucial to the formation of Mendelssohn's difficult poetics. 'Politics devoured her life', Crangle writes, but 'she did not want it to devour her artistry also'. But her commitment to art and politics, Crangle notes, were contradictorily entwined:

> she levied an always leftist assault on the inconsistencies and injustices of political system[s] with the lived reality of the personal, all in the full and certain knowledge of the feminist maxim that the personal is the political, that these realms are inextricable. On the one hand, Mendelssohn's is a self-imposed, irresolvable malediction exacerbated by a gendered double standard that insisted its resilient, condemnatory way into her vanguardism. On the other, the literary – and poetry in particular – offers a way out of this impasse.[8]

Mendelssohn's poetry abjures overtly political messages, but the fragmented details of her life and experiences which feature in the poems are implicitly political. Hers is a self-critical poetry, one which attempts to distance aesthetics from the real, while all the while being drawn back to an examination of material conditions.

Much of Mendelssohn's poetic work is, Crangle observes, 'obsessively attuned to imbalance, inequities', exhibiting a committed 'political rectitude' and a 'high political consciousness'.[9] However, her ambivalence about poetry's efficacy in changing political situations, as well as her sense that, as she puts it, 'a poem is not going to give precise directions' (the poem starts 'to any who wants poems to give them answers'), lead to a dense, syntactically fractured indirect poetic practice.[10] Poems, Mendelssohn puts it in the same poem, 'address a different world', one of aesthetics, not politics. But her poems are not untouched by her sense of political injustice. As such, Mendelssohn repeatedly registers her own and others' experiences of being, as Crangle writes, subject to 'scrutiny of her daily machinations by authority figures'.[11] 'Poverty exerted its daily grind', Crangle continues,

---

[7]   See Anna Mendelssohn, *I'm Working Here: The Collected Poems of Anna Mendelssohn*, ed. Sara Crangle (Swindon, 2020), pp. 28–9 for an account of these events.

[8]   Mendelssohn, *I'm Working Here*, p. 31.

[9]   Mendelssohn, *I'm Working Here*, p. 47.

[10] Mendelssohn, *I'm Working Here*, p. 428.

[11] Mendelssohn, *I'm Working Here*, p. 29.

'as did severe ill health and the stigma of single parenthood'. Mendelssohn
was conflicted about the efficacy of poetry either to describe or to challenge
social and political situations. Hence, in a draft poem for her 1993 collection
viola tricolor, written at the same time as 'to any who want poems to give
them answers', Mendelssohn writes obliquely of her own experience of being
'ground down' by the 'fight for meagre help' from the 'mechanical theatre' of
a welfare state.[12] She describes a 'worn mother', unable to achieve the 'social
lift' required to enable her to keep her children, a feeling of being continually
condescended to and dismissed because of this – and poetry's potential futil-
ity in overcoming such conditions. Pondering the status of her own poetic
protest, in the second stanza Mendelssohn writes:

> whilst I acknowledge criticisms of didacticism levelled against me, I do not
> accept that change has ceased & find that lack of intellectual consciousness
> to be a ploy to hive off life & death onto the vulnerable who may not all be
> as brutal and as vulgar as armies demand they be.

Her political positions in defence of the vulnerable in her poetry may have been
dismissed as didactic, but such 'intellectual consciousness', however stylistically
deployed, is necessary to counter the 'ploy' to categorically contain and dismiss
as 'brutal' and 'vulgar' the vulnerable in society. Without her form of poetic
protest, what Mendelssohn calls 'doggerel' (cheap uncritical language used by
those in power to describe marginalised people) will continue to pass 'for what
untutored people come to be known for and dismissed'.

At the heart of this poem's cryptic argument is a poetically enacted battle
over state discourse and the ways in which such unchecked and uncritiqued
'doggerel' will continue to deny the reality of the vulnerable. The poem ends
with the injunction:

> Why walk away
> & dismiss me. These arguments went on between women. There's nothing more
> convenient
> than to build a wall of pity and support for a new network of power and submission.

Mendelssohn takes aim at the ways in which networks of 'pity and support'
are a veil for increasing the power of institutions and the submission of the
vulnerable. However, as with most of her poetry, her oppositionality is paradoxical. She is cynical about poetry's ability to make anything happen, while

---

[12]   'As soon as a name is to be addressed another child', in Mendelssohn, *I'm
Working Here*, p. 544.

also manically writing poetry with implicit and explicit political messages. She wants to describe and defend women from social marginality and persecution, while also seeming to cynically dismiss the 'arguments [...] between women' as being slightly futile. The deictic 'these' is pejorative, gesturing to potentially frivolous arguments and chatter happening outside of the poem. Mendelssohn's relationship with mainstream feminism and leftist politics was likewise paradoxical. Analysing Mendelssohn's editorial practice in *viola tricolor*, for example, Crangle demonstrates how edits foreground lines which critique unquestioning and mass revolutionary fervour. Thus, Mendelssohn aimed to create a poetics which, contingent and fractured itself, was able to grapple with the state's networks of power and submission.

In the late 1960s and early 1970s, Mendelssohn contributed to a countercultural newspaper, *Frendz*, which satirically discussed politics and covered issues such as prison reform and affordable housing.[13] She also provided investigative journalism on security firms and housing issues for another underground magazine, *Strike* (including attending one meeting about which she was later questioned by police, investigating stolen chequebooks). As such, Mendelssohn was acutely aware, from her own experiences and investigating those of others, of the attacks on housing associations and on those needing help from the state. Poems written during and about this time are veined with, Albinia Stanley writes, 'the dynamics of capitalist exploitation – emotional, sexual and physical', 'the nature of work under capitalism, and the fraught threshold between labour and love'.[14] Writing of Mendelssohn's poem 'friday', Stanley describes her first person voice as 'maligned and insubordinate', a deft summary of the angry and shifting tone and register of several of her poems of this time. In Mendelssohn's poem 'London 1971' (a reference to the place and year of her arrest for her Angry Brigade activity), she wrestles with finding a place of solace despite the constant reminders of precarity and punitive treatment by the state. 'What was that lassitude that never existed before Wit reflected its shortfall in cloudy water', the poem begins.[15] The poem's tone is one of exhaustion, produced by a 'denial' of women's rights to choose to live in comfort and to be housed and looked after. These issues are illustrated by imagery of barren or inaccessible gardens: 'would we climb a staircase with no trace whatsoever of green /

---

[13]   See Mendelssohn, *I'm Working Here*, p. 69.
[14]   Albinia Stanley, '"work with the word that is all"; Politics and Labour in the Poetry of Anna Mendelssohn', *Journal of British and Irish Innovative Poetry*, 12.1 (2020), pp. 1–22 (p. 11).
[15]   Ian Sinclair, ed., *Conductors of Chaos: A Poetry Anthology* (London, 1996), p. 185.

the green in what my poem is not, a paeon to enamelled futures, leafless and formed / between flight and death'. One voice in the multi-vocal poem struggles to find a position of comfort in the liminal space of stark choices: to be housed or to exist in a barren outdoor environment, to flee or to die. Everything seems the 'wrong way round' and it is 'difficult to revolve vertically as a human triangle'. Senses of impossibility and impotence, and of the vulnerable and restless voice not fitting in, are produced by conditions and structures outside of their control. The only option is 'ignoring / advanced unelucidated conditions other than the requisite failure / & further intent to hurt'. The women described in the poem may have the right to vote, but they are denied other human rights and choices: 'aren't the women pleased / to be able to ignore their unfathomability having done them a democratic favour'. Women are denied the right to understand their own position in society; they remain 'unfathomable' and unable to articulate their own experiences in a malign, masculine society, subject to the 'pragmatic expertise' of a welfare system full of 'white torn paper' which produces a society 'full of les disparus'.

Later in the poem, the language of welfare ideology emerges:

> Purpose. Returns. Specific Moments. Voices that never fail to sustain a
>   social dimension.
> Voices that don't trail off into a dyer's land. Voices that don't lounge as
>   precautions to
> exhaustion in siesta time when observations cause disruptions in tedium.[16]

'Purpose. Returns. Specific moments' belong to no direct subject: they are dangling objects of purpose, direction or experience. Abstract 'Voices' (the word repeated three times), either dutifully sustain the social ('do not fail to sustain'), refuse to acquiesce to a collective death drive ('dyer's land') or act as cautionary tales of exhaustion. Such 'observations' (either the poem's or those of the voices) 'cause disruptures in tedium'. These meta-discursive comments highlight her poetic technique. Creating a neologism, 'disruptures', enacts her erupting disruption to any complacency. The language of the poem is opaque and grammatically inconsistent and there is no central authorial control of voice to anchor any stable position.

Mendelssohn's poem registers a felt disruption between what might be called the expectations of the social, of actions and language giving 'voice' to social codes and the marginal and multiple positions of those voices. As Cooper and Lousada suggest, 'societal character is dialectical', existing in 'complex relationships of cause and effect, and of meaning, operating

16   Sinclair, *Conductors of Chaos*, p. 186.

between social structures, the typical patterns of social relationship that produce, reproduce, and also challenge these structures, and the prevailing ideas and beliefs (ideologies)'.[17] In the broadest sense, there are conflicting and conflicted voices in this poem, confusing and unsettling any sense of relational certainty and challenging the ideological interpellation of fixed subject positions. The relative positions of a subject to the state, as well as to others, are, here, destabilised. These ruptures are created and affectively communicated to a reader by radical linguistic practices. To free itself from the ideological classifications sedimented in notions of welfare, radical poetics resists – awkwardly, rebarbatively, aggressively – the language of such. In doing so, it draws attention to the material conditions that create the necessity for welfare.

'Mainstream' Poetry and Austerity Britain

The syntactic and conceptual complexities of Mendelssohn's poetry represent an aesthetic form in combat with social and political marginalisation. But her poetry also actively resists resembling a type of 'mainstream' poetry in the legacy of the postwar, realist and nostalgic Movement poetry by poets such as Philip Larkin, Donald Davie and Thom Gunn. Williams described, in his afterword to the 1977 edition of *Modern Tragedy*, a situation where 'we have been more effectively incorporated into the deepest structures of this now dying order than it was ever, while it was strong, our habit to think or even suspect'.[18] To Williams, this 'order' is a capitalist one which, as he puts it, 'is in the process of defaulting on its most recent contract: to provide full employment, extended credit and high social expenditure as conditions for a political consensus of support'.[19] Williams detects a cultural and social slump to accept capitalism's failure as a new norm. Mendelssohn's poetry registers this despair and attempts to outflank such acceptance of the 'deepest structures' of inequality and loss of social contracts with syntactical and grammatical complexity. But what might a less radical poetic practice grappling with the same issues look like?

Ben Lerner has recently analysed how Claudia Rankine and Maggie Nelson deliberately abjure Language poetry's 'tactical deconstruction of ostensibly natural narrative or lyric'.[20] These poets 'forgo [...] difficulty as a strategy for

---

17   Cooper and Lousada, *Borderline Welfare*, p. 8.
18   Williams, 'Afterword to *Modern Tragedy*', p. 98.
19   Williams, 'Afterword to *Modern Tragedy*', p. 97.
20   Ben Lerner, 'After Difficulty', *The Fate of Difficulty in the Poetry of our Time*,

disrupting subjectivity in order to acknowledge the difficulty of calibrating a responsible self socially'.[21] Lerner suggests that gratuitous grammatical and syntactical strategies of resistance to transparent communication, writing in a singular voice and avoiding being captured by the discourses of capitalism are poetic techniques that are motivated by a now dated belief in the political efficacy of literature as well as by a homogenising sense of bourgeois culture. Referring to Ron Silliman's practice of The New Sentence, Lerner asks: 'Who among us still believes, if any of us ever did, that writing disjunctive prose poems counts as legitimately subversive political practice?'[22] As in the work of Rankine and Nelson, Lerner suggests that we should now aim to be more direct in tackling social issues.[23]

In 2011, Caparison Press published an impassioned anthology of such direct poems, entitled *Emergency Verse: Poetry in Defence of the Welfare State*. The collection began as a 2010 eBook, collected and edited by Alan Morrison, who, in response to the austerity budget of the 2010 Conservative and Liberal Democrat coalition, created 'Poets in Defence of the Welfare State' (PDWS), 'an ongoing literary campaign' (as Morrison writes in the forward to the collection), 'which will continue to oppose the Con-Dem Government's war on the poor and vulnerable in our society'.[24] *Emergency Verse* was the first publication of this group and was followed up in 2012 by *The Robin Hood Book – Verse Versus Austerity*. *Emergency Verse* was endorsed by Green Party MP Caroline Lucas, whose manifesto, entitled 'Invitation to

---

ed. Charles Altieri and Nicholas D. Nace (Evanston IL, 2018), pp. 135–41 (p. 139). 'Language Poetry' is an American experimental poetics movement started in the 1970s in response to mainstream and traditional poetry and forms, particularly the persistence of a lyric voice or the presentation of a singular subject position. Its practitioners, such as Charles Bernstein and Ron Silliman, emphasise the role of the reader in creating meaning, and undertake a political re-thinking of the role of the 'voice' of the poet. Its practices are deliberately political, emphasising communal meaning making and a radical critique of subjective individualism apparently embodied by mainstream lyric poetry.

[21] Lerner, 'After Difficulty', p. 138.

[22] Ron Silliman invented the phrase 'The New Sentence' to describe a paratactic form of prose poem featuring sentences that are discreet units of meaning and which do not have to cohere with their previous or subsequent sentences. The idea was to remove the sentence from being a unit within a larger structure and to make it singularly signifying and the conduit of discreet thoughts. He developed his practice from a reading of Ferdinand de Saussure's linguistics, Ludwig Wittgenstein's philosophical ideas (particularly about 'language-games') and the latter's style of writing.

[23] Lerner, 'After Difficulty', p. 136.

[24] Alan Morrison, ed., *Emergency Verse: Poetry in Defence of the Welfare State* (Bodmin and King's Lynn, 2011), p. v.

the Government to Join the Fair Society: An Alternative Budget and Response
to the Spending Review', opens the anthology. Morrison also created and
maintains the excellent *The Recusant* website, which is an ongoing platform
and resource for 'oppositional poetry, prose and polemic'. [25]

Emergency Verse contains several polemics, bookending a wide range of
poems and poets. The collection is testament to an abiding belief or hope
that poetry is in a unique position to challenge the ways in which we view
people who rely on the welfare state. All the poems show a left-wing critique
of welfare cuts as well as the use of a direct and declarative form of poetry.
Morrison's 'Emergency Forward: Autumn Harvest: Bonfire of the Benefits:
A Response to the October "Cleansing Review"' is a scathing tirade against
what he calls 'the most ethically and politically despicable' Budget in the UK's
national history.[26] He attacks the 'Con-Dem' government's 'indefatigable
top-down ruthlessness in its attempts to rebalance the country's books and
reimburse "the deficit" with the lifeblood of the sick, poor and unemployed,
and half a million public sector workers'. The cuts, he writes, are directed at
the wrong people and should be levelled at neoliberal 'City speculators; or
the parasitic multi-millionaire tax-avoiders' who were the architects of the
2008 financial crash. Morrison highlights 'the tacit criminalising of unemployment' and the 'fiscal fascism' of the Budget.[27] The collection defends
the principles, institutions of the welfare state, such as the National Health
Service, against privatisation and swinging cuts.

The choice of authors is wide-ranging, with contributions from established poets such as Sebastian Barker, Michael Horowitz and Michael Rosen
combined with many poets publishing for the first time. The styles and tones
of the works are varied, but most of them operate in the stylistic realms of
'mainstream' poetry. For instance, Tim Evans's poem 'Do You Want Some?'
takes place in a dole office. It speaks from the perspective of a benefits admin-
istrator asking the claimant ever more absurd questions. It starts with the
familiarly cold greeting: 'Someone from our Office / Will be coming to see
you soon / About your Benefits', adding in the next stanza:

FOR YOUR PROTECTION
All our Visiting Staff
Carry an identity card
ASK TO SEE IT.

---

[25]   <https://www.therecusant.org.uk/>.
[26]   Morrison, ed., *Emergency Verse*, p. i.
[27]   Morrison, ed., *Emergency Verse*, p. ii–iii.

Such humourless and human-less interactions (also glimpsed in Mendelssohn's 'London 1971') are characteristic of brutalising and bureaucratic interactions, with the faux-health and safety messages following an imperative to interact with the office on its terms as recognisable features of such exchanges. As the poem develops, the addressee is told:

> So that there is no further delay
> In calculation and payment
> Of your Benefit
> Entitlement
>
> You must fill in the tear-off part of this form each week.

They are then asked a series of ever-more bizarre personal questions designed to check for the person's suitability for the benefits. These questions range from the plausible ('Are you pregnant?', 'Are you getting Disability Living Allowance?') to the absurd ('Can you walk? / Can you crawl / Can you pick up a half litre carton of milk / Or Special Brew?')[28] Evans's title, 'Do You Want Some?', is double-edged and can be read as a benign request or an aggressive taunt. The poem illustrates this contradictory state: an apparently helpful institution is aggressively reticent to follow through on its stated purpose. Evans reveals what Cooper and Lousada describe as the controlling nature of the welfare system and its in-built reactionary character.[29] To Evans, the system is full of 'tensions, contradictions and inconsistencies, but the immovable system fails to account for these'.[30]

The poet and counsellor Maria Gornell's poem 'Inner city blues' contains similar images of people stuck in the paradoxical and contradictory limbo of benefit administration. The poem starts with an epigraph by Karl Marx ('For the bureaucrat, the world is a mere object to be manipulated by him') followed by these opening lines:

> The air is thick with degradation
> the dole queues haven't been this
> long since the 80's
>
> Greeted by the pitiful smile of administration

---

[28] Morrison, ed., *Emergency Verse*, pp. 65–8.
[29] Cooper and Lousada, *Borderline Welfare*, p. 15.
[30] Cooper and Lousada, *Borderline Welfare*, p. 19.

Trapped in the cycle of poverty
flexed in the frustration of hope
that beats the drum of the welfare state
patterns manipulating the strive to
be free of decay.[31]

Even people are objects to Marx's bureaucrats, stuck in cycles of degradation, looked on with 'pitiful smile[s]' and inexorably tied to the drumbeats
and 'patterns' of hopelessness. As in Evans's poem, Gornell's illustrates the
exhaustion of being subject to a benefits system. The tone is one of enervated
complaint. Cooper and Lousada argue that the state's contract to care for
the vulnerable produces structures of feeling that are expressed through 'a
kind of persistent and inarticulate sense of complaint – complaint about
perpetual change, policy and acronym fatigue, and [...] structural conditions
which engender an atmosphere of professional and moral exhaustion'.[32]
Cooper and Lousada are, in a sense, in the same position as Gornell in diag-
nosing and witnessing these exhausted people. From this situation, the object
of the state's systems can only look on and despair; we can only sadly move
to the 'beats of the drum of welfare'. The poem outlines an exhausted and
disenfranchised state of being.

Elsewhere, in 'Them And Us', Alan Doherty much more explicitly
describes despair:

Housing Benefits slashed
families on the streets
begging for food
food token parcels out of date binned supermarket packages.

Millions of Public sector jobs join the dole line
V.A.T. up to 20%
consumerable goods, shoes-clothing-kitchen bathroom utensils
Dickensian society by the week.[33]

Here, Doherty directly confronts the dehumanising reality of his own experience of living on Incapacity Benefits by listing experiences of destitution and

---

Morrison, ed., *Emergency Verse*, pp. 82–3. The reference can be found in Karl
Marx, 'Contribution to the Critique of Hegel's Philosophy of Law', *Karl Marx,
Frederick Engels: Collected Works, Volume 3: Karl Marx, March 1843–August 1844*
(London, 2010), pp. 3–129 (p. 48).
[32]   Cooper and Lousada, *Borderline Welfare*, p. 21.
[33]   Morrison, ed., *Emergency Verse*, p. 55.

framing these against cold facts. This is the world Vicky Lebeau describes in her analysis of Ken Loach's 2016 film *I, Daniel Blake*: one where people are subject to the 'exposure of the brick wall of the bureaucratic function'.[34] The 'food token parcels' and 'binned supermarket packages' in the poem evoke a landscape of the normalisation of food banks and pervasive, systemic precarity. Austerity under the Tory government recreates a Malthusian logic of the undeserving poor – which Dickens satirises in *A Christmas Carol* – and these poems bear witness to such conditions.

The three poems discussed refer to benefits and the experiences of people on the not-quite-receiving end of a contemporary welfare state. The abiding tone of all of them is disgust and despair. But Evans's poem is also witty and ironic, caricaturing the absurdity of the questioning in a benefits interview. The question about being able to pick up 'Special Brew' also adopts the clichéd, right-wing characterisations of people on benefits found in Hall's poem. These lines remind us of Margaret Thatcher's infamous comments about welfare encouraging, to her, 'illegitimacy', facilitating 'the breakdown of families' and replacing 'incentives favouring work and self-reliance with perverse encouragement for idleness and cheating'.[35] Such characterisations of people on benefits were ramped up under the Cameron-Osborne administration. '[T]he notorious rhetoric of 'welfare benefits as a "lifestyle choice"', writes Lebeau (quoting George Osborne in 2010), 'of the "benefit culture" (David Cameron in 2011), and of a "damaging culture of dependency and worklessness" (Iain Duncan Smith in 2014), has helped create an environment' allowing the 'ruthless reduction of what it means to live a human life'.[36] What unites all the poems are their clear, declarative language designed to make their opposition to cuts in welfare and disgust of Tory policies transparent, their description or caricaturing of bureaucratic discourse, as well as a firm conviction that a reader will and should recognise and empathise with these experiential realities.

These poems offer terrifying glimpses into life under austerity, but they are formally very different from the work of Mendelssohn and the other poems I discuss below. One of the reasons for this is that they are designed for a different readership. What these differences seem to suggest is that mainstream protest poetry retains a faith and conviction that personal witness and what might be called experiential reportage are the best strategies to draw atten-

---

[34] Vicky Lebeau, 'Feeling Poor: D. W. Winnicott and Danial Blake', *New Formations*, 96–7 (2019), pp. 160–76 (p. 173).
[35] David Garland, *The Welfare State: A Very Short Introduction* (Oxford, 2016), p. 107.
[36] Lebeau, 'Feeling Poor', p. 162.

tion to injustice. These poems in defence of the welfare state use personal experiences with the hope of drawing attention to the plight of vulnerable people. To refer to Lerner again, to these poets, 'the subject isn't a dominant bourgeois fiction of inwardness and univocality in need of deconstruction, but an avowedly social and linguistic entity deployed [...] in the space of writing'.[37] In producing vivid images of the social and linguistic entities subject to welfare cuts, the poems aim to elicit a reader's horror and empathy; they do this very effectively. But, as we have seen with Mendelssohn's poetry, there are other poets who still resort to deconstructive strategies, to critiques of socially-produced subjectivity and subjecthood, as well as the employment of radical and difficult poetic strategies in order to draw attention to inequality and welfare precarity. Poets such as Sean Bonney and Fran Lock dispute the notion that such realistic witness is a politically useful aesthetic.

What Remains: Sean Bonney's *The Commons*

The poet Sean Bonney wrote frequently on Mendelssohn's work as a poet-activist. For Bonney, Mendelssohn enacted a poetics of refusal and unrelenting struggle against the assaults of the Thatcher government:

> As far as Mendelssohn's enemies are concerned, and these are many – not only judges but, variously, pompous poets, social workers, narrow-minded politicos and patriarchal imbeciles of all sorts – it [Mendelssohn's work] is a communication that speaks to them in order to deny their ability to read, and to refuse them a place within the poem. It is an outsidedness that also has nothing to do with the easy conformity of the poetry as some kind of rebel. Mendelssohn is no rebel; the content of her refusal to communicate with her enemies is one that demands the possibility of communication, and of the reality of a community that can exist despite the accusations of its incomprehensibility and illegitimacy. In the face of those who would have 'silenced' her, the response is to speak a language to which they have no access.[38]

Bonney sees his own poetry as continuing this resistant poetic project, at a moment when the welfare state was under new strain. This resistant poetics is quite different from the protest poetics collected in *Emergency Verse*, even though it stems from the same starting point; it is less witness and more self-

---

[37]   Lerner, 'After Difficulty', p. 140.

[38]   Sean Bonney, '"Minds do exist to agitate and provoke / this is the reason I do not conform" – Anna Mendelssohn', *Journal of British and Irish Innovative Poetry*, 14.1 (2022), pp. 1–22 (p. 5).

conscious critique. Bonney introduces his collection *Filth Screed* (2003/4) with a credo: 'All poetry that does not testify to an awareness of the radical falsity of the established forms (of life) is faulty [...] No-one has yet spoken a language which is not the language of those who establish, enforce, and benefit from the facts. Language is conservative'.[39] Of course, all language cannot be conservative, but what Bonney aspires to is to produce 'prosody via black bloc tactics', as he puts it, which is perhaps an impossible writing using a 'language which is not the language' of the establishment and to draw attention to the 'radical falsity' of established forms of life.

Bonney's poetic journey began in 'the political context of Thatcher's Britain as an anarchist, anti-fascist and organiser'.[40] As Kashif Sharma-Patel suggests, the coalition 'austerity' budget of 2010, and the subsequent student protests and social unrest, inaugurated a 'more complicated form in Bonney's work, one grounded more explicitly in both hope and defeat'.[41] This period led to the publication of a long sequence, *The Commons* (2011), followed by *Happiness: Poems After Rimbaud* (2011) and *Letters Against the Firmament* (2015). For Bonney and other poets, the 2008 financial crash, and the subsequent Conservative retrenchment of financial inequalities through austerity measures, offered a period of clarification for the type of revolutionary or militant poetics that was required. As David Nowell-Smith puts it in an essay on Bonney's work, 2010 issued in 'a new political conjuncture: the Occupy movement, the student protests, and the mobilisation of hundreds of thousands against a Conservative-led government espousing the very ideology that the financial collapse should have discredited, now seemingly hell-bent on dismantling what remained of the welfare state.'[42] But, for Bonney and others, the solution was not simply for poets to write poems against such conditions, but to attempt to find a language that articulates different logics of collectivity and revolution; to write a poetry that imagines different conditions, one that, to quote Lebeau, 'facilitates, and is facilitated by [...] the mutual imbrication of dependence and mind, care and human creativity.'[43] Bonney's poetry went through a range of dramatic formal changes during

---

[39]   Sean Bonney, 'Filth Screed', *Blade Pitch Control* (Great Wilbraham, 2005), p. 87.
[40]   Kashif Sharma-Patel, 'Bonney's Militant Poetics: Political Aesthetics, Black Poetics and Modernism', *Journal of British and Irish Innovative Poetry*, 14.1 (2022), pp. 1–23 (p. 6).
[41]   Sharma-Patel, 'Bonney's Militant Poetics', p. 7.
[42]   David Nowell-Smith, '"An Interrupter, a Collective": Sean Bonney's Lyric Outrage', *Etudes britaniniques contemporaines*, 45 (2013), pp. 1–12 (p. 1).
[43]   Lebeau, 'Feeling Poor', p. 171.

this time, from direct protest and witness to a more disjunctive poetics. What Bonney envisioned during this period of change, as Robert Hampson writes, was 'a militant poetics, an antagonistic poetry, not protest poetry'.[44]

Bonney's conception of a militant poetics was developed from his close reading of several Black poets, theorists, writers and anarchists – Amira Baraka, Frantz Fanon, Aimé Césaire and the prison writings of George Jackson, in particular – and of Situationist works, Theodor Adorno, the poetry of Arthur Rimbaud and the work of Walter Benjamin. In his 'Notes on Militant Poetics' (originally blog posts, republished in 2022), Bonney offers a range of close readings of revolutionary works and sketches the types of resistant and revolutionary poetics that critique the social and political realities that make welfare necessary. Drawing on Benjamin's writing on hermetic poetry, Bonney reads Rimbaud and other poets' work as 'esoteric' which, to him, confers (albeit obliquely) 'latent content', which is realised 'through a dialectic of poetry and Marxism'.[45] Militant poetics, for Bonney, needs to resist the temporal-spatial locations of capitalist time, a totality enveloping us all, and realise 'a counter-time which is necessarily revolutionary'.[46] For Bonney, 'Poetry does not talk about the world, nor does it create meaning, but rather aims at meanings not yet articulated, meanings not catered to in the currently available aesthetic and social networks'.[47] Such poetry, for Bonney, operates in 'a critical-edge condition', always on the brink of tearing itself apart.

Nowell-Smith captures the impulse of Bonney's work cogently, describing it as expressing 'individual outrage' as well as 'a desire for collective praxis'.[48] Nowell-Smith argues that it 'seeks to cajole its readers into political reflection, and ultimately into collective action', but the collective for Bonney is not simply a question of political efficacy: his entire thinking is united by the belief that human freedom is predicated on collective structures, on the 'commons'. Adjunct welfare institutions and systems of these 'commons' would be socialist and liberating. Bonney's book-length poem sequence *The Commons* (2011) exemplifies his attempt to envisage and mobilise powerful collectivity, particularly a common understanding of the contradictions and

---

44 Robert Hampson, '"Speaking with voices of the dead": Sean Bonney, Amira Baraka, Arthur Rimbaud and Revolutionary Poetics', *Journal of British and Irish Innovative Poetry*, 14.1 (2022), pp. 1–22 (p. 19).

45 Sean Bonney, 'Notes on Militant Poetics', *Journal of British and Irish Innovative Poetry*, 14.1 (2022), pp. 1–16 (p. 7).

46 Bonney, 'Notes on Militant Poetics', p. 5.

47 Bonney, 'Notes on Militant Poetics', p. 10.

48 Nowell-Smith, '"An Interrupter, a Collective"', p. 1.

complicities of writing poetry against the instrumental forces of capitalism in the compromised position of being enveloped by these conditions. As such, each of the fourteen-line sections of the poem features recursive and percussive clots and gobbets of language fractured in a range of voices, tones and registers and which somehow cleave open a space from which we glimpse a hopeful terrain of revolutionary collectivity: 'here is a landscape', Bonney writes, referring to the conditions of living under the conservative government and the 'big constitutional principle[s]' outlined by David Cameron, 'here is "all hell"'.[49] But the next lines shift the focus to the poem itself: 'the distance between each line / some kind of "celestial snarl"' which 'redistributes the city / a strange and bitter crop'. In this landscape 'you live in rigged integers', the codes, symbols and 'alphabets' of the royal family ('gaps in the royal alphabet'), housing benefits ('distort gap / in the housing alphabet'), the police: 'doing "the alphabet" / its secret monarchy, its meaning / its nice dog functions, / its corporate poetry sucks'.[50] Bonney enfolds descriptions of this debased world within language, phrases and voices from a range of perspectives, all united by a rage to change the current system.

Bonney's work registers an acute distrust of the roles assigned to us by a state, and this scabrous scepticism is registered in a refusal to accept the common meaning of words when the consensus of meaning is generated from a bourgeois sensibility. Poetry that expresses this position, as he rather categorically puts it at the beginning of an article on Mendelssohn, is simply 'genteel self-expression' that will be expressed through 'metrical sentimentalities' and contain 'easily digestible liberal homilies that are essentially reports on police reality'.[51] Writing about Mendelssohn's poem 'London, 1971', Bonney argues that its textual strategies are designed 'not simply to counter official discourse' but to 'actively engage in battle with it'.[52] In his essays and poetry, Bonney associates cultural reflections of social and cultural conditions that do not examine their own complicity with such conditions as essentially 'reports' of the conditions as they are. Referring to Mendelssohn's poetry after she came out of prison, Bonney writes that its 'attitude [...] is consistently one of absolute contempt for bourgeois society and its domination by police reality'. Bonney reads the lines 'Serve your own sentences. / In future. / I collect sentences. / I used to have a set of my own' (from Mendelssohn's

[49]   Sean Bonney, *The Commons II* (2009), p. 5. <http://static1.1.sqspcdn.com/static/f/436447/4272776/1254103816363/sean-bonney-the-commons-ii.pdf?token=UOT9GyNfsZra6tOEXWZ7Q3I2EFQ%3D>.
[50]   Bonney, *The Commons II*, pp. 3–9.
[51]   Bonney, 'Notes on Militant Poetics', p. 2.
[52]   Bonney, 'Notes on Militant Poetics', p. 4.

poem 'I do not run the prison system') as battling 'the sentence of the judge'. For Bonney, Mendelssohn's poetry as well as his own create poetic forms that challenge not only prevailing cultural norms but the authorities that are flattered and consolidated within such forms.

Fran Lock and the Trauma of Contemporary Welfare

Fran Lock is a working class, Northern Irish poet of traveller descent. In an article on working-class poetry, Lock outlines the consistent unease, precarity and marginality working-class writers experience in accessing welfare. Lock argues for, and herself writes, a poetry that both reclaims and complicates notions of the individual's experience of marginality. She also explores the fraught nature of trying to speak plainly when such clear and direct language is in the rhetorical control of those who oppress marginalised people. As Lock notes, in writing of poetry by working-class women in particular:

> [A] focus on the materiality of text allows us to use the structural aspects of language to critique the unconscious and invisible organisations of linguistic power: the position of words within linguistic structures echo and evoke the positioning of living subjects within the structures of contemporary society. At a time when working-class visibility within both popular and political discourses is increasingly vexed, this interrogation of positionality assumes a critical importance. Radical poetry, that is poetry alive to the exploitation inherent to working-class existence, can only challenge ideology by first challenging notions about language, for it is through language that ideology is encoded and transmitted.[53]

Lock's poetics of 'enmity' resembles Bonney's 'militant poetics': they are aesthetic practices that absorb, critique and reclaim the language and linguistic practices of power. Her collection *White/Other* offers ongoing questions of 'how will we [create/write/produce a] poem?', as Lock puts it.[54] As such, *White/Other* develops poetic 'style as a singular libidinal fury, erected against destruction', its 'fragmentation [is] a defence against trauma'.[55] But she is compromised and contradictory, as she realises that avant-garde poetic practices are often the province of the middle classes or at least those with significant cultural power. '[I]f fragmentation is the trippy nectar trauma

---

[53]   Fran Lock, 'Thinking the Working-Class 'Aven't Gard', *Journal of British and Irish Innovative Poetry*, 13.4 (2021), pp. 1–25 (p. 7).
[54]   Fran Lock, *White/Other* (London, 2022), p. 41.
[55]   Lock, *White/Other*, p. 25.

makes in language', Lock wryly adds, registering a distrust of the association of 'fragmentation' with what might be called middle-class or elitist avant-gardism. '[R]igour and innovation', Lock writes, 'are solely the fruits of white middle-class literary production'.[56]

The book features recycled, re-imagined, re-coded phrases in a style she describes, embracing playful and often pathologised characteristics, as 'leaden pedantry or manic gabble. verbigeration, perseveration, echolalia-alia-alia.' Perhaps, as she continues, 'it is not the case that trauma is or must remain unspoken, rather, that any attempts at an intelligent representation fail at, or are failed by, the limits of language'.[57] As such, her work is deliberately (at points) opaque: '*opacity* exposes the limits of representation', she says.[58] Taking aim at the types of paucity of welfare help offered by the state, Lock writes:

> what if i don't want to be consoled? or to console in my turn? try to imagine anger as more than a *stage* or a *shtick*. i will not *work through this* internally, politely repress and appease with quiet dignity behind closed doors or in specially sanctioned spaces. you want to draw a *cordon sanitaire* between my dangerous rage and the world, and you keep asking me: *why are you so angry? lament* is not *elegy*.[59]

Lock refuses to play the game of consolation in the performance spaces of those she addresses and who always already address her as needing to be saved and salved from her righteous anger. Like Mendelssohn, instead of speaking through the language of welfare, Lock expropriates such language, squeezing it for irony and contradiction. She continues, describing the death of a close companion,

> i won't write myself well, idealise his dying or his life. i won't dissolve the serial oppressions that beset us in some vague gesture towards empathy, whereby the beauty of my pain functions as a tacit justification for the inequalities that produced it. listen fucker, that deep swell of feeling a poem prompts may *seem* profound to you. may *seem* momentous even. but it is interior, entirely subjective, the opposite of true sympathy, true solidarity. this kind of poetry, and the idea that it connects people through some golden thread of fellow feeling conceals your responsibility for producing the wound. you're a sly shit, you

---

[56]   Lock, *White/Other*, p. 43.
[57]   Lock, *White/Other*, p. 10.
[58]   Lock, *White/Other*, p. 87.
[59]   Lock, *White/Other*, p. 69.

use catharsis to make a fetish out of working-class *resilience*; you tie suffering to a marketable performance of identity.[60]

As Lock declares, a normative appreciation of poetry and culture becomes another way of confining and constraining working-class writing and voices. Words and phrases such as 'momentous', 'fellow feeling', 'catharsis' and even 'identity' are used by Lock's addressees as 'marketable' performances, reifications of real pain that abolish the conditions in which the pain was produced.

Lock's poetry, here, is perhaps one stage further from the descriptions of welfare interviews in the poems of *Emergency Verse*. Like Evans and Doherty, Lock describes the ways in which the people seeking welfare are made to perform the role of the 'identity' of someone seeking benefits. To Lock such capitulation to the common language of sympathy and feeling blocks 'true sympathy' and 'true solidarity'. Lock seems to refuse to even acknowledge such 'reifications' of pain and suffering often expressed in poetry, in a move equivalent to declining to answer any interview questions as an acknowledgement that they are always-already interpolating. For Lock, not only does this transfer working-class experience and writing into a contained thing to witness, but it fails to account for the responsibility for its own production of the conditions that create pain. Lock's response to middle-class commodification of working-class culture and her diagnosis of an ignorance of complicity is to embrace a poetry containing 'dialects and patois', making use of 'multiple linguistic parries and evasions: reversal, metathesis, affixing and substitution'. This is a contemporary, radical lyric that refuses the terms of literature and language underpinned by the state:

> We drop or transpose consonant clusters. We alliterate and metaphoricalise; we play and pun. We incorporate the bejesus out of Romani, Polari, slang. We cultivate and remix idiolects. We force literary and historical allusions up against pop culture; our clipped and cantering rhythms, our t-stopped compressive poetry against iambic pentameter. We take the 'garbled' and we play it against the eloquence of the contemporary lyric.[61]

Lock's last point in her essay is important in framing her resistant poetics against a backdrop of the type of lyric poetry found in *Emergency Verse*. Unlike Bonney, Lock wants to reclaim the lyric mode as an expression of an individual's perspective, but she will do this using her own idiolectic, incorporating playing and punning as well as slang-full and garbled language prac-

---

[60]   Lock, *White/Other*, p. 70.
[61]   Lock, 'Thinking the Working-Class 'Aven't Gard', p. 22.

tices. Lock's poetry demands that it be read on its own terms and, as such, it creates its own space. To approach her poetry, and to enter this space, readers must confront their own comfortable or stable positions in relation to it.

Conclusion

In his afterword to the 1977 edition of *Modern Tragedy*, Raymond Williams registers 'a very deep stasis' in contemporary art's confrontation with social, cultural and political crises. The prevailing conditions, Williams notes, have induced a sense of torpor that literary form struggles to challenge. In 1977, for Williams, the progressive hope that he had charted in tragic form had dwindled; he found the cultural forms representing or expressing such moods were concomitantly despairing. For Williams, it was only by enfolding the inchoate thoughts and voices of immanent collusion within a debased system (as he saw in Beckett's work) that aesthetic forms can 'understand their intricate and diverse formation' to 'see, through and beyond them, the elements of new dynamic formations'.[62]

Williams's description of the shifts from the 1960s to the 1970s detected the beginnings of what Stuart Hall has described as 'the long march of the Neoliberal Revolution'.[63] Since the late 1970s we have moved from a postwar state, offering what Carolyn Steedman describes as 'structure[s] of care and affection', with their concomitant feeling of safety, into a neoliberal society that privileges individualism and the abolishment of caring social and political contracts.[64] Recent analyses of the current British welfare state from psychoanalytic perspectives paint a compelling picture of the ways in which welfare institutions and their attendant discourses have increasingly marginalised and demonised forms of 'dependency'.

For Cooper and Lousada, seemingly progressive changes in the welfare system since the 1970s have created a culture of 'ruthlessness in attempting to *control* rather than *enable* the workforce'.[65] For Lebeau, a comparable breaking of trust between the state and its citizens is understood in the framework of an erasure and demonisation of D. W. Winnicott's psychoanalytic formulations of mutual human imbrication, dependability and care. Using Winnicott's terms, Lebeau argues that neoliberalism's ideological

[62]   Williams, 'Afterword to Modern Tragedy', p. 105.
[63]   Stuart Hall, 'The March of the Neoliberals', *The Guardian*, 21 September 2011. <https://www.theguardian.com/politics/2011/sep/12/march-of-the-neoliberals>.
[64]   Carolyn Steedman, *Landscape for a Good Woman* (London, 1986), p. 123.
[65]   Cooper and Lousada, *Borderline Welfare*, p. 15.

abolishment or criticisms of 'dependence as a living fact' has produced the conditions whereby the complex and individual needs of vulnerable people are literally not seen or recognised by and in the language of welfare.[66] As Lebeau puts it, adjustments to the welfare state no longer provide a 'holding environment' for vulnerable people.[67] While all the poets discussed in this article demand a radical rethinking of the current welfare state, Mendelssohn, Bonney and Lock use a range of poetic tactics in order not to capitulate to a system that has, as Lock writes, working-class people's 'failure as part of the design'.[68] Rather, as Nowell-Smith says of Bonney's poetics, these forms 'contribute to working through what [...] collectivity might look like.'[69]

---

[66]   Lebeau, 'Feeling Poor', p. 167, referring to 'The Theory of the Parent-Infant Relationship' (1960), *The Collected Works of D. W. Winnicott, Volume 6: 1960–1963*, ed. Lesley Caldwell and Helen Taylor Robinson (Oxford, 2017), pp. 141–58.
[67]   Lebeau, 'Feeling Poor', p. 171.
[68]   Lock, *White/Other*, p. 19.
[69]   Nowell-Smith, '"An Interrupter, a Collective"', p. 5.

5

How to Be a Marxist Thief: How Raymond Williams Read T. S. Eliot

BECI CARVER

This essay begins with a cover-up. When Marxist critic Raymond Williams first wrote his monograph of 1961 on drama, its title was *Drama from Ibsen to Eliot*, but when the book reappeared in 1968 it had become *Drama from Ibsen to Brecht*.[1] Eliot had mysteriously vanished. Williams's acknowledgements in the new edition circle a ghost, with two-thirds devoted to Valerie Eliot and the other to copyright owners of Eliot's plays. Where had Possum gone? The argument of this essay is that, appalled by Eliot's increasingly marked shift to the far right in middle age, especially on the theme of welfare, Williams set out to purge the author's influence from his work. Harold Bloom writes of Shakespeare in *The Anxiety of Influence* that 'he will not allow you to bury him', but Williams could not afford for the same to be true of Eliot.[2] Three years after his death it was time to pour cement over T. S. E.

Williams had tried to bury Eliot before. It was then 1948. Eliot's *Notes Towards a Definition of Culture* had, Williams told a *New Left Review* interviewer, 'quickly acquired great influence', and Williams had found himself swept up among the intoxicated.[3] Eliot had begun that book with the grandiose announcement that to 'rescue the word [culture] was the extreme of his ambition', and, echoing him in his own monograph, *Culture and Society*, Williams promised to do the same.[4] However, rather than admitting to the echo, Williams invited his readers to imagine a free-standing epiphany. He had been browsing the basement of Seaford's Public Library, he tells us, when he

---

[1]   Raymond Williams, *Drama from Ibsen to Brecht* (London, 1987), front matter.
[2]   Harold Bloom, *The Anxiety of Influence: A Theory of Poetry* (New York, 1997), p. xviii.
[3]   Raymond Williams, *Politics and Letters: Interviews with New Left Review* (London, 2015), p. 97.
[4]   T. S. Eliot, *Notes Towards a Definition of Culture* (New York, [1948] 1949), p. 17. '[O]n the strength of his path-breaking *Culture and Society 1780–1950* [Williams] was appointed to a lectureship at Cambridge and later to a Chair': Terry Eagleton, *Critical Revolutionaries* (New Haven, 2022), p. 259.

found himself 'look[ing] up "culture" almost casually' in *The Oxford English Dictionary*, and there it was, the word whose connotations would, long after, 'force [themselves] upon [his] attention', asserting their 'significance and difficulty.'[5] 'Almost' here *almost* admits to a more than casual inclination to care about a word that, famously, had been Eliot's keyword first.

I understand Williams's preoccupation with Eliot to have begun in the mid-1940s, when he returned to Cambridge after active service to resume his undergraduate degree in English Literature. It was the heyday of the Labour Party, largely to be credited with the creation of the welfare state and the ascendancy of Aneurin Bevan, the foremost parliamentary champion of the National Health Service. In 1939, Eliot had snuck into *The Family Reunion* a cameo for a character named 'Mr Bevan' who exists simply to hassle his upper-class cast about their 'taxes.'[6] At the time, Bevan was a familiar pit bull character in the House of Commons, noisily defending his constituency's welfare needs to one chronically frail 1930s government after another. He was an easy – because loud yet comparatively harmless – target for Tory mockery. But a few years later, following Bevan's appointment as Labour's Minister of Health and the slow but sure emergence of welfare, attacks on the Welshman, and upon socialist reform more generally, began to stand out. It was at this point that Williams became conscious of Eliot as an anomaly in the reading interests of his socialist peers: did they not see that Eliot could be bad for them? He tells a *New Left Review* interviewer that '*The Four Quartets* completely dominated reading and discussion in Cambridge at the time [...] I recall coming out of one of these discussions, not with enemies but with friends who considered themselves active socialists and yet were endorsing Eliot's work'.[7]

Not least among Williams's worries on this score was his own susceptibility to Eliot's word-music. He admits to the same interviewer: 'I said to myself – a ridiculous expression that must have been some echo of an Eliot rhythm – "here also the class struggle occurs".'[8] Eliot had become an earworm for Williams by 1946, and would remain so at least until 1966, when an echo between *The Family Reunion* and Williams's egalitarian theory of tragedy in *Modern Tragedy* reveals him to have been mouthing another 'Eliot rhythm.' In *The Family Reunion*, Eliot's chorus chants: 'We *know* about the railway

[5]   Raymond Williams, *Keywords* (London, 1983), p. 13.
[6]   Amy reminds Harry, 'Mr Bevan – you remember – wants to call tomorrow / On some legal business, a question about taxes', T. S. Eliot, *The Complete Poems and Plays of T. S. Eliot* (London, 1969), p. 292.
[7]   Williams, *Politics and Letters*, p. 67.
[8]   Ibid.

accident / We *know* about the sudden thrombosis / And the slowly harden-ing artery'.[9] Williams sings back in the well-known opening lines of *Modern Tragedy*, as if improvising an Anglican call and response: 'I have *known* what I believe to be tragedy in many forms [...] I have *known* tragedy in the life of a man driven back into silence [...] I have *known* this tragedy more widely since [...] I have *known* also, as a whole culture has *known*, a tragic action framing these worlds, yet also, paradoxically and bitterly, breaking into them' (my italics).[10] My interest in this essay lies in the story of Williams's relationship with Eliot's words: how they haunted him, how at times they seemed even to align with his own politics – and even to push the egalitarian cause further than welfare could – and how they let him down. I will track here Williams's romance with an author he ostensibly shunned.

Eliot and Bevan

One reading of *The Family Reunion* may allow us to imagine Eliot and Bevan singing from the same song-sheet. The lines quoted above belong to a larger meditation by Harry on why the experience of human suffering, as soon as it is put into words, may become mutual and communal. Harry reasons that *because* 'the particular has no language', 'We *know* about the railway acci-dent / We *know* about the sudden thrombosis / And the slowly harden-ing artery.'[11] Subsequent theorists, most notably Elaine Scarry in *The Body in Pain*, have argued the contrary: 'intense pain' is 'language-destroying', since 'as the content of the world disintegrates, so the content of one's lan-guage disintegrates; as the self disintegrates, so that which would express and project the self is robbed of its source and its subject.'[12] Pain is solitary because it destroys the self that might communicate it. But, for Harry and Eliot through him, pain is *public* because our words make it so: you cannot have your own entirely unique 'thrombosis' because there is a shared word that connects your experience to that of others. Language compels us to suffer together. For Eliot, this became a reason to revive the ancient Greek chorus as a device for pooling expressions of pain, while his plays and poems consistently hinge on shared grievances. '*We* are the hollow men'. Bevan, too, believed that suffering was intrinsically a public matter. From 1928, when he

---

9   Eliot, *Complete Poems and Plays*, p. 301.
10   Williams, *Modern Tragedy*, p. 33.
11   Eliot, *Complete Poems and Plays*, p. 294.
12   Elaine Scarry, *The Body in Pain: The Making and Unmaking of the World* (Oxford, 1985), p. 35.

surfed into office on a wave of Welsh working-class support – from a mining village close to Williams's hometown of Panty – and throughout his parliamentary career, he earned national backing for the principle that personal medical illness was the state's responsibility.

Bevan's socialist mission to involve society at large in the suffering of individuals was sparked in the first instance (or so he claimed) by the loss of his father, a collier, to emphysema or 'black lung'.[13] David Bevan's treatment proved too costly either for his family or for the fund created by his workmates, the Tredegar Workingmen's Medical Aid Society, meaning that while the nature of his illness was legible to all, he died undiagnosed and untreated.[14] To his son, the injustice seemed blatant, and he began to say so in the House of Commons, using his father's example to fuel the case for a national health service. Susan Sontag would write in 1964, casting her eye back over the dramatic output of recent decades, that 'self-exposure is commendable in art only when it is of a quality and complexity that allows other people to learn about themselves from it'.[15] Perfectly exemplifying these criteria, Bevan's 'self-exposure' in Westminster improvised autobiography into a lesson in collective, taxable responsibility. He was good theatre by Sontag's standards, as well as embodied proof that 'the particular has no language'.[16]

The idea that my thrombosis is your thrombosis, that tragedy may invite not just sympathy but communion, goes back to ancient Greece and to the tragic convention of the *chorós* – a group of up to fifteen choral singers and dancers (and twenty-five in comedy) whose role was to reflect on the unfolding drama, absorbing its crises into their song.[17] We have long believed we could co-suffer. However, until the twentieth century there had been no substantial political endeavour – in the United Kingdom, at least – to correlate the humane intuitions upon which art rested with government policy. And even after the embedding of national welfare provisions in the state machine, something remained wanting. Lecturing on the Bloomsburyans in Canterbury in 1978, Williams depicts a group who, for all their socialist talk, displayed no real 'solidarity' or 'affiliation' with those whose cause they took up.[18] What motivated them, Williams argues, was not comradeship but a felt 'obligation' to dissent from the 'dominant majority' in opposing 'the cruelty

---

[13]   Martin M. Krug, *Aneurin Bevan: Cautious Rebel* (New York, 1961), p. 86.
[14]   Ibid.
[15]   Susan Sontag, *Against Interpretation and Other Essays* (London, 2009), p. 141.
[16]   Eliot, *Complete Poems and Plays*, p. 294.
[17]   Graham Ley, *A Short Introduction to the Ancient Greek Theatre* (1997; Chicago, 2006), p. 30.
[18]   Raymond Williams, *Culture and Materialism* (London, 2005), p. 154.

and stupidity of the system' towards those who were 'relatively helpless.'[19] They were radical in speech rather than sensibility, as though tragedy had taught them nothing.

That British society was divided in spirit seemed reflected in the Cambridge degree programme to which Williams returned in 1945. For it was now, upon reaching Part II of what is called 'Tripos', that he started work for the 'Tragedy Paper', as well as for another paper designed to enhance his close reading skills, 'Practical Criticism.' 'Practical criticism' had, for Williams, the makings of an egalitarian course, which by focussing on 'unseen' texts and aiming to sharpen students' spontaneous responses, potentially offset 'the element of collusion in [the] tradition of appreciation: the informed, assured and familiarized discourse of people talking among themselves about works which from a shared social position they had been privileged to know'.[20] But if 'Practical Criticism' levelled the playing field, 'Tragedy' reintroduced its hills and holes, both superficially, by rewarding students who knew their classical allusions, and more profoundly, by reframing tragic experience in elitist terms. For in 'tragedy' as Cambridge taught it, only the socially high-ranked were understood to be capable of tragically significant pain. 'Your thrombosis' was not 'my thrombosis' if either of us happened to outrank the other. Appalled at this bigotry, Williams, with extraordinary ambition – as if carrying to the furthest extreme what John Guillory calls criticism's 'overestimation of aim' – set out in *Modern Tragedy* to *change his readers' ideological settings*, making a collectivist tragedy possible.[21] In other words, Williams meant to expose the gap between tragedy's reliance on our instinct for humane fellow-feeling and British culture's broader commitment to class inequality.

Some of the blame for Cambridge's elitist perception of tragedy may be assigned to A. C. Bradley, whose classic 1904 monograph, *Shakespearean Tragedy*, dictates as a non-negotiable rule that 'A tale [...] of a man slowly worn to death by disease, poverty, little cares, sordid vices, petty persecutions, however piteous or dreadful it might be, would not be tragic in the Shakespearean sense.'[22] We do not know for certain that Williams read Bradley at Cambridge. Yet his role as a touchstone throughout *Modern Tragedy*, both

---

[19] Ibid.
[20] Raymond Williams, 'Cambridge English, Past and Present', *Writing in Society* (London, 1991), pp. 177–91 (p. 182).
[21] John Guillory, *Professing Criticism: Essays on the Organization of Literary Study* (Chicago, 2022), p. xii.
[22] A. C. Bradley, *Shakespearean Tragedy: Lectures on Hamlet, Othello, King Lear* (New York, 1992), p. 3.

in explicit allusions and more oblique responses to his work, suggests a level of retention characteristic of the student. Another Cambridgean, William Empson, recalls an eerie sensation when writing his essay on *Lear*'s Fool, that his argument was 'unconsciously borrowed' from Bradley, as though his memory of *Shakespearean Tragedy* were so familiar as to have become indistinguishable from thoughts he knew to be his.[23] In the introduction to this book, Williams paraphrases a Cambridge colleague who seems in his turn to be paraphrasing Bradley: 'I once heard it said that if you or I got run over by a bus, that would not be tragedy.'[24] This pronouncement at the time left Williams aghast; he says he did not to know 'how to take this', whether as conscious insult or mere insensitivity.[25] But, in a way, it did not matter which alternative was right, but simply that Bradley's view, resounding through at least two 'unconscious borrowings', required a robust ideological refutation. Wanting not only to correct his colleague but the entire half century of wrong thinking he represented, Williams wrote his *Modern Tragedy*.

But while Cambridge's dons were teaching Bradley, their students were reading Eliot. And in Eliot's own 'modern tragedy' of 1935, *Murder in the Cathedral*, it is not only the Archbishop Thomas Beckett who is accorded tragic status, but Canterbury's 'poor women.'[26] Eliot's obvious inspiration here was the ancient Greeks; but his intervention could not help but resonate in the welfare era too. Was this a kind of socialism, warring against his professed aversion to what he inelegantly calls 'equalitarianism' in *Notes Towards a Definition of Culture*?[27] Williams became fascinated with the play, finding in its story of an archbishop's treason on behalf of his diocese, and subsequent, brutal execution in his own church, a collective and working-class vision of tragic suffering. In this play, the 'us' of the opening lines includes everyone, even *us*:

> *Chorus*: Here let us stand, close by the cathedral. Here let us wait.
> Are we drawn by danger? Is it the knowledge of safety, that draws our feet
> Towards the cathedral? What danger can be
> For us, the poor, the poor women of Canterbury?[28]

---

[23]   Adrian Poole writes that 'he had gone back to Bradley and been struck by how much he had unconsciously borrowed': 'A. C. Bradley's *Shakespearean Tragedy*', *Essays in Criticism*, 55.1 (2005), pp. 58–70 (p. 58).

[24]   Williams, *Modern Tragedy*, p. 71.

[25]   Ibid.

[26]   Eliot, *Complete Poems and Plays*, p. 239.

[27]   Eliot, *Notes Towards a Definition of Culture*, p. 16.

[28]   Eliot, *Complete Poems and Plays*, p. 239.

'What danger can be / For us?' asks: 'What tragedy may be for ordinary people?' The answer: the entire content of the play to come. 'For' bestows a universal entitlement, which at first seems questionable: 'There is no danger / For us.' Yet the church-ward motion of the women's feet and their clairvoyant dread tell another story. The danger faced by Beckett is very much theirs too, since they will lose their bishop and spiritual leader. And it is also *our* tragedy, since we as audience members and readers inhabit their collective vantage point, becoming a (silent) chorus within a chorus, who are likewise, as Eliot writes of them, captively 'compelled to witness' what follows. Forty years after the play's publication, Williams would lecture in Canterbury on the lack of 'solidarity' felt by Bloomsburyans with the lower classes. But in *Murder and the Cathedral*, Eliot's opening presupposes our ability to number ourselves among Canterbury's 'poor women.'

Crucially too, though, and with an irony that may not be wished away, collective feeling in Eliot is ultimately a bleak matter. For there are no full agents in the worlds he constructs, only vehicles of historical destiny: there is no graduation from 'collective' to 'collecti*vist*'. Williams writes of the ancient Greeks that 'their tragic action was not rooted in individuals [but] in history'.[29] Eliot argues along similar lines, in 'Tradition and the Individual Talent', that the 'individual' artist is only a medium for history: 'You cannot value him alone; you must set him, for contrast and comparison, among the dead [...] The existing monuments form an ideal order among themselves, which is modified by the introduction of the new.'[30] The most an individual may do is 'modify' tradition, and this modification is made on behalf of history, whose overarching motion then becomes visible through him. Williams writes frustratedly of *Murder and the Cathedral*: 'the structure of the play pushes Beckett towards a heroic death which is in fact irrelevant. It is [...] a historical death, and thus in a sense indifferent.'[31] Beckett was no 'hero' in any sense that Williams would grant, since history had already spoken: he was to be 'murdered in the cathedral' in punishment for a crime against King Henry II that could not be proved, was to abandon his congregation because this – though manifestly unfair – was his historical destiny. Eliot's version of collective solidarity was grist to the mill of his play's dark mood. His Canterburyans for all their tragic stature were limp.

29   Williams, *Modern Tragedy*, p. 113.
30   T. S. Eliot, 'Tradition and the Individual Talent', *The Complete Prose of T. S. Eliot, Volume 2: The Perfect Critic, 1919–1926*, ed. Anthony Cuda and Ronald Schuchard (Oxford, 2014), pp. 105–14 (p. 107).
31   Williams, *Modern Tragedy*, p. 196.

Underestimated Ghost

Empson once said: 'I do not know how much of my own mind Eliot invented, let alone how much of it is a reaction against him or indeed a consequence of misreading him'.[32] Williams would have sympathised with this view while wincing at the corollary that literary influence, or any influence for that matter, could be permitted to be passive. And Eliot himself, too, insisted that writers should impose themselves upon their ghosts, that 'Immature poets imitate; mature poets steal'.[33] My title is a riff on this statement, and takes as its premise that, when Williams became conscious of Eliot's influence on him, he sought to assert mastery over it; he set out to be a Marxist thief.

Eliot's account of literary theft may in its turn be accused of naivety. For, if Empson is right and influence can mean merged minds, how do you know what belongs to whom? Theft relies on a boundary between 'yours' and 'mine'; with the lights off, how can I know I am stealing? Writing on Bloom's professed critical endeavour to take control over his influences, Adam Phillips asks: 'What is the fantasy of autonomy a fantasy about?'[34] For Phillips, there can be no such thing as autonomy – no theft because you cannot know where your own thoughts start. To the extent that selves are constituted by their influences, we already have lost control. Influence is a losing game. So what are we nostalgic for, when we want autonomy? The answer in Eliot's case might be the sensation of originality, in Williams's, the sensation of volition. However, for Williams the stakes are raised by his sense that to accept, unchallenged, Eliot's intellectual legacy is to follow the trudge of his chorus towards social injustice. If the cost of influence was the loss of political agency, one had a moral obligation to learn how to steal.

Williams's commentary on contemporary culture, developed throughout his work, never loses sight of the lens through which what could have seemed like whims of the moment showed up in aggregate as historical patterns. He was Fredric Jameson's predecessor in believing that the accumulated past would eventually harden into the larger history of capitalism. It was dangerous to let historical 'destiny' run the show. Joseph North writes of Eliot that 'His mystique was of such a kind as to conceal the real contours of his position, which allowed his name to be used to authorize the pursuit of quite

---

[32]   Cited in John Haffenden, *William Empson: Among the Mandarins* (Oxford, 2005), p. 110.
[33]   T. S. Eliot, 'Philip Massinger', *Selected Essays* (London, 1999), pp. 205–20 (p. 206).
[34]   Adam Phillips, 'Bloom's Freud and Bloom's Anxiety', unpublished paper (2023).

opposite ends.'[35] Yet Williams's own experience tells another story, in which Eliot's 'position' lurked insidiously in all his writing, an underestimated ghost. When a writer like Eliot became so familiar as to be like an 'ideology', a 'condition of [one's] conscious life', his politics thus posed a serious risk by becoming intellectually intangible: 'you wonder who is ever going to analyse [them].'[36] An unwatched, 'unconscious' Eliot (to borrow Empson's word about Bradley) might penetrate our only armoury, critical analysis.

Williams was determined to be as conscious as he could be of Eliot's influence. Yet the distance needed for objectivity was not always possible for him with this particular ghost. Again, reconstructing his first encounter with *Notes Towards the Definition of Culture* in *Keywords*, he attempts to tidy the book away between dashes:

> My year in Cambridge passed. I went off to a job in adult education. Within two years T. S. Eliot published his *Notes Towards the Definition of Culture* (1948) – a book I grasped but could not accept – and all the elusive strangeness of those first weeks back in Cambridge returned in force.[37]

The rhetoric of the brief, parenthesised review, '– a book I grasped but did not accept –', depends on our finding sufficient opposition between 'grasp' and 'accept' to imagine an effect of neutralisation, whereby the incorporative logic of the first verb is resisted by the second. But on a closer look, the verbs' meanings may slide into each other. In Eliot's own rhetoric, for Beckett to 'grasp' that he will be executed is the same as 'accepting' that it must happen; for his chorus (and audience), to know they are one of 'us' is to succumb to what follows. What if to 'grasp' *is* in a way to 'accept'?

Twenty years earlier, Williams had introduced the word 'grasp' into a similar syntactical see-saw. The hero of his 1960 novel, *Border Country*, is an economic historian named Matthew, engaged in 'measuring' the 'population movement into [a] Welsh mining valley in the middle decades of the nineteenth century.'[38] On leaving the sphere of numerical measurement to consider a more amorphous, qualitative change, Matthew finds that his subject eludes his 'grasp':

---

[35]   Joseph North, *Literary Criticism: A Concise Political History* (Cambridge, 2017), p. 214.
[36]   Williams, *Writing in Society*, p. 207.
[37]   Williams, *Keywords*, p. 12.
[38]   Raymond Williams, *Border Country* (Cardigan, 1960), p. 6.

It's hardly a population movement from Glynmawr to London, but it's a change in substance, as it also must have been for them, when they had their villages. And the ways of measuring this are not only outside my discipline, they are somewhere else altogether, *that I can feel but not handle, touch but not grasp* [my italics].[39]

The scenario evoked here may be compared to that associated by Empson with Eliot's voice in his thinking life: a presence which, like gas or gossamer, asserts itself by coming close, almost of its own accord. It is as though you may 'grasp' only that which is within range, when 'touch' becomes something more. On a scale of haptic inches forward, 'touch' occupies an initial position and 'grasp' an intimate one, as though understanding were done to you by an object coming close. And the upshot, metaphorically at least, is an abandonment of distance: to 'grasp', when it happens, is to exchange the minimal agency of a reaching 'touch' for a condition that cannot be altogether voluntary.

When Williams writes that he 'grasps but could not accept' Eliot's argument, he may be accused of indulging in a 'fantasy of autonomy.' Wanting to have his cake and eat it too, to 'grasp' Eliot's meaning without getting close to it or him, he wishfully scripts a moment prior to the first 'touch' when the moves in the relationship are all his. If we read 'accept' and 'grasp' as relative synonyms too, as Eliot invites us to do in *Murder in the Cathedral*, 'I grasped but could not accept' may imply 'I grasped but could not grasp' – a transparent contradiction. In my reading of him, Williams found himself haunted, at a moment when Britain seemed ripe for a new welfarist politics, with the worry that he had gone further with Eliot than was safe.

Romantic Absentees

Empson's exposure to Eliot differed from Williams's, in that it began with his presence. Eliot lurked in person in Empson's Cambridge of the 1920s; he turned up to I. A. Richards's lectures to listen, gave his own Clark Lectures at Trinity (Williams's college), and returned, too, for Thursday 'visits', when students were invited to call in.[40] Empson forsook the lectures but emerged on Thursdays instead to pester Possum, exposing his mind to 'reinvention' at the closest possible range. However, though Williams likewise drew close

---

[39]   Ibid.

[40]   'On his visits to Cambridge, Eliot was prepared to receive undergraduates after breakfast on Thursdays [actually Wednesdays], Empson was to recall years later', Haffenden, *William Empson Among the Mandarins*, p. 111.

to Eliot – and in a welfarist era, when clarity of mind mattered more than ever – his own conundrum owed nothing to geography. As Williams puts it in 'Cambridge English', he had a 'habit of turning up too late for Golden Ages', and by the time he arrived at Trinity, the nymph had departed.[41] Eliot was by then even more of a ghost than F. R. Leavis, who, just down the road at Downing College seemed as far away as though he were in 'Oxford or Toronto'.[42]

Williams had, already, a tendency to erect as major influences people who were absent from his world. Stefan Collini pictures him as a stalker of the animate dead, bored by the living, recognising only the past as 'active.'[43] Collini's theory is supported by Williams's use of Brecht (deceased by 1956) as a modern-day partner for Ibsen in his revised title, *Drama from Ibsen to Brecht*. In my own reading of Williams, moreover, it is not only the histori-cally remote who charm Williams but the physically distant. Space could be as effective a seducer as time. The romance of his work on Lucien Goldmann lay for him in the quirk of their intellectual similarity although they derived 'from very different traditions', Goldmann being Swiss and Williams Welsh.[44] They had crossed the miles in their heads without ever meeting. In *Modern Tragedy*, the only fellow Briton in his cast of sixteen modern tra-gedians, D. H. Lawrence, was forty-years dead by 1966, and had been buried thousands of miles away from Cambridge, in San Cristobal, New Mexico. And the Anglo-American Eliot was, of course, underground.

Treating the absent as though they were 'active' in one's own world is a famous habit of Eliot's too – and a notorious one, as well, since the release in January 2020 of his almost twenty-year correspondence and love affair with Boston-based Emily Hale.[45] For Eliot though, it was not only individu-als who could become ubiquitous in their absence but whole communities of thinkers, whose thoughts had been transferred into our common lan-guage by centuries of reading and criticism. As he explains in 'Tradition and the Individual Talent', it seemed to him that the only appropriate way to proceed as an author was with a 'sense of history' sunk into 'his bones'.[46] In

---

[41]   Williams, *Writing in Society*, p. 177.
[42]   Raymond Williams, 'Our Debt to Dr Leavis', *Critical Quarterly*, 1.3 (1959), pp. 245–56 (p. 245).
[43]   Stefan Collini, *The Nostalgic Imagination* (Oxford, 2019), p. 158.
[44]   Williams, *Culture and Materialism*, p. 11.
[45]   T. S. Eliot, 'Statement by T. S. Eliot on the Opening of the Emily Hale Letters at Princeton'. <https://tseliot.com/foundation/statement-by-t-s-eliot-on-the-opening-of-the-emily-hale-letters-at-princeton/>.
[46]   Eliot, *Complete Prose*, p. 107.

his Cambridge lecture series of 1926, *The Varieties of Metaphysical Poetry*, Eliot goes as far as to assert that his own era's most innovative poets were re-voicing the 'dissociation of sensibility' that had created the seventeenth-century's metaphysical poets.[47] Modernism was a matter of ghost visitation.

Curiously, although Williams could not have attended these lectures of Eliot's, his *Modern Tragedy* echoes their thesis. Influence happened without the co-operation of geography. For, in *The Varieties of Metaphysical Poetry*, a revolution in social history *produces* an echoing revolution in art, resulting, in Eliot, in a 'dissociation' from which 'we have never recovered'; in Williams, too, a 'violent internal conflict and substantial transformation' in the social world *created* Shakespearean tragedy.[48] In both cases, it is seventeenth-century society that shudders so profoundly as to generate a new aesthetic sensibility. For both authors, this shudder carries through into modern-day art; as Williams writes in *Modern Tragedy*, 'the context, finally, is ourselves.'[49] Perhaps even, to the extent that Eliot's view aligned with Williams's own positive conception of the effect of social revolution on literary history, he helped carry Williams further than a welfarist vision of the reformable state could? Eliot could, intermittently, be good for Williams's politics.

Eliot and Williams were alike disinclined to affiliate their criticism with what was then becoming known as academic literary criticism, just as they were each staunchly unconvinced by mainstream politics (albeit for opposite reasons). They were interested in history, they said, although Williams is right to comment that Eliot's historical narratives are 'arbitrary' and over-'generalis[ed].'[50] Williams too, according to Collini, failed to interest trained historians even when claiming to be most historical, in *Culture and Society*: 'few books [have done] as much to shape the wider understanding of modern British intellectual history as *Culture and Society* [...] that barely registered on the thinking of modern British historians of [their] time'.[51] If Eliot's type of critical writing has no name – it was not quite cultural history, not simply analysis, not freewheeling theory – the consistency of his style and interests nonetheless give it a broad coherence. Applying this paradox to himself, Williams was wont to say that he had no subject, only questions. In *The Long Revolution*, he presents himself as a scholar with nowhere to put

---

[47]   T. S. Eliot, *Varieties of Metaphysical Experience*, ed. Ronald Schuchard (London, 1993), p. 536.

[48]   Eliot, *Varieties of Metaphysical Experience*, p. 536; Williams, *Modern Tragedy*, p. 77.

[49]   Williams, *Modern Tragedy*, p. 191.

[50]   Raymond Williams, *Culture and Society* (London, 1958), p. 231.

[51]   Collini, *Nostalgic Imagination*, p. 158.

his words: 'there is no subject within which the subject which I am interested in can be followed through'.[52] To the *New Left Review*, he said: 'I ceased to see work in criticism as the sort of book I wanted to produce'.[53] Like Eliot, Williams drifted; he could not settle down in one medium. Aiming for a 'brilliance and nervous energy of definition', like Eliot's, what made him himself was a firework quality, coming into focus for moments.[54] The critical temperament that led him to question the optimism of fellow socialists under welfare found an echo in the jerky blaze of his prose.

Williams was not alone in the 1960s in recoiling at critical convention. Likewise professing not to know what manner of thing her work might be, Susan Sontag in the preface to her 1966 essay collection, *Against Interpretation*, offers 'metacriticism' as an approximate term.[55] Yet Sontag's solution was too suave for Williams; he could not reconcile himself at a distance, as she seemed to do, to a vision of a modern tragedy in which 'Nihilism [became] our contemporary form of moral uplift.'[56] Indeed, he could not pronounce on anything at a distance: his political passions were always involved. And it was an irony of both his own work and Eliot's that, although they were drawn to authors beyond their own space and time, they could not be disinterested about them. They were each, always, too close to their subjects: hence, in part, the uneven historical narratives of which Collini complains, as well as their typically open-ended close readings of individual lines. Williams wrote on *Murder in the Cathedral* twice, once in *Drama from Ibsen to Brecht* and again in *Modern Tragedy*, as though pulled back by an unsolved problem. In both instances, he quotes the chorus's chant: 'For us, the poor, there is no action, / But only to wait and to witness.'[57] In neither context could his argument explain how the principle of tragic action was flipped into a vow of despair; could he only grasp the anomaly by believing it?

Eliot's turn to drama in the 1930s is mirrored in Williams's turn to drama criticism. Drama appealed to them both because of its 'collective function', how its success relied on the live and unfolding responses of an audience.[58] This unique characteristic was, Williams told the *New Left Review*, in danger

---

[52]   Raymond Williams, *The Long Revolution* (Harmondsworth, 1965), p. 10.
[53]   Williams, *Politics and Letters*, p. 243.
[54]   Williams, *Culture and Society*, p. 231.
[55]   'I am aware that little that is assembled in this book counts as criticism proper […] most of it could perhaps be called "metacriticism"': Sontag, *Against Interpretation*, p. x.
[56]   Sontag, *Against Interpretation*, p. 149.
[57]   In *Drama from Ibsen to Brecht*, p. 180, and *Modern Tragedy*, p. 194.
[58]   Williams, *Politics and Letters*, p. 189.

of being 'cut [...] off' as the medium became more and more bourgeois, a private drawing room writ large.[59] When invited in 1961 to accept a Cambridge lectureship, Williams thus chose drama as his field in the hope of restoring its social power. This choice of specialism is evident in *Modern Tragedy*, while his influence upon drama's academic fate may be gleaned from the subject's slow rise to popularity at Cambridge in the period. 1971 saw the creation of the university's first Professorship in Drama, to which Williams was the natural appointment. However, because his understanding of drama was so informed by Eliot, there remained in his vision of the genre a nagging rumour of political impotence. In *Modern Tragedy*, he suggests that the hope of tragedy may reside in its 'unresolved meaning', which could imply an unmade socialist future, one linked in its broad positivity to the welfarist present, in which parliamentary socialism had revealed a mandate for change.[60] But non-resolution is also, in a way, another borrowing from Eliot, whose own take on the unresolved was to elevate it to a verdict: Beckett could not defend himself, and died because he would not try to.

Break-Up

Kafka wrote in 1907 to his friend Max Brod about the novel the latter was then writing, and had read aloud to Kafka:

> A person who assents to your novel [...] – 'assent' meaning here to grasp it with all the love he can muster – a person who assents to your novel must all the while he is reading it increasingly long for a solution of the kind you have presented in the half chapter you read aloud.[61]

I understand Williams to have 'assented' to Eliot's work *because* he 'grasped' it in the sense given above, where 'to grasp' involves a two-way advance between oneself and the object of knowledge, and 'love' describes a process of sympathetic attunement to a rhythm of knowledge distribution. Reading in these cases is a way of wanting what the text wants. But Kafka's theory of 'assent' also raises the possibility that, just as you may want what comes, you may resent surprises. Because your loyalty is to a train of thought rather than an author, the disappearance of the train effectively ends the relationship.

---

59   Ibid.
60   '[I]t offers as absolutes the very experiences which are now most unresolved and most moving': Williams, *Modern Tragedy*, p. 89.
61   Franz Kafka, *Letters to Friends, Family and Editors*, trans. Richard Wilson and Clara Wilson (1977; New York, 2016), p. 62.

In Eliot's *Murder in the Cathedral*, we have another version of Kafka's evoked scenario. Again, we know where the narrative is heading: the title could not be more of a spoiler. However, the perspective we now enter is that of the chorus – since it is they rather than Beckett who inscribe the play's emotional centre – and they do not want the 'solution' towards which everything drives. They chant 'We do not wish anything to happen', as if they might by sheer effort of imagination rip themselves from their fictional condition.[62] It is my understanding of Williams, too, that, despite his 'grasp' of Eliot, a Kafkaesque sleepy submission to his spell, Williams rebelled like a doomed cast member against the logic in which he was immersed. Bound in a way to 'assent' by the motion of his reading mind and quoting memory, he simultaneously also sought exits. In *Modern Tragedy*, he writes, after several anxious pages on Eliot, 'We need not pursue Eliot further'; and in *Culture and Society*, he terminates a chapter with the rebuke 'Eliot has closed almost all the existing roads.'[63]

I want to consider Williams's two break-up statements above each in turn, taking the second first. Williams has, when he abandons Eliot in *Culture and Society*, just been quoting from a passage in *The Idea of Christian Society*, where Eliot denounces societies 'organised for profit' in which 'the public were influenced by any means except their intelligence'.[64] So far, so Marxist. Indeed, more so than the British socialist governments of the 1940s through to the 1960s, whose welfare programmes, Williams told the *New Left Review*, had left the 'deeply undemocratic state machine' wholly intact.[65] Williams had, in the 1950s, attempted to persuade the Labour Party to support cultural initiatives that promised to reinvigorate British political thinking on an organic level. But he got nowhere. Unexpectedly, Eliot agreed with Williams that the only way to maintain a society's health was by nourishing its culture. For Eliot, culture implied a whole way of life, just as for Williams it meant a 'structure of feeling'.[66]

Yet the next step in Eliot's argument about culture was a complete betrayal of its socialist embryo. Williams knew this was coming – as Eliot's chorus knows what is coming – but also instinctively rebelled against an

---

[62]   Eliot, *Complete Poems and Plays*, p. 243.
[63]   Williams, *Modern Tragedy*, p. 200; Williams, *Culture and Society*, p. 243.
[64]   Cited in Williams, *Culture and Society*, p. 230.
[65]   Williams, *Politics and Letters*, p. 368.
[66]   Cited in Williams, *Culture and Society*, p. 237, and reintroduced throughout the second half of the chapter on Eliot. For Williams, the 'structure of feeling' was the element of a text that belonged to the 'intangible' thinking atmosphere of the culture it came from, *Politics and Letters*, pp. 164–5.

inevitability that seemed to him evil nonsense. For how could the same Eliot who believed that culture should include everyone *also* commend the British class system for 'help[ing] to preserve the [upper] class and select the elite'?[67] How could Eliot's wish to 'preserve' a genuinely national culture rationally take this form? Eliot would in theory not even have accepted Williams's own admission to Cambridge University, and by implication, Williams's first encounter with Eliot and the reading romance that ensued. How could you make peace with a writer whose politics were predicated on not letting you read them? The Eliot of *Notes Towards a Definition of Culture* was opposed even to national education; Williams's academic success, despite his working-class background, was already freakish in the era before welfare. Eliot would have preferred that he remain obscure.

The second break-up statement is a response to *Murder in the Cathedral*, a play that, at the same time that it irked Williams, crystallised an effect which seemed to him in *Drama from Ibsen to Brecht* to be unique to drama: namely, 'assent.'[68] In a play, you could be made to believe that the actors were in the North Pole or that two men were a horse, not because this was what you saw but because you 'assented' to its being the case. As Williams writes of drama: 'We accept, we agree, these are the conventions.'[69] Dramatic convention asked that your understanding be equivalent to acceptance, and you said yes. *Murder in the Cathedral* is designed to be set, Williams reminds us, in a cathedral. You do not need to assent to the existence of a cathedral in this play: you are there. But now your assent has a different, more difficult duty: to 'collaborate' in 'celebrati[ng] the murder of the archbishop.'[70] You go from accepting an optical fiction to accepting martyrdom, or from submitting to seeing what you cannot see to enacting through your presence a belief in what follows. Eliot wrote in 1928's 'Dialogue on Poetic Drama', 'A devout person, in assisting at Mass, is not in the frame of mind of a person attending a drama, for he is *participating* [his italics]'.[71] Dramatic convention in *Murder in the Cathedral* ups its demand upon the audience, floats without warning into a dimension where the stakes of complicity are infinitesimally higher. We are not now spectators *of* a play but 'participants' *in* an execution. And the ensuing crisis in ideological pressure upon *us* is the atmosphere into which Eliot's archbishop then walks, being himself also stripped of the freedom to do as he wants.

67   Eliot, *Notes Towards a Definition of Culture*, p. 100.
68   Williams, *Drama from Ibsen to Brecht*, p. 14.
69   Ibid.
70   Williams, *Drama from Ibsen to Brecht*, p. 179.
71   Eliot, *Selected Essays*, p. 49.

'Dogma', protests Williams, is Beckett's reason for submitting himself to his fate, making the tragedy a mechanical inevitability.[72] 'Resignation' replaces any possibility of rebellion, of any meaningful action, even by the protagonist.[73] Nevertheless, dogma is what the convention of dramatic assent, when carried into this nightmare zone of exaggerated duty, requires. The aesthetic experiment needs blood. Yet, at the same time – and I think this is what Williams means in writing of the play's 'tragic challenge' – the text maintains a constant low-level hum of outrage against its own unchangeable chain of events.[74] What then ends up being most horrific about the play is that it cannot lucidly describe its horror, because there are no words granted to it that it would not be heresy to say. It is not even allowed to call itself a tragedy. Eliot's chorus reflects, 'Every horror had its definition / Every sorrow had a kind of end.'[75] A comforting thought, but only if you can name your horrors and sorrows. Eliot had taught Williams that, by defining their sufferings in cultural works, individual members of a society could lift themselves out of their personal insignificance, endowing a communal 'way of life' with the prolonged existence of art. If they could not save themselves, at least their words could last. The shock of *Murder in the Cathedral* lies in its suggestion that there are tragedies that, by the incidental, cruel accident of their being too subtle or delicate for words, may mean nothing.

Some great writers steal. For others, theft, or imaginative re-appropriation, may not be enough. Finding himself more haunted by Eliot than was ideologically safe, I understand Williams to have attempted to make it all stop. Absorbing his influence uncontrollably at first and even starting to sound like him, at least to his own mental ear, I see Williams, when engaging with the poet directly in the examples above, as having been compelled to pull away when Eliot's attitudes slanted to the far, far right. The cathedral had been ready for Mass, but on learning that he was not to be a spectator but a participant, Williams said no. Professionally committed to promoting drama but convinced that this was not drama anymore, or even argument (what was it when it got into your veins?) he left the church, got out into the street and took a deep breath.

---

[72]   '[T]he action of sacrifice, a giving of life to renew a general life, is limited in Eliot to dogma': Williams, *Modern Tragedy*, p. 207.
[73]   Williams, *Modern Tragedy*, p. 189.
[74]   Williams, *Modern Tragedy*, p. 200.
[75]   Eliot, *Complete Poems and Plays*, p. 276.

Aftermath

Standing at a Cambridge podium in 1983 at the dawn of his retirement, Williams provocatively chose to say of the university:

> Many friends have told me I have never distanced myself enough, but they were wrong. The distance is entire, the conflicts absolute. My only community and inheritance in Cambridge is with some of the questions then posed and with the campaigning energy and seriousness that were brought to them. As these are now pushed away, disregarded even when they are nominally honoured, their largeness of spirit is indeed worth recalling.[76]

Williams leaves us to guess what his 'community and inheritance in Cambridge' amount to, what it is he seeks 'distance' from, but among the most likely answers is its legacy of practical criticism, and with it the hard-wired reflex of attention to the granular matter of Eliot and other modernists' work. As Williams writes to an *New Left Review* interviewer, 'the force of the new criticism in the twenties was directly related to the new poetry and prose of Eliot and Joyce.'[77] Arguably, too, Eliot is also personally relevant to Williams here, as the author whose work he himself *kept* close reading, long after the books were closed. Eliot was what Cambridge had done to him.

The problem with the Cambridge tradition of 'practical criticism', as Williams saw it in 1983, was that it clashed with his Marxism. He had recently told the *New Left Review* that the reading method 'suspended you mid-air', ironically making you so 'intensely active' as to be 'passive', like a hoverfly consumed by the agitation of stasis.[78] Williams had become convinced by the late 1970s that such absorption was not conducive to Marxist critique, and he had also always suspected this to be the case. Across the Atlantic in 1981, the young Jameson of *The Political Unconscious* had similarly worried that the 'libidinal' charge of poetry, especially in tragedy's cathartically opiate, determinist narratives, could flatten readerly response to a swoon.[79] Distance was vital for critique, yet in attending closely with their full sensitivity to texts, readers exposed themselves to the subtlest manipulations. If you listened to the 1980s' foremost Marxist literary critics, you might thus never dare to close-read at all. Williams for his own part was ready to lay down his

[76] Williams, *Writing in Society*, p. 190.
[77] Williams, *Politics and Letters*, p. 239.
[78] Williams, *Politics and Letters*, p. 121.
[79] Fredric Jameson, *The Political Unconscious: Narrative as a Socially Symbolic Act* (1981; London, 2008), p. 206.

microscope in 1983. A 'conflict' that is 'absolute' is one beyond healing: it was time to go.

But could he leave? Was it his decision to make? It has been one of the working theories of this essay that the authors about whom and with whom we are most moved to think begin to influence us long before we recognise their presence for us. The very language that Williams used to steer his Cambridge peers away from *Four Quartets* synced to Eliot's cadences; he was speaking in 'some echo of an Eliot rhythm', always. To speak of total 'distance' or 'absolute' severance was even by then an exercise in fantasy. And Williams's problem may be ours too. For his conundrum over Eliot is to a degree formative to all reading. The enchantment necessary to reading – of abandoning oneself to a curiosity that could go anywhere and that we expect to deepen – is the feature of our relation to literature over which we have least control. It happens before we know it, and has access to our unconscious in its most suggestible, because pleasure-seeking state. Close reading describes an act of seduction that is underway long before we find words for it. Yet even so, surely Williams must retain his right to say no. There must be boundaries to a reading relationship, as to all human relationships, and those boundaries must be able to be asserted even after they have been breached.

The trick played in *Murder in the Cathedral* is a darkly capricious one. We enter a theatre ready to 'assent' to whatever we are told is the case; and Eliot uses this dramatic convention to enlist our involvement in a murder. Not an execution but a murder: a death that bloodies our hands, while lifting to a sacred pitch a verdict of despair. Beckett's manifestly unfair trial and wrongful accusation are to be meekly accepted by him, the 'poor women' of his congregation, and by us. On the eve of welfare, Eliot's play preaches that there is, and should be no recourse for the victims of a corrupt state. In the contemporary era, we speak of 'problem faves' and 'cancellation' as though these were genuine options for us, but what if we are already in the cathedral? The example of Williams and Eliot may suggest an alternative response, a gestural break-up. Williams could not disentangle his mind from Eliot's, and yet saying he could do so mattered. We cannot speak for the unconscious but we may fight with it. Williams stood in a lecture hall in Cambridge in 1983, his profession's equivalent of a theatre, and announced with the automatic assent of his audience that, whatever their eyes told them, he had gone.

6

The Ethics of Attention in Christine Brooke-Rose's Out

SARAH BERNSTEIN

In her 1967 essay 'The Aesthetics of Silence', Susan Sontag considers the 'reduction of means and effects in art, whose horizon is silence', to be characteristic of much postwar art and literature.[1] Sontag links this reduction of means and effects to the faculty of attention, since 'in one of its aspects, art is a technique for focusing attention, for teaching skills of attention'.[2] She suggests that

> [p]erhaps the quality of the attention one brings to bear on something will be better (less contaminated, less distracted) the less one is offered. Furnished with impoverished art, purged by silence, one might then be able to begin to transcend the frustrating selectivity of attention, with its inevitable distortions of experience. Ideally, one should be able to pay attention to everything.[3]

Literature, like the visual arts, provides a frame for ways of looking at the world, for focusing attention and interest on specific objects. Writing engaged in the project of a silent or 'impoverished' art invites a new kind of attention: what Sontag terms a 'stare', as opposed to a 'look'.[4] The stare 'allows – at least in principle – no release from attention, because there has never, in principle, been any soliciting of it'.[5] As a form of extended contemplation that 'entails self-forgetfulness on the part of the spectator', the 'stare', Sontag argues, enables a more expansive attention to the world that might produce new forms of knowledge.[6] 'Silence', she writes, 'administered by the artist, is part of a program of perceptual and cultural therapy' whose new modes of

---

[1]   Susan Sontag, 'The Aesthetics of Silence', *Styles of Radical Will* (New York, 2009), pp. 3–35 (p. 13).
[2]   Sontag, 'The Aesthetics of Silence', p. 13.
[3]   Sontag, 'The Aesthetics of Silence', p. 13.
[4]   Sontag, 'The Aesthetics of Silence', p. 15.
[5]   Sontag, 'The Aesthetics of Silence', p. 16.
[6]   Sontag, 'The Aesthetics of Silence', p. 16.

attention – of looking – might help to uncover ways of knowing and 'thinking that we don't know about yet'.[7]

This essay focuses on the forms of attention in Christine Brooke-Rose's 1964 novel *Out*, using Sontag's notion of silent art and its affordances for thinking about the work of care. *Out* takes place in a future society that has just undergone a politically transformative event in which the present system of white supremacy has been upended and replaced by a Black ruling class. In this world, many members of this 'Colourless' (i.e. formerly white) underclass are afflicted by the effects of a 'malady' related to the effects of radiation. The novel's unnamed protagonist, through whose consciousness much of the text is organised, is an unemployed 'ex-Ukayan' Colourless man; he is married to Lilly, who works at the 'Big House' under the direction of its proprietor, Mrs Mgulu. Over the course of the novel, the protagonist moves from their shack to the Labour Exchange, and subsequently to the Big House, where Mrs Mgulu eventually finds him some menial work. These scenes of home and work are the focal points of the narrative, which proceeds by a logic of repetition and recursion rather than by linear plotting.

Central to the world of *Out* is a welfare state in a state of severe attrition. Social welfare is dispensed and mediated primarily by the Labour Exchange, where Dole Pills are handed out more frequently than employment opportunities, and medication for those afflicted with the malady is haphazardly allotted and in short supply. Alongside the institutions of the novel's welfare state, there is an informal system of patronage in which members of the upper classes, such as Lilly's employer Mrs Mgulu, 'take an interest' in those less fortunate. Through textual strategies such as repetition, recursion and elision, the novel ironises these traditional approaches to social welfare, administered through the state or individual charity, as failing to provide meaningful support to any of the characters. Insofar as *Out* presents an alternative to these systems, it is through its representation of attention as care: both within the text, that is, how it is represented thematically, and at the level of form, as something that the style asks of the reader, namely a refiguration of readerly attention.

Critical work on *Out* has focused primarily on its style. Considered by critics to be Brooke-Rose's first 'experimental' work, the novel's narration is marked by the repetition and recursion mentioned above – what Adam Guy has referred to as its 'metafictional architecture'.[8] These stylistic innovations have usually been read as evidence of the author's engagement with

[7]   Sontag, 'The Aesthetics of Silence', pp. 23, 18.
[8]   Adam Guy, '"That's a Scientific Fact': Christine Brooke-Rose's Experimental Turn,' *The Modern Language Review*, 111.4 (2016), pp. 936–55 (p. 950).

poststructuralist theory, although Guy has suggested they more accurately mark her interest in quantum physics and in the nouveau roman. In this chapter, I want to focus more directly on the dimensions of social welfare in the novel as they relate to Brooke-Rose's use of form. In some ways, a discussion of Brooke-Rose and the welfare state might seem incongruous, not least because of the way *Out* draws attention to its own construction as a text. The novel challenges any easy identification with character or even, in some cases, with the 'real world' of the text. Insofar as there is a 'literature of the welfare state', it is usually associated with the realist texts of the 1950s by writers like Kingsley Amis, Shelagh Delaney and Alan Sillitoe, where the world of the text acts as a mirror of the world outside of it. This sort of association is an extension of the aesthetics versus politics debate of the 1930s, which connects committed political engagement with realist style and a focus on aesthetics with more bourgeois concerns. And yet, *Out* challenges this easy binary by complicating the boundary between text and world. The novel's commitment, at the level of both form and theme, to attention as it relates to the operations of care, in fact, suggests that the novel's anti-realist form can enable us to think more experimentally about the politics of welfare. Specifically, this chapter argues that Brooke-Rose's experimental style in *Out*, because of the ways it refigures attention, approaches something like an ethics of care.

Welfare States

Brooke-Rose's work is most frequently read in relation to the philosophical and scientific concepts that animate her play with language and form. Her experimental novels are less frequently read in terms of their socio-political context, for the reason that this context is not always clear, in the same way that the goings on of the novels are often obscured, at least on first reading, by narrative style. Debra Malina has argued that 'politics per se do not become central to Brooke-Rose's project until her science fiction *Intercom Quartet*', although she acknowledges that even Brooke-Rose's prepositional series (comprised of her novels *Out*, *Between* and *Thru*) seems 'to grant the postmodern condition a clear historico-political context', and cites *Out*'s representation of the racial hierarchy as an example of this preoccupation.[9] Malina suggests that the primary site of *Out*'s politics is in the way it 'stresses the psychic violence inflicted by both the construction and deconstruction of

---

[9]   Debra Malina, *Breaking the Frame: Metalepsis and the Construction of the Subject* (Columbus, 2002), p. 66.

the novel's hierarchies'.[10] But the novel's political engagement is in evidence elsewhere, too, not least in its representation of one of the engines of this new hierarchy, a barely functioning welfare state. The strong institutions negotiated in the United Kingdom in the postwar settlement (which culminated in the welfare state's official foundation in 1948, when the National Assistance, National Insurance and National Health Service Acts came into force) have been dismantled in the novel's present, with an attenuated version of 'care in the community' as the last vestige of a broader social safety net. Even in the 'golden age' of the welfare state, *Out* already registers the cracks in the postwar consensus.

In *Out* the primary interface of the state and its citizens in this regard is the Labour Exchange, where 'Daily from 8 a.m [...] a name will be called out and the thigh will slope up in a vertical position, slowly or suddenly' and will be asked about their ex-nationality (Ukayan, in the case of the protagonist), their ex-occupation (humanist and Ph.D., according to his identity cards, which appear at the start of the novel) and any re-training undertaken at the Resettlement Camp. More often than not, the agents of the Labour Exchange find no work for the unemployed, partly due to 'an irrational fear of the Colourless that lingers on' that is 'justifiable' since it arises from the association of Colourless people with the malady, which renders the Colourless 'unreliable'.[11] These are familiar tropes of the racialised 'Other': the fear of contagion, the accusation of unreliability with regards to work (even though the system itself is passively and actively keeping these same people from work), the assertion, in spite of this, by the ruling classes that 'we have no prejudice that's an article of faith'.[12]

But it is difficult to understand the ends to which this tidy inversion of the racial hierarchy is put. The world of *Out* has suddenly and completely changed but only for the Colourless, who have arrived in a new country whose native population seems to be living much as before. Malina argues that the upending of white supremacy has taken away the protagonist's framework for understanding the world, which would suggest that the novel recognises how foundational whiteness is to the construction of the self. The novel's inverted racial hierarchy also serves to underscore how the welfare state works primarily to regulate, or even control, the behaviour of a given society's most vulnerable people, partly as a way of shoring up the foundations of that hierarchy. At the same time, however, rather than highlighting

---

10   Malina, *Breaking the Frame*, p. 66.
11   Christine Brooke-Rose, *Out, The Christine Brooke-Rose Omnibus: Four Novels – Out, Such, Between, Thru* (Manchester, 1986), pp. 11–198 (p. 51).
12   Brooke-Rose, *Out*, p. 51.

the question of race as central to its construction, or of pointing to this hierarchy as being clearly rooted in white supremacy, the novel's representation of race, and the inversion of its hierarchies, seems rather to evade or sideline the key issues.

On the Dole Pills

At the Labour Exchange, should no work be available – which is the case more often than not – the unemployable are dispensed Dole Pills. The pills are intended to make the unemployed 'employable' again.[13] One agent at the Labour Exchange explains to a recalcitrant applicant that:

> As far as I am concerned you must take this pill, and I am entitled to insist that you take it here in front of me. We're only trying to prevent unemployment apathy frustration, you know, which are the seeds of crime. But it's for your own good mainly. Don't you see that you must keep yourself fit and cheerful just in case a job does turn up?[14]

The paternalistic attitude in evidence in this passage reflects some of the thinking surrounding the establishment of the United Kingdom's welfare state at mid-century. In 1946, the sociologist Richard Titmuss outlined some of the most important objectives of welfare programmes:

> To raise worker productivity, to increase worker reliability and economic growth [...] To insure and protect the worker against the risks and hazards of industrialisation [...] To increase or decrease the birthrate [...] To integrate all citizens into society [...] to increase or decrease inequalities in the distribution of incomes.[15]

Titmuss reflects a central ambivalence of institutional welfare, namely that it is poised between the mechanisms of care and control.

For Titmuss, welfare policy aims to nurture and regulate simultaneously, so that the 'postwar settlement' does come to seem like a compromise, or what Melinda Cooper describes as an imposed 'reciprocal obligation', where

---

[13] Brooke-Rose, *Out*, p. 154.
[14] Brooke-Rose, *Out*, p. 154.
[15] Richard Titmuss, 'The Relationship Between Social Security Programmes and Social Service Benefits: An Overview', *Commitment to Welfare*, 2nd edn (London, 1976), pp. 59–71 (p. 64).

welfare services are received in exchange for checks on individual freedom.[16] The balance between care and control, freedom and security, is figured as fundamental to the operation of social welfare programmes in Brooke-Rose's novel as well, with the Labour Exchange in *Out* being key to disciplining and controlling the Colourless population. That the Dole Pills are meant to keep the unemployed 'fit and cheerful' suggests they may even be designed to have a sedative effect on the people who take them, rendering them unable to protest against their treatment. This is the view of one character that the protagonist meets at the Labour Exchange, who says to him: 'can you honestly say that you haven't been feeling steadily worse since you started taking the pills? [...] More and more debilitated!'[17] The protagonist responds that he 'won't believe that. If I did I couldn't go on living'.[18]

The question of whether the Dole Pills are deliberately debilitating the unemployed remains an open one in the novel. What is clear is that they represent one of the ways control over the (non)working classes is extended. Like the required daily attendance at the Labour Exchange, the requirement to take the pills in front of the agent serves to humiliate and diminish the dignity of people who are ostensibly the subject of care. The anxiety evinced in *Out* about the welfare state's balance of care and control, freedom and security is characteristic of other mid-century novels that employ a not-quite-realist form.[19] For writers like Brooke-Rose, Angela Carter and Muriel Spark, this ambivalence is a product of the dominant ethos of planning, efficiency, order and rationalisation at mid-century, what we might call the 'administered life'. These novelists register state administration at once as a good after the chaos of wartime and the Depression, and as an oppressive, conscriptive intrusion into private life, particularly in the context of the Cold War. In Brooke-Rose's text, this anxiety relates specifically to how a mechanistic attitude to dispensing welfare privileges efficiency of delivery and degrades the quality of care.

The novel's representation of psychiatric treatment, in the form of something called 'psychoscopy', functions in a similar way. Though it is not clear whether the procedure definitively makes the patient worse, the process is as opaque as it is humiliating. In her role as patron, Lilly's employer Mrs Mgulu 'takes an interest' in Lilly and her husband's sorry situation and helps

[16]   Melinda Cooper, *Life as Surplus: Biotechnology and Capitalism in the Neoliberal Era* (Seattle, 2008), p. 8.

[17]   Brooke-Rose, *Out*, p. 156.

[18]   Brooke-Rose, *Out*, p. 158.

[19]   See, for example, Sarah Bernstein, 'The Social-Scientific Imagination: Muriel Spark's *The Ballad of Peckham Rye*', *Modern Fiction Studies*, 68.2 (2022), pp. 298–319.

him find employment on her estate. That Mrs Mgulu 'takes an interest' is a refrain in the text, repeated in variations that seem earnest or ironic in turn. Mrs Mgulu takes an interest in the sense that she believes she is helping, but she also takes an interest in the sense of making a profit off the people she employs. The novel never makes clear what Lilly or her husband are offered in terms of remuneration beyond Mrs Mgulu's cast-off medications and tins of food, while Lilly's husband is employed to assist in the construction of a hair salon to be run out of Mrs Mgulu's estate. The question of care as it relates to this kind of patronage is, therefore, rendered null: the overall effect of the phrase, repeated every few pages throughout the novel, is to empty it of meaning.

Mrs Mgulu's intervention is necessary to get the protagonist a job because, in the world of the novel, employment is strictly regulated by a kind of guild system, whereby only people given a specific job title are allowed to undertake certain tasks. Lilly recounts to her husband Mrs Mgulu's account of her own reasoning: 'it's not charity, it's not philanthropy, Lilly, you must understand, it's a basic right [...] but when a thing gets out of hand, like this, and for reasons beyond anyone's control it becomes impossible to give a large number of men their basic rights one can but do one's bit to help one individual case whenever it comes one's way'.[20] The passive structure of this passage, and the use of the indefinite pronoun 'one', combine to occlude who is responsible for giving 'a large number of people their basic rights'. What Mrs Mgulu leaves open (her gentility preventing her from stating it outright) is her view that the Colourless themselves have made the safeguarding of those rights impossible.

The protagonist is eventually hired as an 'odd-job man', and tasked with breaking up slabs of pink marble as part of a transformation of a room in Mrs Mgulu's house into a hair salon. Working in a hot attic, with the doors and windows closed to keep the disturbance of noise and dust to a minimum, the protagonist faints. In a conversation that seems to be both actually happening and partially imagined between the protagonist and Mrs Mgulu, she refers him for psychoscopy where they 'will restore equilibrium. They will weigh you in the balance and find you wanting'.[21] Psychoscopy attributes the protagonist's general enervation and possibly even his illness to a problem of attitude. Like the Dole Pills, the diagnosis is designed to return the patient to a sense of balance and proportion, which presumably includes feeling grateful for the scraps that he is offered. There is an echo here of *Mrs Dalloway*'s Dr

20 Brooke-Rose, *Out*, pp. 70–1.
21 Brooke-Rose, *Out*, p. 126.

Bradshaw and his twin 'goddesses' of proportion and conversion; reinstilling a sense of 'proportion' in the patient – an acceptance of their social situation and its limitations – is seen as a way to bring about a kind of conversion from an intractable personality into an obedient and pliable citizen of the state.[22] As I discuss below, in *Out* the process of restoring 'equilibrium' involves limiting the characters' imagination of a different kind of world.

In the course of the protagonist's psychoscopic treatment, a series of either/or questions are posed, for example: 'Would you rather support medical treatment of criminals or medical treatment of politicians?'[23] The protagonist thinks he knows the desired answer to this question and responds, 'Er ... politicians', but the technician asks: 'What do you have against criminals, don't you think they need medical treatment as much as anyone else?' His answers to these apparently pointless questions are undermined and criticised throughout the procedure, and over the course of the scene, the exchanges become more outlandish, suggesting that the protagonist has stopped relating the events directly and has moved back into his own imagination. When the ordeal comes to an end, the protagonist asks about a follow up appointment, assuming that the quiz he is administered is part of an intake interview. The technician mocks him and explains that:

> Psychoscopy's an extracted absolute of analysis. We don't need transference any more. We're not only able to telescope a dependence that used to take years to build up, we telescope the let-down as well. You'll see, the wrench will be fairly painless [...] You'll have to renew your drugs, though, we haven't quite solved that one yet, but there's an automatic dispensary outside, you just feed in your prescription each time. Goodbye.[24]

Here, patient care has been outsourced to an algorithm, and the interaction between therapist and patient rendered unnecessary. The apparently pointless contradictions of the subject's answers are in fact deliberate and are geared toward 'telescop[ing] a dependence' that used to form the basis of the therapeutic relationship, as well as accelerating the process of the 'let down'.

In *Out*, treatment of a vaguely defined and unlocatable problem, whose origins may be social, psychological or biological is reduced to a chemical imbalance (disequilibrium) that can be fixed only by medication. The novel here reflects a contemporary debate about mental health policy in the 1960s, specifically relating to inpatient care versus care in the community.

---

22 Virginia Woolf, *Mrs Dalloway* (London, 2019), p. 91.
23 Brooke-Rose, *Out*, p. 136.
24 Brooke-Rose, *Out*, p. 141.

New health policy, which was still being worked out in the early part of the decade, recognised different possibilities for treating mental illness, which included the use of community care, day centres, out-patient clinics and domiciliary social work, alongside hospitals and psychiatric wards. In the ideal scenario, different treatment options would be integrated under the National Health Service, with mental health or psychiatric social workers helping to streamline the process by operating at a local level. It is a model that never came to fruition: within three years of the Mental Health Act of 1959, Conservative policy would derail these initiatives with its campaign to dismantle the asylums.

While, in fact, both the welfare state and the new Conservative policy focused on community care for mental health issues, this focus meant different things in each context, due in part to different understandings of the efficacy of psychotropic drugs. When the psychotropic drug Largactic was introduced in Britain in the winter of 1953/4, there was a surge of optimism that illnesses like schizophrenia had been cured. By the early 1960s, however, this initial optimism had worn off, and clinicians had come to see these drugs as useful palliatives rather than cures, which needed to be paired with on-going therapeutic treatment. Conservative politicians, on the other hand, continued to view the psychotropic drugs as cures. Even though the welfare model was still being worked out in the early sixties, and involved the range of treatments outlined above, politicians would pose the problem of mental health services, from this point on, as a conflict between institutional and decentralised care.

The elision and conflation of the biological, the social and the psychological, in evidence in *Out*'s psychoscopic treatment, is reflected also in the protagonist's representation of the malady, which serves as a hinge between the denuded care offered by the institutions of welfare and patronage in the novel, and those offered by more informal networks of care and attention. The novel's first descriptions of the malady are physical: it is attributed to exposure to radiation in the air, to which the Colourless seem more susceptible:

> This is how the malady begins. The onset is insidious, well advanced before diagnosis. Anaemia, progressive emaciation, fatigue, tachycardia, dyspnoea, and a striking enlargement of the abdomen due to splenomegaly and hepatomegaly.[25]

The focus is on the malady's effects on the body and the way that it weakens the body. A few sentences on, however, part of this final clause is repeated

---

[25]   Brooke-Rose, *Out*, p. 66.

with a new addition: 'The imagination increases in size progressively and usually painlessly until it fills most of the abdomen'; it is the imagination, rather than swollen organs, which causes the enlargement of the abdomen.[26] This observation introduces, for the first time, the notion that the malady is connected to the psyche, a connection that is reinforced in a scene where the protagonist reflects on how he feels knowing that his line manager, Mr Swaminathan, will never nod to him:

> The absolute knowledge has entered the body at the back of the neck somehow, in the medullary centres, down the glosso-pharyngeal nerve no doubt, or the pneumogastric, at any rate forward and down into the throat, which tightens as enlargement of the lymphatic glands occurs and the knowledge spreads into the chest and down into the stomach, nauseous. Sooner or later it will reach the spleen, which will increase in size until it fills most of the abdomen, though remaining firm and smooth on palpation. Anaemia, fatigue, pyrexia, tachycardia, dyspnoea, cachexy.[27]

The language parallels the initial description of the malady: anaemia, fatigue and so on, but attributes these symptoms to the knowledge, and its attendant pains, that the protagonist will never be treated as an equal, or even with a little bit of dignity, by his superior. In this context, the idea that the 'imagination' is perhaps at the root of the malady, or at least is as responsible for the experience of its effects as the radiation itself, suggests that what afflicts the characters is an awareness of a possible world where care is figured as a reciprocal and ongoing relation between people, and the knowledge that such a relation is beyond reach. The protagonist's appeals to Mr Swaminathan to recognise him as human are as sure to fail as his attempts to persuade the Labour Exchange agents to find him work, as they only make recourse to a system whose existence is based on the exclusion of people like him.

The Mechanics of Attention

Critics of Brooke-Rose's novels, and of *Out*, in particular, have commented on her interest in the mechanics of observation.[28] They argue that some of

---

[26]   Brooke-Rose, *Out*, p. 66.

[27]   Brooke-Rose, *Out*, p. 107.

[28]   For Hilary White, Brooke-Rose's focus on vision highlights her interdisciplinary engagement with contemporary visual arts, 'The Limits of Looking: Conceptualising the Frame in Ann Quin's *Berg* and Christine Brooke-Rose's *Out*', *Angles*, 13 (2021), pp. 1–17. Guy argues that the way Brooke-Rose thematises observation relates to her

the ways the novel obsessively refigures views, objects or scenes, already represented in a particular way, connects it to cubist art, or to texts like Gertrude Stein's modernist literary portraits, which approach people, objects, food and rooms from all angles simultaneously. From the first pages, it is clear that *Out* is preoccupied by seeing things clearly and attending to things carefully. Brooke-Rose has referred to the narrative as using a narrator-less present tense; the text is, nevertheless, consistently tethered to the protagonist's consciousness. The novel opens with an observation of a pair of flies mating on the protagonist's knee, related in some detail: 'the fly on top is [...] jerking tremulously, then convulsively, putting out its left foreleg to whip, or maybe to stroke, some reaction out of the fly beneath'.[29] The level of detail does not seem to satisfy, though. The next line imagines that 'A microscope might perhaps reveal animal ecstasy in its innumerable eyes, but only to the human mind behind the microscope'. The acknowledgement that such ecstasy would only be recognised 'to the human mind behind the microscope' suggests an awareness of the difficulty of anything like objective observation: the human mind is always interpreting and mediating. The line acknowledges the final impossibility of interpreting, or of understanding, the inner life of the fly. Instead, the narrative focuses primarily on the moment of perception.

In his 1890 work *Principles of Psychology*, William James writes that 'everyone knows what attention is. It is the taking possession by the mind, in clear and vivid form, of one out of what seem several simultaneously possible objects of thought. Focalization, concentration, of consciousness are of its essence'.[30] In *Out*, in moments of heightened perception, the object of perception and the area of concentration is not determined in advance: the narrative brings it into focus. In one scene, as the protagonist looks out the window, his eyes alight on a neighbouring shack:

A red and white blob floats in the darkness behind the verandah window, grows big and becomes presumably Mrs Ned, though without a head [...] Mrs Ned grows unmistakeably into Mrs Ned, who is ironing in the small front room. She bends her white face downwards, more than is perhaps necessary for ironing, and shows therefore mostly the top of her brown head, with the thin untidy hair emerging now from the dark background.[31]

---

interest in the principles of physics, and in particular the observer principle: '"That's a Scientific Fact"', p. 942.

[29]   Brooke-Rose, *Out*, p. 11.
[30]   William James, *Principles of Psychology* (New York, 1890), p. 227.
[31]   Brooke-Rose, *Out*, p. 29.

The neighbour Mrs Ned gradually comes into focus, becoming 'unmistake-ably' herself, as the narrator's attention fixes on a point beyond his window. There is a sense of pathos in the gaze: first, the 'red and white blob' realises itself into the human figure of Mrs Ned, who is understood to be undertak-ing her daily chores and a sense of her human vulnerability enters into the description: her 'thin untidy hair' showing as she leans over her ironing. This moment of sustained attention, which takes place in the neighbourhood of Colourless shacks, in which different colours and disparate parts assemble into someone, is different to the kind of attention that occurs in the novel's public sphere, where the protagonist's gaze can only register individual body parts, a leg, say, or a foot. In these public scenes, at the Labour Exchange or at the Big House, the disjointed descriptions of body parts do not tend to resolve into a whole.

Out's central character approaches attentiveness by framing and refram-ing the people, objects and world in his line of vision. Early on we are given a description of a fig tree, seen from the window of the protagonist and his wife's home:

> The dark grey trunk leans along the edge of the bank at an angle of forty degrees, inside which, from a standing position, the road may be seen. One of the branches sweeps downwards out of the trunk, away from the road, forming with the trunk an arch that frames the piece of road within it.[32]

A number of different observational positions are posited simultaneously: first, the tree is seen from the window of the shack; second, a scene is pro-jected further away – the road, which 'may be seen' 'from a standing position' underneath the angle of the tree; and finally, a further frame of the road itself is created by one of the branches. The kind of attention here is both atten-tive and distracted: limited to a specific scene (the tree) but also expansive, moving beyond it. The description of the tree is returned to several times in the novel, with slight variations in description. This approach to atten-tion frames it as a practice: not something that can be achieved or sustained, but something that must be returned to, and always refigured according to the object of one's attention. In this way, attention, as it is represented in Brooke-Rose's novel, escapes the imperative of efficiency which is central to the novel's welfare system and becomes a kind of unproductive, non-instru-mental practice of maintenance: a practice, in short, of care.

It is possible to read the descriptions of the observer's gaze (referred to as a 'blue squint'), as they evolve over the course of the opening account of

---

[32]   Brooke-Rose, *Out*, p. 22.

the flies, along these lines. In this scene, the protagonist and his wife Lilly exchange a brief dialogue, and he draws her attention to the flies: 'Look,' he says, 'two flies are making love on my knee'.[33] We are then told, 'The squint seems bluer today, and wider'. Because this squint (this gaze) observes the flies, it is unclear at first to whom it belongs. But tracking descriptions of the blue eye and its eyelids across the scene, it seems likely that this gaze belongs to Lilly, and that her husband is observing her closely. Right before Lilly asks for the flyswatter, 'the mobile eye shifts towards the knee and back', though the flies appear not to notice 'that extra light of awareness briefly on them'.[34] Similarly, as Lilly's interest turns from the flies to the old medications her employer Mrs Mgulu has given her, 'The winter flies lie quite still, dead to the removal of that light of awareness briefly upon them'.

The protagonist's observation of his wife's gaze turns at a certain point in this scene to care and concern: 'The skin around the eyes, both the mobile eye and the fixed eye, is waxy, but the eyelids are the right colour'.[35] A few lines down, we are told 'The waxiness is due to a deficiency in the liver', and on the next page, 'The waxiness could even be due to cancer':

> If the waxiness were due to cancer then the eyelids would not be the right colour, but of course the colour of the eyelids might have reflected the luminosity from the rectangle of rippling light. On the other hand, the luminosity thrown by the rectangle of light would also have affected the waxiness of the skin elsewhere around the eyes.[36]

The narrative wheels through the possible causes of the waxy skin, at times giving partial reassurance (the eyelids were the right colour, after all); at times refusing such reassurance (perhaps it was only the light making the eyelids look healthful). These comments are interspersed with the protagonist's usual framed observations of the space around him (lines of dialogue that may or may not be spoken) but the waxiness of the skin around the eyes, the colour of the eyelids, are returned to again and again throughout this scene. This reads like worry, like a practical concern for a person one cares about. This concern is reciprocated by Lilly, who always ensures the protagonist has his bowl of gruel or, when possible, something more enticing from their dwindling stock of tinned food. The protagonist feels this care: whenever he leaves the house for the daily degradation of the Labour Exchange, or the

---

33 Brooke-Rose, *Out*, p. 13.
34 Brooke-Rose, *Out*, p. 14.
35 Brooke-Rose, *Out*, p. 17.
36 Brooke-Rose, *Out*, p. 18.

menial labour at Mrs Mgulu's, he thinks to himself of how 'At home there would be a remedy'.[37] This phrase is another of the novel's refrains and acts as a kind of talisman for the protagonist when he is among strangers, providing comfort for him and leading him home.

The Affordances of Form

Martin Buber suggests that a practice of attention 'can suspend our tendency toward instrumental understanding - seeing things or people one-dimensionally as the products of their function - and sit with the unfathomable fact of their existence, which opens up towards us but can never be fully grasped or known'.[38] Although Brooke-Rose's narrative cycles through various scientific modes of observation, its constant reframing of perspective suggests that no single approach will be able to grasp, comprehensively, the Other who is the focus of this attention, whether the Other is another person or the world itself. This model of attention is different from 'the process of "understanding" people and ideas from the perspective of Western thought', Édouard Glissant writes.[39] In the place of the requirement for transparency, Glissant argues for acknowledging the Other's 'right to opacity'.[40] In terms of the novel's approach to form, the recursive structure, its structural reliance on repetition, and repetition with or without variation, suggest this sense of opacity. The protagonist's refrains, his repeated phrases and attempts to describe particular scenes, far from trying to pin down meaning, are a form of praxis rather than of teleology. As Sontag puts it, 'Verbosity and repetitiveness [...] in the temporal arts of prose fiction [...] cultivate a kind of ontological stammer – facilitated by their refusal of the incentives for a clean, anti-redundant discourse supplied by beginning-middle-and-end construction'.[41] Such textual strategies, which Ellen E. Berry has referred to as a 'negative aesthetics', involve the refusal of linear plotting, the refusal of closure, and instead insist on a kind of indeterminacy. Berry argues that literary experiment along these lines demonstrates how experience can 'only be represented accurately through the experimental *un*making of dominant

---

[37]   Brooke-Rose, *Out,* p. 48.
[38]   Cited in Jenny Odell, *How to Do Nothing: Resisting the Attention Economy* (Hoboken, 2021), p. 104.
[39]   Édouard Glissant, 'For Opacity', *Poetics of Relation*, trans. Betsy Wing (Ann Arbor, 1997), pp. 189–94 (p. 189).
[40]   Glissant, 'For Opacity', p. 190.
[41]   Sontag, 'The Aesthetics of Silence', p. 27.

structures of rationality', and constitute 'an aesthetics of negation in which style supports antisocial forms of radical refusal'.[42]

The sort of attention such a text demands 'could be described as establishing a great "'distance"' (between spectator and object, between the spectator and his emotions)'.[43] But, as Sontag writes, 'psychologically, distance is often linked with the most intense state of feeling, by which the coolness or impersonality with which something is treated measures the insatiable interest that thing has for us'.[44] Distance, in other words, suggests a relation of proximity as well: it describes a partiality that holds connection in a dialectical relation. Just as a presumed connection is necessary to initiate a practice of distance, so is a kind of distance necessary to maintain these connections. Again, distance does not suggest a position of objectivity; rather, like its related concept, detachment, distance is always only 'a temporary vantage, unstable achievement, or regulative ideal', Amanda Anderson argues.[45] For Anderson, detachment is a practice that is 'intimately related to the sociological, novelistic, and political project of understanding and potentially transforming the social totality'.[46]

The transformative potential of distance reflects Brooke-Rose's thoughts on her 'anti-novels' and her aesthetic practice more broadly. As Natalie Ferris suggests, Brooke-Rose defined the 'anti-novel [...] as an act of literary radicalism, in both form and content', which, per Brooke-Rose, would 'turn the form inside out, hold it up, perhaps, to ridicule, and give it a thorough beating, or at least an airing'.[47] Brooke-Rose cited the works of Samuel Beckett as exemplary anti-novels, and she was especially interested in their 'self-mocking purpose; the "desire to break forms"; the dwelling on every detail of a situation or gesture; the "mathematical style;" the "carefully mundane language to describe either incredible things in an ordinary context or, more usually, ordinary things in an incredible context"'.[48] For Brooke-Rose, Ferris comments, 'the "point" of the anti-novel was "to force the reader to read actively not passively," so as to address the "representational impasse"

---

[42]   Ellen Berry, *Women's Experimental Writing: Negative Aesthetics and Feminist Critique* (London, 2017), p. 1.
[43]   Sontag, 'The Aesthetics of Silence', p. 26.
[44]   Sontag, 'The Aesthetics of Silence', p. 26.
[45]   Amanda Anderson, *The Powers of Distance: Cosmopolitanism and the Cultivation of Detachment* (Princeton, 2001), p. 32.
[46]   Anderson, *The Powers of Distance*, p. 32.
[47]   Natalie Ferris, '"I think I preferred it abstract": Christine Brooke-Rose and Visuality in the New Novel', *Textual Practice*, 32 (2017), pp. 1–20 (p. 228); Brooke-Rose, cited in Ferris, '"I think I preferred it abstract"', p. 228.
[48]   Cited Ferris, '"I think I preferred it abstract"', p. 228.

that the novel was thought to have reached'.[49] In this regard, Brooke-Rose's avant-gardism works in similar ways to that of another 'experimental' writer: Gertrude Stein. Dana Cairns Watson sees Stein's interventions into the grammar of the sentence as also intervening in the grammar of looking: they work to 'condition [...] readers to understand words differently than they have before' and '[O]nce we hear differently, we can see differently. We then treat words differently ourselves, altering how others can hear'.[50] Stein's strategy, like Brooke-Rose's, helps readers to become more attentive to the multiple possible valences of language, as well as to the power that language has to create and recreate the world. Debra Malina has argued that Brooke-Rose's metaleptic games trouble 'the very distinction between representation in "fiction" and reproduction in "reality"'.[51] Brooke-Rose has in fact suggested as much herself, writing that one of her aims is 'never allowing the stock response to materialize in fact. The moment the reader feels secure, you just make him think again'.[52]

Out, as many critics have pointed out, draws attention to its construction as a text: the novel's organising consciousness shows the protagonist forming perspectives and then remaking them again, writing imaginary letters and rewriting them. Likewise, the detachment implicit in the approach of the novel's focalizor-framer, who is both the protagonist and something more than the protagonist, challenges any easy identification with these characters or the 'real world' of the text.[53] Malina, for instance, writes that the 'focalizors' of Brooke-Rose's prepositional novels, *Out*, *Between* and *Thru*, lack 'the sorts of realistic attributes that generally define novels' actors or even narrators'.[54] A 'focalizor', she suggests, 'is a functionary, a lens, a perspective – at most, the projection of a subject behind the observations made possible by a certain *position*'.

The combination of *Out*'s thematic and formal focus on attention, together with the lack of access granted to any of the characters' emotional lives, is reminiscent of a position Deborah Nelson characterises as being 'alone together'. For Nelson, the stance is adopted by writers of the late twentieth century who are preoccupied by one of the era's 'greatest dilemmas': 'how to confront the scale of painful reality [...] Scale itself, the sheer

---

[49]   Cited Ferris, "'I think I preferred it abstract"', pp. 229–30.
[50]   Dana Cairns Watson, *Gertrude Stein and the Essence of What Happens* (Nashville, 2004), p. 7.
[51]   Malina, *Breaking the Frame*, p. 68.
[52]   Cited Malina, *Breaking the Frame*, p. 68.
[53]   Malina, *Breaking the Frame*, p. 69.
[54]   Malina, *Breaking the Frame*, p. 64.

imponderability of the size of the problem, became one of the psychic, social, aesthetic, and political challenges of the postwar era'.[55] Nelson argues that, in response, the work of such writers as Sontag, Simone Weil and Hannah Arendt, evinces a commitment to attention that 'take[s] precedence over the writer's relationship with the reader or the reader's relationship to the thing described'.[56] Their committed focus on what Nelson calls 'reality' is unsentimental and refuses shared feeling. For these writers, 'the greatest form of compassion is attention which is not precisely sympathetic or empathetic'.[57] This is because, as Nelson explains, they viewed the politics of empathy 'as *anaesthetic*'.[58]

In *On Revolution*, Arendt writes about the ways in which pity or empathy maintains a relationship to power. In empathising, we incorporate someone else's suffering into our world view. Arendt asks for responses from readers that are thoughtful rather than sympathetic.[59] It is an ethical stance to the other that looks outward rather than in and that challenges instead of consoles. At issue here is a devotion to the concrete, which Lyndsey Stonebridge argues is an attempt to build blueprints or frames for understanding experience that is not ours, and that cannot be incorporated into our worldview.[60] It is the kind of attention that Brooke-Rose's writing asks of the reader. In upending conventional forms in the context of a novel 'about' care and caring institutions, Brooke-Rose's formal strategies point us to the potential affordances of an experimental style for reading welfare and for thinking about, and giving, care. In refusing the reader the usual consolations of narrative, character and plot, the novel asks for a different kind of reading, a different way of looking at the text and, by extension, at the world. As expansive as *Out*'s vision appears to be, it remains inevitably constrained by the logics of whiteness, but its novel ways of knowing and seeing, the space it creates for opacity, might nevertheless constitute a crack in these structures of thought.

---

[55]   Deborah Nelson, *Tough Enough: Arbus, Arendt, Didion, McCarthy, Sontag, Weil* (Chicago, 2017), pp. 3–34 (p. 6).
[56]   Nelson, *Tough Enough*, p. 31.
[57]   Nelson, *Tough Enough*, p. 37.
[58]   Nelson, *Tough Enough*, p. 68.
[59]   Nelson, *Tough Enough*, pp. 9–10.
[60]   Lyndsey Stonebridge, 'The Moral World in Dark Times: Hannah Arendt for Now', *On Being Podcast* (2017). < https://onbeing.org/programs/lyndsey-stonebridge-the-moral-world-in-dark-times-hannah-arendt-for-now-jun2018/>.

7

Dreaming of Welfare: Doris Lessing, the Good Neighbour and the Sociological Imagination

JESS COTTON

You shall love your crooked neighbour
With your crooked heart

—W. H. Auden, 'As I Walked Out One Evening'[1]

Mrs. Thatcher did not at any point link her praise of Victorian values with an explicit attack upon the values of the welfare state. But many among both her opponents and supporters instantly assumed that this was in fact what she meant.

—Jose Harris, 'Victorian Values and the Founders of the Welfare State'[2]

In 1983 Doris Lessing sent a manuscript, which would become the first part of *The Diaries of Jane Somers* (1984), under a pseudonym to her publisher Jonathan Cape and to Granada, both of which rejected it. The editors at Cape viewed it as not commercially viable. Granada called the book 'too depressing to publish'.[3] Eventually Michael Joseph, who had published Lessing's first novel, *The Grass is Singing* (1950), agreed to take it on, but in its first year of publication it sold only around one thousand five hundred copies in England and around three thousand copies in the United States.[4] The précis of the first 'Jane Somers' novel, *The Diary of a Good Neighbour*, as sent to publishers, reads as follows: 'Magazine editor "comes of age" and finally matures through involvement with and caring for three old women

[1]   W. H. Auden, *Collected Poems* (London, 2007), p. 134.
[2]   Jose Harris, 'Victorian Values and the Founders of the Welfare State', *Proceedings of the British Academy*, 78 (1992), pp. 165–82 (p. 165).
[3]   Doris Lessing, *The Diaries of Jane Somers* (1984; London, 2002), p. vii.
[4]   Lessing, *The Diaries of Jane Somers*, p. ix.

and helping them to maintain at least some kind of control over their lives and deaths'.[5] One of the reviewers at Lessing's agent Jonathan Clowes assessed the novel accordingly:

> this is not not not the familiar U.S. story of sweet old lady becomes friends with young boy girl [...] The relationships between selfish Jane and difficult Maudie is not sweetness and light: Jane spends much time washing, cleaning, emptying commodes. But they also talk – Maudie of her working-class life in the early 20th century, while Jane works out her own problems. What amazes Jane is Maudie's unwillingness to die: she does not want to and right up to the end never accepts death [...] I find the book wholly (and often upsettingly) credible. It is not the Hollywood treatment – it is old age in all its fear, filth, pain and anger. The style is easy, readable. But the subject is, obviously, gruelling, and by no stretch of the imagination could the book be described as commercial or popular.
>
> If this were by an unknown writer, one could congratulate her, encourage her and probably reject the book as being too 'difficult'.[6]

In drawing our attention at once to the easy, readable style of the novel, its commercial unviability and its difficult subject matter, the anonymous reviewer evidences the literary conundrum presented by Lessing's pseudonymous novel, which most likely would not have been published if she had not revealed her authorship. In a slightly embarrassed apology several decades later, the writer James Lasdun confessed in the *New Yorker* to being the young reader at Cape who rejected Lessing's submission. '"Good" for me', he explains, 'at that time meant tight and clever and stylistically showy. The idea that failing to see the merit of "The Diary of a Good Neighbour" might have been a reflection of my own limitations rather than the book's had no resonance for me at all. My mechanism of judgement was as ruthless as it was narrow'.[7]

In this chapter I want to consider the question of literary value and the form of social realism that is presented by the publishing hoax in relation to the representation of welfare. *The Diary of a Good Neighbour* documents a period in the life of the protagonist Jane Somers and the care she provides for a ninety-year-old woman named Maudie Fowler. While documenting this care in diary form, and noting her reflections on her life and career at

---

5   Doris Lessing Papers, 'The Diary of a Good Neighbour (as Jane Somers, 1983)', 13.2 Harry Ransom Center, University of Texas.

6   Doris Lessing Papers, 'The Diary of a Good Neighbour (as Jane Somers, 1983)'.

7   James Lasdun, 'Doris Lessing and the Perils of the Pseudonymous Novel', *New Yorker*, 23 July 2013.

a women's magazine, Jane is also at work on a novel of historical fiction, a work that is nostalgic and sentimental, and which is presented in contrast to the diaristic transcription of the present. *The Diary* is, then, the literary realism that does not get published about old age, welfare and the provision of care because there is no literary market for it. In writing a novel as Jane Somers, within a diary that is also narrated by her, Lessing uses the diary form to show a reality and a fictional production of that reality simultaneously, as she does through the diaristic structure of her earlier work, *The Golden Notebook* (1962). The literary experiment exposes how certain subject positions and publishing contexts push certain authors into certain genres that are expected of them.

The publication circumstances of the Jane Somers hoax alert the reader, then, to the relationship between authorship, genre, subject matter and what Lessing refers to as 'the literary machine'.[8] Jane Somers, a fictional authorial creation, establishes a complex relationship to Lessing's own 'serious' authorship. The Jane Somers novels are not stylistically sophisticated; they seem to consciously inhabit the realm of the middlebrow and are rarely spoken of in the same context as Lessing's other novels, although they have received more critical attention recently.[9] The novels are distinctive amongst Lessing's body of work not only in their subject matter but in their tone; they expose 'the difficult, anxious eighties' without the irony that informs Lessing's other Thatcher-era novels, *The Good Terrorist* (1985) and *The Fifth Child* (1988).[10] Their moralism is left ambiguous as they open up questions about the relationship between welfarist ideology and the deserving subject of care. In her preface to *The Diaries*, Lessing writes that her ironic perspective *is* her conscience. '[A]s Jane Somers I wrote in ways that Doris Lessing cannot. It was more than a question of using the odd turn of phrase or an adjective to suggest a woman journalist who is also a successful romantic novelist: Jane Somers knew nothing about a kind of dryness, like a conscience, that monitors Doris Lessing whatever she writes and in whatever style'.[11]

---

8   Doris Lessing, *Conversations*, ed. Earl G. Ingersoll (Princeton, 2000), p. 163.
9   See Susan Watkins, 'The "Jane Somers" Hoax: Aging, Gender and the Literary Marketplace', *Doris Lessing: Border Crossings*, ed. Alice Ridout and Susan Watkins (London, 2009), pp. 75–91; Nonia Williams, '"No Hip Muffs": Female Ageing in Doris Lessing's Fiction and Correspondence', *Critical Quarterly*, 63.1 (2021), pp. 67–81; Fiona Tolan, 'The Politics of Cleaning in Doris Lessing's 1980s Realist Fiction: *The Diary of a Good Neighbour* (1983) and *The Good Terrorist* (1985)', *Critical Quarterly*, 63.1 (2021), pp. 89–97.
10   Lessing, *The Diaries of Jane Somers*, p. 145.
11   Lessing, *The Diaries*, p. vi.

If Lessing locates her conscience in her irony, then, how are we to judge her relinquishment of both her irony and her authorship, and locate value in a novel that is consciously less stylistically sophisticated than her early novels, though not markedly so from those that followed? Irony is, moreover, hardly absent from the novel, but the irony is seemingly not directed at Jane herself but rather at her relation to literary convention – at the way she negotiates a particular form of realism in relation to her own role as a romantic novelist. In withholding her signature irony, Lessing shows the work that an individual can do in contributing to the welfare of others, an idea that is central to her 1957 essay 'A Small Personal Voice', which is widely considered her most programmatic statement on realism. In allowing Jane Somers to narrate her own experience of welfare, Lessing allows us to see both the value of that care and the split between the representation of reality and welfare and the readerly world in which that reality and welfare is conceived. One of the affordances of Lessing's writing is that she alerts us, Philip Tsang observes, to a 'constant sense' that 'reality is coming from elsewhere'; her writing 'invites readers to reconstruct a historicist mentality with which to view their own societies and individual selves as historical products'.[12] The formal ambivalence of the Jane Somers novels directs our attention to the tension between welfare provision, realism and the sociological imagination. In her autobiography, Lessing reflects, accordingly, on the 'golden age' of welfare:

Mass observation, particularly during the war, was the first manifestation of an attitude towards ourselves now common. Sociology was being born, the ability to look at our society, our own behaviour, as an alien might see it. Now this seems to me the important thing, but it was welfare that filled our imaginations.[13]

In this chapter I consider the movement between welfare and the sociological imagination in Lessing's novels *In Pursuit of the English* (1960) and *The Diary of a Good Neighbour* (1983). I am interested, specifically, in the representation of kinship and neighbourliness in relation to the promises of the postwar welfare state. In both novels Lessing uses the microworld of the novel's community to test the possibilities and limits of solidarity that emerge in relation to narratives of welfare. She shows how these micro forms of welfare interact and counterbalance the disciplinary aspects of the welfare state as embodied by the welfare officer, a character who becomes more sympathetic in the later novel insofar as she is seen not simply as an instrument

[12] Philip Tsang, *The Obsolete Empire* (Baltimore, 2021), p. 163.
[13] Doris Lessing, *Walking in the Shade: Volume Two of My Autobiography, 1949–1962* (1997; London, 2013), p. 90.

of the state but as a low paid female worker. At stake in both novels is the question of communal living, loneliness and the inadequacy of welfarist ideology to account for the dreams, wishes and needs of the postwar British subject. In the layered referentiality of Lessing's welfare fictions, we see how individual dreams and needs align and conflict with the collective narrative of welfare. Where sociological studies such as Michael Young and Peter Willmott's *Family and Kinship in East London* (1957) present a nostalgic vision of working-class people's attachment to place, Lessing presents a more complicated vision of uprooted communities in postwar London, so that we see how characters' frustrated (not merely benevolent) attachments coincide with Britain's own imperial contraction.

In my reading of Lessing's novels, I draw lines of comparison between her narration of working-class communities and welfare provision in relation to the social realism that was generated by the publications affiliated to the Institute of Community Studies, the Bethnal Green-based social research organisation founded in 1953. The institute is best known for Young and Willmott's *Family and Kinship*. The publication sold more than half a million copies in its 1962 Penguin paperback edition, influencing a generation of scholars, social workers and other professionals.[14] Young and Willmott's study sought to show the importance of the extended family and neighbours in the everyday care of the young and old, care structures that, they argued, would be jeopardised by new housing policy, particularly policy that displaced working-class communities to new towns. Their defence of working-class inner-city communities was, in part, founded on the idea that neighbourly relations and kinship structures were 'the building blocks for a mutualistic socialism'.[15]

This focus on the work of kinship and neighbourly ties was intimately related in Young's thought, Pat Thane observes, to his advocacy for a localised, 'decentralised, participatory system' of welfare that would provide a 'space to express [workers'] wishes, needs or complaints', desires, which he saw, had little space for articulation in the welfare state's attachment to grand narratives and national programmes.[16] Young had first articulated this idea to the Labour government in 1948 as the need for a 'neighbourhood democracy'.[17]

---

[14]   Jon Lawrence, 'Inventing the "Traditional Working Class": A Re-Analysis of Interview Notes from Young and Willmott's *Family and Kinship in East London*', *The Historical Journal*, 59.2 (2016), pp. 567–93 (p. 569).

[15]   Lawrence, 'Inventing the "Traditional Working Class"', p. 570.

[16]   Pat Thane, 'Michael Young and Welfare', *Contemporary British History*, 12 (2005), pp. 293–9 (p. 294).

[17]   Michael Young, 'Small Man: Big World: A Discussion of Socialist Democracy',

Family and Kinship is divided into two halves: the first part documents the kinship structures and the sense of place in Bethnal Green, which 'helps to keep alive a very personal sense of history', and which 'reinforces the feeling of attachment (just as it does in a regiment, a university, a trade union, or a political party) to the community and to its inhabitants'.[18] The second part contrasts this sense of attachment and historical belonging with the isolation of the new town in Greenleigh, where there is little sense of communal feeling and where neighbourliness is defined by forms of surveillance, imitation and envy. Young and Willmott's focus on neighbourly and kinship relations, as their final chapter concedes, conceals both a historical shift in ways of organising social life and the way that social mobility under the welfare state complicates class-based forms of attachment. As the historian Jon Lawrence has shown, it also depends on leaving out testimonies which contradicted its coherent picture of working-class inner-city life.[19]

Lessing's mediation of two levels of referentiality in her fiction allows us to see, then, how contemporary sociology produced a form of realism that influenced the perception of welfare, class and neighbourliness in postwar Britain. In the split between the representation of reality and the desire for readerliness, we find a fantastical, nostalgic vision of neighbourliness that is passed off as reality. Lessing's sociological realism reveals the complex historiography that emerges within the myths of postwar London that were central to the remediation of nineteenth-century urban neighbourhoods in *Family and Kinship*. Young and Willmott drew on a sustained engagement with testimony from people whose lives had been re-engineered by successive postwar governments committed to large-scale slum clearance and the dispersal of overcrowded inner cities. The book was also, Lawrence notes, 'in many respects the definitive statement about class as community in post-war Britain'.[20] Lessing complicates Young and Willmott's sociological approach to personal testimony by focusing on the sociological gaze and the fictions that the welfare officer and the sociologist alike expect to encounter when they visit working-class communities.

Published seven years after the collection of its research data, *Family and Kinship*'s vision of Bethnal Green's working-class communities was already a historical object that was being passed off as a contemporary reality. Narrating

---

Towards Tomorrow, 4 (London, 1948); Young Papers YUNG 2/1/1, Churchill Archives Centre, University of Cambridge.

[18]   Michael Young and Peter Willmott, *Family and Kinship in East London* (1957; London, 2007), p. 114.

[19]   Lawrence, 'Inventing the "Traditional Working Class"', pp. 567–93.

[20]   Lawrence, 'Inventing the "Traditional Working Class"', p. 568.

austerity Britain from the perspective of 1960, Lessing is interested in how the period had already been historicised. *In Pursuit of the English* makes us aware of sociology's role in constructing a historically fictitious present and of the role of the good neighbour in this idealised vision of working-class community. In seeking to evidence their vision of neighbourly community, Young and Willmott edited out complex accounts of neighbourly ties in favour of the 'public accounts' of community, which 'people reproduced', Lawrence writes, 'almost as clichés'.[21] The vision of the good neighbour in *Family and Kinship* is coextensive with the vision of social care undertaken by the privatised family unit, a concept that Lessing insistently interrogates in her welfare fictions.

Welfare's Late Realism

When Doris Lessing arrived in London in 1949, on a month-long boat journey with her young son from South Africa, the England that she encountered on her arrival was quite unlike the image of British prosperity that she had envisaged while growing up in southern Rhodesia. On her arrival she found herself in a grey city filled with lonely neighbours, imposing landlords and airless lodgings. It was a state recorded by many émigré writers in the period, who recall the itinerant life of bedsit and boarding house living, and the ominous fogs that would engulf the city, where 'some areas [were still] all ruins'.[22] Nonetheless, London still promised a new life for Lessing, as it did for thousands of emigrants in the postwar years: a 'clean slate, a new page – everything still to come', as she puts it in her autobiography.[23] This sense of change was propelled by the optimism of the image of postwar Britain as a new Jerusalem, a vision that was outlined by the Beveridge Report, published in December 1942, which gave a blueprint for a postwar system of social security.

Designed by William Beveridge and implemented by Clement Attlee's Labour government, the welfare state guaranteed social provision and opportunities regardless of one's economic position, and so created the vision of a postwar collectivity and social aspiration that would make permanent the wartime's 'real feeling of community'.[24] But the reconstruction of Britain was to be a slow process, and, in the late 1940s, the mood for many was one

---

21 Lawrence, 'Inventing the "Traditional Working Class"', p. 572.
22 Lessing, *Walking in the Shade*, p. 4.
23 Lessing, *Walking in the Shade*, p. 3.
24 Raymond Williams, *The Long Revolution* (London, 1961), p. 363.

of austerity and deprivation rather than hope for a bright new future. 'What was perhaps most depressing about the early postwar period was not that it felt so much like wartime', Marina MacKay observes, 'but that conditions were sometimes even worse'.[25] *In Pursuit of the English*, which is set in a war-damaged London boarding house, is situated in the stilled time of reconstruction; it represents welfare and the sociological imagination in relation to the stalled promise of welfare.

Lessing always saw herself at a distance from metropolitan literary culture, and she insistently alerts her reader to that distance: to the way that the parochialism of English realism is created in relation to empire.[26] Lessing's conviction, as she outlines in her essay 'A Small Personal Voice,' that realism can '"enlarge one's perception of life" had', Philip Tsang argues, 'strong geopolitical resonances in the 50s'.[27] Lessing complicates the parochialism of English realism to bring it into alignment with complex realities across Britain's empire. By presenting a social reality simultaneously with a fictionalised version of it her reader becomes aware of how reality is constantly being produced elsewhere. *In Pursuit of the English* is an ironised homecoming narrative which exposes the uprootedness of postwar British communities caused by the inadequacy of housing provision under the welfare state, and exacerbated by the disciplinary aspects of welfare. In the novel, characters indulge in 'the forbidden pleasures of nostalgia' rather than identifying with a vision of community.[28] Through the material constraints of the boarding house, which is suffused with an atmosphere of stasis, Lessing reveals the difficulty of transcending the class and gendered division of labour that has historically informed the British empire.

Lessing fictionalises her arrival in the imperial metropolis on several occasions as a demystifying process, one which at once allows her to understand the imaginary space that England occupied in her father's imagination and to articulate her own ambivalence about national belonging. *In Pursuit of the English* opens in this vein:

---

[25]   Marina MacKay, 'Slender Means: The Novel in the Age of Austerity', *British Literature in Transition 1940–1960*, ed. Gill Plain (Cambridge, 2018), pp. 37–51 (p. 38).

[26]   For more on this idea see Cornelius Collins, '"In that Other Voice:" Doris Lessing's Ironic "Return to Realism" in the 1980s', *Critical Quarterly*, 63.1 (2021), pp. 98–109.

[27]   Tsang, *The Obsolete Empire*, pp. 150–1.

[28]   Doris Lessing, *A Proper Marriage* (New York, 1964), p. 129.

I came into contact with the English very early in life, because as it turns out, my father was an Englishman. I put it like this, instead of making a claim or deprecating a fact, because it was not until I had been in England for some time that I understood my father.

I wouldn't like to say that I brooded over his character; that would be putting it too strongly, but I certainly spent a good part of my childhood coming to terms with it. I must confess, to be done with confessions right at the start, that I concluded at the age of about six my father was mad.[29]

This prelude about the idiosyncrasies of the narrator's father stands in for the madness of colonial life, prompting the reader to think metonymically about the relation between the formation of the self and empire. This psychoanalytic understanding of attachment (one that goes far beyond British psychologist John Bowlby's fixation on maternal care) that accounts for the madness of colonialism, establishes a complex relation to the sociological fiction that unfolds in the subsequent pages.[30] Only, Lessing suggests, by understanding the complexity of such attachments to England can one hope to understand how a reality is produced which is at odds with the sociological reading of postwar British communities. *In Pursuit of the English* reveals emotional attachments as historical products, and the realities of English life as intimately related to realities produced elsewhere in the empire.

I read *In Pursuit of the English* as part of a trajectory of what Tsang refers to as Lessing's 'late realism', which 'frames her famous "pursuit of the English" as a restless pursuit of literary form'.[31] 'Arrival in the metropolis', Tsang writes, 'fails to remedy the predicament of colonial untimeliness', and the ideals of Englishness are exposed as a home that no one comfortably inhabits in the novel.[32] The pursuit of literary form, the pursuit of the British and the pursuit of the welfare state are intimately entangled in this formally and tonally ambivalent book. Over the course of *In Pursuit of the English*, Englishness and the working class recede the nearer Lessing approaches the colonial centre. As she comes to cohabit with the English, she finds that its forms of community and its housing are built on precarious foundations (forms are submitted to the government to repair the bomb-damaged building, but welfare appears to have little material reality in the boarding house). As her fellow resident Rose explains to Lessing, 'the English' is a term that

---

[29]   Doris Lessing, *In Pursuit of the English: A Documentary* (London, 1980), p. 5.
[30]   For more on the legacy of Bowlby's attachment theory, see Denise Riley, *War in the Nursery* (London, 1983).
[31]   Tsang, *The Obsolete Empire*, p. 151.
[32]   Tsang, *The Obsolete Empire*, p. 173.

only works to describe those in the past or those at a geographical distance from the metropolis: 'I'm from London, as I told you. That's what I mean when I say I'm not English. Not really. When I talk of English, what I mean is, my granddad and my grandma. That's English. The country [...] They were shut off, see?'[33] If Englishness no longer has the coherence that it once did (now imagined as an isolated community that is untouched by the material reality of empire), the lack of this English communal feeling, Lessing shows, generates a mood of nostalgia that informs the stasis of the boarding house and the residents' hostility to the promises of welfare. 'People liked each other well [during the war, but] they don't now, do they?' Rose tells Lessing, 'And so don't talk to me about your socialism'.[34] A suggestion that the recent founding of the National Health Service might be one reason to see the advantages of a Labour government falls on deaf ears in the boarding house, which has the social markers and claustrophobia of nineteenth-century urban British fiction.

During *In Pursuit of the English* Lessing satirises her own pursuit of the working class as being the primary subject of social realism:

> My life has been spent in pursuit. So has everyone's, of course. I chase love and fame all the time. I have chased, off and on, and with much greater deviousness of approach, the working-class and the English. The pursuit of the working-class is shared by everyone with the faintest tint of social responsibility: some of the most indefatigable pursuers are working-class people. That is because the phrase does not mean, simply, those people who can be found by walking out of one's front door and turning down a side-street. Not at all. Like love and fame it is a platonic image, a grail, a quintessence, and by definition, unattainable.[35]

The irony of the pursuit gives way in the novel to her subject's elusive pursuit of welfare, and to the dreams of reconstruction in postwar Britain that seem to falter from the perspective of the ruinous boarding house. In the place of the idealised working-class community that Lessing goes in search of, we find instead a community of lonely, depressed subjects, who provide one another with forms of companionship, unsentimental care and provisionally urban – though markedly not English – forms of belonging. The community of the novel is determined by the scope of their shared housing, and their relations

---

[33] Lessing, *In Pursuit of the English*, p. 106.
[34] Lessing, *In Pursuit of the English*, p. 115.
[35] Lessing, *In Pursuit of the English*, p. 115.

are informed by their states of tenancy that are interrupted rather than sustained by visits from the welfare officer.

Neighbourhood Fictions

In Pursuit of the English, which sits somewhat ambiguously between autobiography, fiction and sociological study, exposes a far less romanticised vision of working-class communities, kinship and neighbourly relations than does Young and Willmott's study. Lessing's novel allows us to see not only the schisms in neighbourly ties but how those schisms result from the internalisation of welfare policy. If the welfare state failed to assure the forms of belonging required to build a vision of the 'neighbourhood democracy' which Young made a case for in 1948, the women in the boarding house nonetheless provide some form of solidarity and communal belonging, as Lessing recounts of Rose:

> She knew I did not like the Corner House, but tolerated my dislike. She was only exerting her rights as a neighbour, exactly as I might go into her and say: 'I'm depressed, please come and sit with me'. At such times she put aside whatever she was occupied with, and came at once; she recognized a tone in my voice; she knew what was due to communal living.[36]

The figure of the neighbour assumed a central role in sociological studies of the 1950s, particularly of urban working-class communities. Young and Willmott had documented working-class communities with strong neighbourly ties in Bethnal Green, but this vision failed to address Commonwealth immigration in the period. Lise Butler argues that a nostalgic view of neighbourliness expressed an idealised 'parochialism of the working-class communities'. The value placed on '"extreme localism and parochialism, and local patriotism"' hid 'not only [...] its limitations for women, but also [...] the xenophobia we might have guessed was there'.[37]

Young's idealist view of community, which drew on Bowlby's theories of separation anxiety, valorised working-class people's powerful attachment to place, kinship networks and the values of neighbourliness. Not incidentally, the maternal figure was important to this vision of attachment and 'gave rise', Ann Oakley observes, 'to generations of specious ramblings about kitchen

---

[36] Lessing, *In Pursuit of the English,* pp. 96–7.
[37] Lise Butler, *Michael Young, Social Science, and the British Left, 1945–1970* (Oxford, 2020), p. 226.

matriarchs'.[38] However, it is a fantasy absent from Lessing's boarding house where forms of idealised attachment and place are viewed in the context of economic relations: the landlady Flo is of Italian heritage, and her neighbourliness is coextensive with her desire to extract maximum rent from her fellow residents. In the novel, Lessing contrasts this fraught relation between women who are lonely in their lack of collectivity with her experience of living 'in similarly crowded places in that other continent', Africa, where 'the women and children flowed together like tadpoles the moment the men left for work'.[39] It is not only that the English boarding house, and the welfarist emphasis on the importance of attachment, is not designed for structures of collectivity, but that the possibility of collectivity is also curtailed by visits from the welfare officer, which polices working-class women's subjectivities. Something of this vision is glimpsed in the mock-sociological lens through which Lessing relates her journey with Rose to the 'slum' where the latter grew up:

> She was happily nostalgic. Passing these familiar places, which knew her, acknowledging her by a gleam from a lit window or the slant of a wall, like so many friendly glances or waves of the hand, reinstated her as a human being with right of possession in the world.[40]

In performing a nostalgic form of political ethnography, and in personifying the buildings through a dated literary trope, Lessing suggests how the fixation on place is instrumental to the sociological view of postwar London. The mock-sociological visit, which recalls Henry Mayhew's ethnographic gaze in *London Poor* (1861), at once alerts us to the nostalgia that couches sociological narratives about working-class communities and acknowledges a sense of dispossession amongst those communities.

The archive of the Institute of Community Studies allows us to see the more complex historical reality behind the narrative of *Family and Kinship in East London*. Documents show how Young approves of sociological case studies, such as the Damsons in Debden, who had 'excellent relations with neighbours. Have made real friends with their contemporaries. No apparent fear of my seeing into their home or their family life'. Young recounts how during his visit, two neighbours dropped by [...] If these had been siblings of

---

[38]   Ann Oakley, *Father and Daughter: Patriarchy, Gender and Social Science* (Bristol, 2014), p. 58.

[39]   Lessing, *In Pursuit of the English*, p. 123.

[40]   Lessing, *In Pursuit of the English*, p. 70.

the [Damsons]', he writes, 'they could not have been more at ease in [their] home'.[41] Lawrence's account of this case study reveals how a priori ideals of neighbourhood democracy inform the vision of community that underwrites Young and Willmott's study.[42] *In Pursuit of the English* demonstrates a recurrent pantomime that Flo must perform for the welfare officer. The novel shows the welfare state to be a bureaucratic institution that operates as a disciplinary force:

> At regular intervals a woman referred to by Flo as 'that interfering busybody from the Welfare' would descend, to find Flo, bland as butter, serving tea and her wonderful cake, and [her daughter] Aurora dressed to kill in organdie and white ribbons. If anyone was there, Flo would direct, over the woman's head, a profound and cynical wink [...] Once she asked Welfare if Aurora could go to a council nursery. But the reply was that Flo had a nice home and it was better for small children to be with their mothers. Besides, the council nurseries were closing down. 'Women marry to have children', said the official when Flo said she was trained for restaurant work and wanted to go back to it – the truth was she planned to help with Bobby Brent's night-club.[43]

The 'truth' about women's lives, Lessing suggests, evades the sociological case study. In excluding Flo from its nursery provision, the welfare state also excludes her from a communal structure of feeling that she could believe in. After this visit, Flo becomes envious of the other women residents who have access to nursery care, and parrots the welfare officer's view that 'a decent woman looks after her children herself'.[44] In this way, Lessing shows how welfare policy generates new states of dispossession and unfulfilled desire. The visit from the welfare officer mediates a mother's relation not only to her child but to other women, generating isolating effects which counteract the forms of care and neighbourliness that are possible under the welfare state.

In their study, Young and Willmott had set out to provide a political argument that the government needed to attend more carefully to ordinary people's lives, before it sought to construct better lives for them. The investigation of close-knit inner-city ties was designed to provide a stark contrast to the isolation of suburban life which relocated residents would have to

[41] Case D14 (Damson), 1953, CAC, YUNG 1/5/1/1, Institute of Community Studies, University of Cambridge.

[42] Lawrence, 'Inventing the "Traditional Working Class"', pp. 588–9.

[43] Lessing, *In Pursuit of the English,* pp. 124–6.

[44] Lessing, *In Pursuit of the English,* p. 126.

contend with in new towns. In their concerns about the alienation of new forms of housing that emerged in the wake of the war, Young and Willmott engaged with contemporary anxieties about the rise of 'suburban neurosis'.[45] Like many contemporary sociologists, they argued that the isolation of suburban life resulted in alienation amongst people who had been naturally sociable, even gregarious in the familiar surroundings of their old neighbourhoods. The idealisation of former close-knit working-class communities produced a historical narrative that, Lawrence observes, is complicated by 'surviving interview transcripts' which 'cut across' the narrative of '"moving out" as a great social and cultural rupture'.[46] The focus on place has the effect of depoliticising women's discontent in the domestic sphere, and of seeing their isolation as a response to redevelopment rather than as a response to the limited mobility – especially for working-class women – under the welfare state.

In her autobiography, Lessing recounts how, while canvassing for the Communist Party in the mid-1950s, she encountered isolated women in large blocks of flats who were cut off from a sense of political belonging; they did not want information, she writes, about political parties but 'advice about hire purchases and child allowances'. 'They did not know what was due to them', Lessing writes, 'or how to obtain it'. [47] In Lessing's account, the alienation arises less from the location of the new housing development than the political isolation of women. Lessing's short story 'To Room Nineteen' (1963), a portrait of a 1960s middle-class suburban marriage, is written in the vein of a sociological case study of suburban neurosis. The short story charts the isolation of its protagonist Susan from the psychological constraints of her suburban domesticity to an 'absolute solitude', a state of suicidal despair.[48] Susan is observed with the detached, clinical distance of the sociological observer, and we consequently see how, in viewing her own life with the certainty of a sociological fact, she is unable to move outside it. Susan's tragic fate – her desire for an 'absolute solitude'

[45]   See Rhodri Hayward, 'Desperate Housewives and Model Amoebae: The Invention of Suburban Neurosis in Inter-War Britain', *Health and the Modern Home*, ed. Mark Jackson (London and New York, 2007), pp. 42–62, and Alison Haggett, *Desperate Housewives, Neuroses and the Domestic Environment, 1945–1970* (London, 2012).

[46]   Lawrence, 'Inventing the "Traditional Working Class"', p. 593.

[47]   Lessing, *Walking in the Shade*, pp. 105–6.

[48]   Doris Lessing, *To Room Nineteen* (London, 2002), p. 352.

that would remove her from her state of alienation – is a condition that we only glimpse, like the sociologist, from the outside.[49]

'To Room Nineteen' is unusual amongst Lessing's body of work in that it comes so close to the sociological imagination as seemingly to confirm it. The reader is not given an alternative layer of referentiality that would allow them to understand the construction of Susan's reality in relation to the case study's production of knowledge, or to consider her fate in relation to the marriage plot and the history of women in realist fiction. It is perhaps unsurprising, then, that Lessing remained ambivalent about the merits of the short story. In a 2008 letter to Margaret Drabble, Lessing recounts how a group of anarchist students in Berlin took issue with what they saw as the story's fatalism, criticizing Lessing for not sending 'the couple to a marriage councillor'.[50] In allowing her protagonist to succumb to her sociological fate, as they saw it, Lessing had relinquished her authorial responsibility; she had seemingly adopted the distanced narration of the sociologist. The students' critique of Lessing's authorial role adopts the social scientific literalism of the story's narrative voice, so that rather than observing Susan's lack of agency as a product of a sociological way of thinking, they seek to resolve it through the psychosocial rationale of 'marriage welfare' services, a form of psychosocial provision that was state-supported in Britain in the postwar years.[51]

The Somers Experiment

In 1957, Peter Townsend (who was affiliated to the Institute of Community Studies) published *The Family Life of Old People*, a companion study to Young and Willmott's *Family and Kinship in East London*, which focuses on the effects of weakening neighbour and family ties amongst old people in Bethnal Green. Townsend's account sets out to respond to a growing sociological concern about the rising number of single elderly people and the effects of their social isolation on the welfare state. Isolation begins to be seen as a health concern in relation to the dispersal of communal and familial relations. Like Young and Willmott, in his interviews, Townsend observes an attachment to home and place; he notes how the majority of old people

[49] Lessing, *To Room Nineteen*, p. 370.
[50] Letter from Lessing to Margaret Drabble (12 December 2008), DL/2008/ Drabble, M 0011, Doris Lessing Archive, University of East Anglia.
[51] See Teri Chettiar, '"More than a Contract": The Emergence of a State-Supported Marriage Welfare Service and the Politics of Emotional Life in Post-1945 Britain', *Journal of British Studies*, 55.3 (2016), pp. 566–91.

who lived alone preferred it as long as they were within reach of relatives.[52] 'Most people living alone', he writes, 'considered themselves part of a family circle spread over neighbouring streets in Bethnal Green, or sometimes over great distances'.[53] Townsend notes that an 'exchange of services' between the young and old 'seemed to be an essential feature of the relationship between generations', and prevented the loneliness that he observes in the childless and the unmarried, who were far more likely to be lonely.[54]

The study concludes 'that desolation, or the loss of someone who is loved, is more important than social isolation in explaining the loneliness of old people' and he cites one woman whose husband had died eight years previously and who had no children as saying that she got 'so lonely [she] could fill up the teapot with tears'; she also notes that the neighbours had not even realised her husband had died.[55] *In Pursuit of the English* features a similar figure from the East End, 'an old man on the old-age pension, who was reading for the first time in his life', and who, since the death of his wife, 'was now half-crazy with loneliness and the necessity to communicate what he had so slowly and belatedly learned'.[56] Townsend views a sense of loss or desolation as a more influential factor in loneliness than architectural and geographical structures of isolation, and recognises the pressure of the old on the welfare state. But his response to this shifting social reality is to see the family as the primary safeguard against the dependence of the old on the state.

The loneliness of old age and the provision of care would continue to pre-occupy sociologists in the postwar years, given the rising number of elderly people living outside family structures. By the early 1980s, increased mobility, longer life expectancy and the breakdown of the family had put pressure on the capacity of the welfare state's provision of elderly care and particularly on the amount of care that was absorbed by kinship structures. Since more women were employed in the workforce, this also reduced the number of voluntary care roles. During the postwar years, Pat Thane observes, 'the traditional reservoir of voluntary labour' provided by 'middle-class married women' dwindled, as they entered the paid workforce. 'Older organizations gradually followed the new model, taking on more professional staff, becoming more inclusive of the people they spoke for and more publicity conscious. The change was symbolized by name changes for many of them, e.g. the Old

52   Peter Townsend, *The Family Life of Old People* (1957; London, 1980), p. 42.
53   Townsend, *The Family Life of Old People*, p. 58.
54   Townsend, *The Family Life of Old People*, p. 192.
55   Townsend, *The Family Life of Old People*, p. 198.
56   Lessing, *In Pursuit of the English*, p. 124.

People's Welfare Committee (founded 1940) became Age Concern'.[57] Other welfare institutions such as Home Help, operating since the early days of the welfare state, continued to provide care for elderly people.

A wave of sociological studies by feminist scholars in the late 1970s and 1980s drew attention to the ways that scripts of old age were conditioned by the few available narratives about elderly lives. In her 1981 study on the significance of friendship for women in later life, Dorothy Jerrome observes that narratives about ageing are dictated 'by the few who need to be rescued by the welfare state, or other agency', thus framing old age as a state of exception. Jerrome remarks on the erosion of care systems in the early 1980s, when welfare provision was stripped back at the same time that family values were prioritised, a fantasy of privatised care relations that failed to account for the weakening of kinship ties. 'One of the aims of decreasing public services in the late 1980s', Eve Worth contends, 'was to reinvigorate civil society and family life'.[58] Given a 'decline in secondary relationships outside the workplace and the growing emphasis on the family as the main source of intimacy and companionship', those 'with neither work nor close kin' are liable, Jerrome writes, to experience loneliness as a physical state of isolation and stigma, which compounds its psychosocial effects.[59] In a study of elderly women in Hastings in 1984, Jerrome argues that friendship is a more reliable and valuable attachment structure in countering the loneliness of old age than the family, since friendship 'provides continuity of experience and confirmation of a self which is valued by the ageing woman'.[60] Where the family insures against social belonging, 'friends', Jerrome notes, 'provide protective isolation in managing confrontation with the wider society'.[61]

The Diary of a Good Neighbour is concerned with the relationship between realism and the representation of subjects of care. It is a novel about the care that is possible outside of kinship structures, and the limitations of the welfare state to account for the emotional needs of its citizens from 'the cradle to the grave', outlined in the 1942 Beveridge report. In *The Diary of a Good Neighbour*, the value of realism is entangled with the possibility of

---

[57] Pat Thane, 'The "Big Society" and the "Big State": Creative Tension or Crowding Out?', *Twentieth Century British History*, 23.3 (2012), pp. 408–29 (pp. 426–7).

[58] Eve Worth, *The Welfare State Generation: Women, Agency and Class in Britain since 1945* (London, 2022), p. 112.

[59] Dorothy Jerrome, 'The Significance of Friendship for Women in Later Life', *Ageing & Society*, 1.2 (1981), pp. 175–97 (pp. 175–6).

[60] Dorothy Jerrome et al., *Hastings Women's Study Group: Women and Loneliness* (Brighton, 1984), p. 54.

[61] Jerrome, 'The Significance of Friendship for Women in Later Life', p. 179.

imagining the inner life of Maudie Fowler, a ninety-year-old working-class woman who lives alone, has no immediate family of her own and who refuses to go into a home. Maudie, who would ordinarily be reduced to a minor character in a realist novel, is brought into the foreground in *The Diary of a Good Neighbour*, though the foreground is still mediated through the first person of Jane's diary. The diary is at once a record of Jane's experience of providing voluntary care for Maudie, a coming to terms with the lack of friendship in her own life, and a growing recognition of the value of socialist medical care at a moment when governmental cuts were making the provision of that care increasingly precarious.[62] It is also a space to reflect on how states of singleness and loneliness affect women's lives. Jane comes to recognise the privilege of her solitude, its relation to health, and to contrast it with that of with her friend Joyce who, terrified of being alone, cannot imagine life outside her marriage, as well as with the destitute shape of Maudie's loneliness. The company the women offer one another, whilst not as overtly a political force as in *The Golden Notebook*, nonetheless acknowledges the work of companionship in a political climate that was increasingly hostile to forms of state-sponsored care and community. The novel allows us to see the ethics of neighbourly relations and the spirit of philanthropy that runs through volunteer and welfare provision.

In the preface to the novel, Lessing acknowledges that 'another influence that went to make Jane Somers was reflections about what my mother would be like if she lived now: that practical, efficient, energetic woman, by temperament conservative, a little sentimental, and only with difficulty (and a lot of practice at it) able to understand weakness and failure, though always kind'.[63] Jane's approach to care is seen in the novel as, in part, the product of a late Victorian philanthropy, a position that was to become particularly important in the Thatcher government which further dismantled the cuts to the welfare state that had begun in the 1970s. Before she meets Maudie, Jane describes how she, a philanthropist, and an old lady 'had tea together in a little flat in Kensington'; she had found the experience 'false and awful'. She subsequently sets out to find a more realistic form of care, one which might emerge spontaneously from public life.[64] But she ends up far from acting spontaneously: Jane seeks out Maudie because she reminds her of the women whom Jane had left unrepresented in an article she had written on stereotypes of women (for the magazine *Lilith* that she edits).[65] Maudie, then, becomes a social experiment

---

62   Lessing, *The Diaries*, p. 133.
63   Lessing, *The Diaries*, p. vi.
64   Lessing, *The Diaries*, p. vi.
65   Lessing, *The Diaries*, p. 145.

for Jane. But by withholding her signature irony in describing the relationship, Lessing also allows for the possibility of interpreting, in her tonal ambivalence, a genuine human connection between the two women.

Pat Thane contends that the argument that justified the rollback of the state, that welfare 'crowd[s] out' non-governmental action, is not only historically inaccurate but fails to recognise how the welfare state emerged in close proximity to institutions of civil society.[66] In the novel, Jane's care supplements rather than replaces welfare work; it is viewed at once as a more unstable and sentimental form of emotional provision than that provided by welfare workers, who are obliged by the demands of labour to consider people as cases. It gradually transpires that Jane is not only interested in Maudie as a friend, and as someone she can provide care for, but also makes Maudie serve a literary purpose. Whilst providing voluntary care, and diaristically documenting Maudie's faltering health, Jane is at work on a historical novel, *The Milliners of Marylebone*, which is a nostalgic, fictionalised account of Maudie's life – written without the latter's permission. Jane moves Maudie into the centre-ground of realism, then, but only to fictionalise her and to make her part of a nostalgic vision of the working class. Musing on her desire to romanticise history, Jane also plans to write a 'serious' historical novel, to represent the 'ward maids, the Spanish or the Portuguese or Jamaican or Vietnamese girls who', she concedes, 'work for such long hours, and who earn so very little'.[67] But this project does not come to fruition. 'Reality is clearly too much for me', Jane whimsically reflects when asked about her abandoned writing project.[68]

Towards the end of *The Diary of a Good Neighbour,* Jane recalls a moment in Leo Tolstoy's *War and Peace* that focuses on the figure of the old Countess:

> in that household [...] an old woman, sitting in a corner in a chair, or propped in bed, would be assimilated. I cannot think of any household I know where Maudie could be accommodated now, we all work too hard, have too much responsibility as it is; our lives are pared down to what we can fit in, we can all just cope and no more.[69]

Young, Willmott and Townsend's response to this growing sense of social isolation and the weakening of kinship ties was to emphasise housing structures which would make it easier for the family to absorb that care. In attend-

---

[66] Thane, 'The "Big Society" and the "Big State"', p. 408.
[67] Lessing, *The Diaries*, pp. 248–9.
[68] Lessing, *The Diaries*, p. 318.
[69] Lessing, *The Diaries*, p. 230.

ing to the affective relations and the possibilities of community outside the
family romance, Lessing reveals a more complex picture of the reality that
emerges between housing structures and neighbourly relations. In her 1957
essay on realism, Lessing critiques 'the Victorian charitable view' that 'the
poor are always with us, suitable objects for uplifting emotions' in relation
to individualist trends in contemporary fiction.[70] Taking issue with sceptics
who argue that communal concern is always driven by self-interest, she notes
that 'most of the people I have known during the past 15 years have devoted
themselves to causes against their self-interest', and that this political responsibility has restored her faith in humanism.[71] *The Diary of a Good Neighbour*
occupies an ambivalent space between self-interest and humanism, historical
romance and social realism; it at once shows the literary and social effects of
a Victorian charitable view in generating realist fictions of working-class lives,
and the role of the individual in transforming social reality. In interleaving
a nostalgic historical fantasy with an unadorned diaristic documentation of
old age in the present, *The Diary of a Good Neighbour* is an experimental
realist narrative about the costs of welfare work that shows the complicity
between realism, welfare and narratives of class. The capacity to create new
welfare narratives depends, for Lessing, on experiments in realism that com-
plicate the immovable reality of the sociological case study.

[70]   Doris Lessing, *A Small Personal Voice: Essays, Reviews, Interviews* (New York,
1974), p. 18.
[71]   Lessing, *A Small Personal Voice*, p. 18.

8

Welfare Fictions and the Brixton Uprising: Beryl Gilroy's Black Teacher and Caryl Phillips's The Final Passage

LARA CHOKSEY

The transformation of national care in post-1945 Britain involved a change in subject and vista: from the detailed genealogies of national trees to panoramas of barren and bombed-out settings. The Beveridge Report's expansion of aspirational possibility to all British subjects promised to transform vertical lines of descent to horizontal trajectories of influence, and bring the submerged lateral relationship between England and other parts of the Empire into sharper focus in the metropole. Was this new social infrastructure enough to include migrant subjects of the colonies in a rejuvenated, modern Britishness? In practice, the welfare state attempted to manage a volatile hybrid of English specificity and immigrant ubiquity amidst a political cacophony of opposing values: the valorisation of nostalgic forms of inclusion and mobility (the parish pastoral as the origin environment for *Bildungsroman* trajectories in English cities), and the amalgamation of colonial newcomers into a generic and static category of immigrant. These hostile beginnings were overwritten in the 1990s in another nostalgic genre, when the idea of Windrush as a pivotal moment for Black presence in Britain historicised the emergence of Black Britain as a twentieth-century phenomenon. *Empire Windrush* was a 'huge fiction', and this fiction centred the successful integration and assimilation of migrant diasporas into modern Britain through the premeditated creation of a thriving multicultural society in the postwar period.[1]

The British welfare state had its own narrative structure, a model for national development that relied upon various approximations of how certain characters were likely to use and abuse it. Narrating a system that has not been designed around their protagonists, Beryl Gilroy's *Black Teacher* (1976) and Caryl Phillips's *The Final Passage* (1985) are formal realist experi-

---

[1]   Jackie Kay, 'Out of Hand: A Short Story', *Soundings*, 10 (1998), pp. 97–103 (p. 103).

ments that foreground the vexed proximity between social literacy and socio-economic mobility for colonial migrants. Between the two is a complex story about the welfare state that looks back on how Caribbean migrants experienced it during its golden era. Gilroy and Phillips set an elusive welfare architecture against a climate of neglect for its migrant workers and their extended communities. This system was not designed around the new arrivals from Britain's colonies; these were the subjects who helped to construct it from imperial funds. Gilroy and Phillips depict post-imperial unity as a thin compromise, where the Caribbean's geography, aesthetics, and cosmologies intervene at the limit-points of British national care. To borrow from Caroline Levine's recent revival of structural approaches in literary analysis, this essay considers the exceptional fabulations that function as 'social structuring principles' and 'by necessity reshape the core plot' of meritocratic inclusion in these texts, and which expand the plot to the history and folklore of Caribbean plantation societies.[2]

The structures of exclusion, dependency and reciprocation that characterise migrant experiences of the welfare state take the protagonists of these texts back and forth in time over England's relation to the Caribbean, spreading this long history across the spaces of postwar London. Between their publication dates lay the Brixton Uprising of 1981. The Uprising stood in for a failure of inclusion for postcolonial subjects in the socio-political life of the post-imperial nation. 'Brixton' became a metonym for the rebellions across England in 1981: St Pauls in Bristol, Toxteth in Liverpool and Handsworth in Birmingham. These riots took the spectacular, collective form of empty burning buildings: twenty-eight in London and 150 in Liverpool. These emptied, burned buildings stood against the lives lost in the New Cross fire a few months earlier, when thirteen young Black people were killed after a fire started at a house party on Sunday, 18 January 1981. It was also a month after the Black People's Day of Action, in March, when tens of thousands marched through London to demand an inquiry into the fire. The Brixton Uprising evoked a visual memory of anticolonial resistance, recreating the large-scale destruction of the Roehampton Estate on Jamaica in 1831, and recalling the economic catastrophe that ricocheted from Jamaica to Britain which led to the 1833 Slavery Abolition Act. The Brixton Uprising was a turning-point for race relations and citizenship in the United Kingdom, and a limit-point for the welfare state, foreshadowing the project of multicultural inclusion that followed in the 1990s and 2000s. The Uprising was initiated by people who were no longer migrants but part of a growing second- and

---

[2]   Caroline Levine, 'Structures All the Way Down: Literary Methods and the Detail', *Modern Language Quarterly*, 84.2 (2023), pp. 129–46 (p. 139).

third-generation diaspora. This restive diaspora owed very little to the state; it was able to co-opt and instrumentalise its Caribbean connections to interrupt flows of capital in the imperial metropole through property damage.

Black Teacher and *The Final Passage* were also published on either side of economic reforms that were instrumental to dismantling and defunding the class consensus, political implementation and governmental protection of the welfare state. Both texts register this transition, as the increasingly elusive complicity between horizontal promises of state care and vertical barriers of private capital frustrates their characters' upward progress. In *Black Teacher*, Beryl observes this process in younger generations of Black children, and in *The Final Passage*, Leila experiences it directly.[3] Surviving the system means acting in one's own interests in a variety of minor and incidental ways. Against this individuated aspiration, Gilroy's and Phillips's lateral retellings of the welfare state through the relationship between the Caribbean and Britain narrate this transition as a process of collective expansion into a sense of diasporic mobility.

The postwar period saw an expansion of English literature into literature of the British Commonwealth and the transition of the nineteenth-century Ur-texts of social mobility into new spatial and economic forms: from the housing estate to the semi-detached, from doctor's surgery to hospital, from school to university, from the job centre to the white-collar office. In the 1980s, the fiction of economic migration as a golden opportunity for British Caribbean subjects was over. Their role had been to supplement welfare provision for both the target recipients of welfare and for those who were considered burdens on the system, as well as to defend the myth of meritocratic parity. Both novels draw on folklore and fire to invoke a longer history of plantation rebellion which informs the varying compliance of their immigrant subjects in relation to the welfare state. These figures reshape two key characters of welfare's golden age: in Gilroy's memoir, the scholarship boy working hard to reciprocate the state's investment in his future; and in Phillips's novel, the undeserving, deviant subject dependent on state resources and unwilling to reciprocate.

The Prodigal Plot

The class consensus of postwar liberalism never arrived collectively for colonial subjects, because of the dependence of the early welfare state on low-paid labour and practices of informal exclusion in street-level welfare

---

[3]   I refer to the protagonist of *Black Teacher* as Beryl, and to its author as Gilroy.

decisions.[4] Caribbean migrants were not granted immediate access to the inclusion/exclusion model of welfare provision, for which reliable and aspirational working-class families were the target recipients. The Beveridge Report was the latest in a long line of arguments, most famously between William Godwin (1793) and Thomas Malthus (1798), over the responsibility of government in ensuring human happiness and better-functioning societies. The consensus on a national insurance scheme collated earlier models of social reform: free school meals (1906), against cruelty towards children (1908), pensions for the over-70s (1908), employment agencies (1909) and the 1911 National Insurance Act on free medical treatment and sick pay. The Beveridge Report outlined five obstacles to social mobility: poverty (want), unsafe and inadequate housing (squalor), unemployment (idleness), a lack of education (ignorance) and a lack of healthcare (disease). Above all, it was a consensus on the government's responsibility towards its national population to provide the basic blocks of social security and to facilitate social mobility. As well as seeing off the Soviet influence, the early welfare state also attempted to bridge a birth-right conservatism and an upwardly mobile socialism. Some of the looser seams of this compromise were exposed in the latent Malthusianism of some of its social categories and guiding principles. Bruce Robbins writes that the welfare state has from the outset been 'a set of imperfect institutions, produced in part by management from above and in part by pressure from below, which also enters into the unfinished project of "social citizenship"': an aspirational model that aspires to its own aspirations, while hastily constructing its ideal subjects.[5]

The system was designed around a nuclear family unit of employed parents and hardworking children. Women held primary responsibility for establishing a stable domestic environment. To decide who deserved state care, the welfare system produced a cast of characters that a social worker might encounter at street-level: the scholarship boy from a poor but hardworking family, and the problem family that refused to cooperate. Scholarship boys would pay back into the system by stimulating national development, while the problem family was a social unit unwilling to reciprocate or contribute. As Clare Hanson puts it, 'Almost all discussion of meritocracy and postwar educational chance focused then (as, to a large extent, now) on the opportunities being offered to [white] working-class boys'.[6] The problem family was

---

[4]   Michael Lambert, '"Problem families" and the Post-war Welfare State in the North West of England, 1943-74', Ph.D., Lancaster University (2017).
[5]   Bruce Robbins, *Upward Mobility and the Common Good: Toward a Literary History of the Welfare State* (Princeton, 2007), p. 25.
[6]   Clare Hanson, *Eugenics, Literature and Culture in Post-war Britain* (London,

an object of exclusion from welfare, and these exclusions were determined through street-level decisions by welfare officers about who would and would not be eligible for benefits, and decisions made at street-level later fed into policy, establishing social categories.[7] The problem family fiction centred on white mothers' failure to facilitate the flourishing of male family members – husband, son, brother – through the foundations provided by the state.

Social workers cast the communities under their regimen into roles for official policymaking. The child of the problem family might access the infrastructure of rehabilitation, but only through hard work. The core plot to be preserved and transmitted by this new system was a model of the English family as the environment of national cultivation. The scholarship boy-problem family nexus contains both the horizontal radicalism of Godwin's vision of political justice and the vertical anti-statist arguments of Malthus. This nexus recalled a story much older than either: the prodigal son of the Old Testament who, having fled his father's house and his familial obligations, returns, and is welcomed back with a feast, while the elder brother has been toiling in the fields without thanks, but with the everyday protection and provision of his father. Immigrants were not included in welfare's prodigal plot. The presence of these communities was tolerated by welfare institutions, but they fell outside its core provisions. In the state's role as 'gatekeeper', Michael Lambert writes, housing allocation was based on racial determinations and allocation for non-white applicants was withheld.[8] Irish Catholic, Black, and mixed-race families were separated into separate areas of British cities, falling beyond the problem family paradigm: 'Officials were anxious over the permeation of racial boundaries with new families and the children of such unions constituting a problem'.[9] The distribution of welfare was premised on racialised determinations of which racial groups required state support, and which did not.

In a comparative study of European welfare states at the turn of the twenty-first century, Carl-Ulrik Schierup, Peo Hansen and Stephen Castles identified the UK's adoption of a neoliberal model of social policy: restricting migrants' access to social citizenship and using migrants as a flexible reserve army of labour, with undocumented workers permitted only minimal claims.[10] More recently, Gurminder Bhambra and John Holmwood have discussed the

---

2013), p. 26.
[7]   Lambert, '"Problem Families" and the Post-war Welfare State', p. 4.
[8]   Lambert, '"Problem Families" and the Post-war Welfare State', p. 25.
[9]   Lambert, '"Problem Families" and the Post-war Welfare State', p. 30.
[10]   Carl-Ulrik Schierup, Peo Hansen and Stephen Castles, *Migration, Citizenship, and the European Welfare State* (Oxford, 2006).

welfare state's colonial and racial origins: colonial enclosure created displacement and destruction of indigenous populations, the need for a workforce to produce cultivated commodities (sugar and cotton) and, with this, the figure of the commodified labourer.[11] Gilroy and Phillips rewrite the problem family as a fiction created by a paternalistic ethos of welfare that needed to create undeserving subjects to rehabilitate them into the prodigal plot of welfare, but from which colonial migrants were excluded. While the immediate historical period of the authors is the late 1970s to the mid-1980s, the texts go further back in time, to the early years of the welfare state, and further still – across the Atlantic, to histories of resistance on the plantation.

Windrush Fictions and Mythic Play

If the welfare state was modelled on the country parish, then its ideal community was what Raymond Williams calls the 'knowable community' of the early nineteenth-century novel, 'an epitome of direct relationships [...] within which the novelist can find the substance of a fiction of personal relationships'. Williams finds knowable communities in the novels of Jane Austen, where to be 'face-to-face' is 'already to belong to a class', beyond which no other community is knowable. Later in the century, in *Adam Bede*, George Eliot looks back in a nostalgic key at this moment on the cusp of industrialisation, and 'restores the real inhabitants of rural England to their places', but, Williams observes, this restoration of country folk makes them into 'a landscape', a set of already-read plurals (the Poysers, the Gleggs, the Dodsons).[12] Eliot navigates this great transformation of national priorities and imperial expansion by making this nostalgic form the stable environment against which the protagonists' conduct can be judged.

A similar logic might be applied to the way the welfare state was structured to produce particular subjects and dispositions. In the narrative structure of welfare provision, the people arriving in Britain from the Caribbean at the end of the 1940s were neither a nostalgic plural form, nor a group of differentiated protagonists. The Windrush story had underwhelming beginnings: the ship arrived in Kingston *en route* to Britain from Australia in 1948. It was the same year that the British Nationality Act made commonwealth residents into British citizens to attract a new workforce to the country who would

---

[11] Gurminder Bhambra and John Holmwood, 'Colonialism, Postcolonialism, and the Liberal Welfare State', *New Political Economy*, 23.5 (2018), pp. 574–87.

[12] Raymond Williams, 'The Knowable Community in George Eliot's Novels', *NOVEL: A Forum on Fiction*, 2.3 (1969), pp. 255–68 (pp. 255–8).

carry out the labour of its reconstruction. Royal Mail Lines saw an opportunity to fill the ship, and passage was advertised at £48 for cabin class and £28 to travel in the troop deck. Hannah Lowe has tracked the HMT *Empire Windrush*'s 'belated rise to fame' in the 1990s as part of 'New Labour's project exalting a multi-ethnic Britain; the sanctioning of this project by state institutions; and the efforts of Black community groups'.[13] In a much-quoted interview on his 1998 Windrush documentary, Mike Phillips said, 'Before we created it, nobody had a coherent story about Windrush. I made the story up. History is about fact, but it is also about narration. I created a narrative that had coherence'.[14] As well as a narrative about Windrush, Phillips's documentary also created a version of Black Britain through its roster of successful public personalities from across the arts, sport, media, government and academia: Lenny Henry, Charlie Williams, Valerie Amos, Stuart Hall, Diane Abbott, Darcus Howe and Linton Kwesi Johnson. Windrush was not just a fiction of first contact, the belated and excited arrival of Black Caribbeans to the imperial metropolis, but also of the creation of a Black British community with the aspiration to settle and contribute to the mother country. Windrush was a fiction of aspiration, and 'A Very British Story'.

Windrush, then, was a retrospective fiction, a celebration of modern aspirational Britain granting the colonial diaspora access to some of its benefits. The professional arc of Gilroy's memoir takes her from a position as domestic help and protégée to an aristocrat, the formidable Lady Anne, to becoming headteacher of a state primary school. A trained teacher, Beryl travels to London from Skeldon in Guyana during the mid-1950s. She is initially barred from entering the profession in England on the grounds of race and instead finds administrative work in a small office. She is the only Black woman in the office and, while she gets on with her colleagues and often goes out of her way to help them in moments of crisis, she is constantly reminded of her racial position. In her next job, Lady Anne instructs her about art, manners and the value of service and encourages Beryl to make something of herself. Her employer's encyclopaedic knowledge of 'everything English' makes Beryl 'feel a little ashamed of my scant knowledge of my Guyanese

[13]   Hannah Lowe, 'Remember the Ship: Narrating the *Empire Windrush*', *Journal of Postcolonial Writing*, 54.4 (2018), pp. 542–55 (p. 543).
[14]   Cited in Barbara Korte and Eva Ulrike Pirker, *Black History White History: Britain's Historical Programme between Windrush and Wilberforce* (London, 2011), p. 73. See also Eva Ulrike Pirker, *Narrative Projections of a Black British History* (London, 2011), and Simon Peplow, '"In 1997 nobody had heard of Windrush": the Rise of the "Windrush Narrative" in British Newspapers,' *Immigrants & Minorities*, 37.3 (2019), pp. 211–37.

heritage'.[15] The books she read as a child in Guyana were English classics. After this cultivation into a white upper-class sensibility, Beryl eventually works her way back into primary school teaching. Working with children from low-income families, Beryl is often required to negotiate the unevenness of welfare distribution, which is manifested by her students' hunger and sleeplessness. Frequently, the frustrations of their parents are meted out on her. The children hide under desks and the parents tell her that she is not fit to teach them. There are lonely lunch breaks while other teachers ignore her, or else look for 'Black' reactions while provoking her. In the end, the work pays off: she becomes Britain's first Black woman headteacher.

Gilroy's memoir charts a shift from solo migrant subjects to diasporic communities from the 1950s to the 1970s. Gilroy's memoir begins in this key; it is a variation on the scholarship boy, the good immigrant who contributes to state institutions. She is always working, or looking for work, always helping, and always finding ways to contribute, making up for failures or gaps in state care. 'Gilroy maintains her composure', Bernadine Evaristo writes in her 2021 foreword to the book, casting Gilroy as a quieter kind of radical than the young soul rebels that came after her.[16] Hers is a story of meritocratic achievement against the odds: work has been rewarded by a gradual rise in professional position.

The list of chapter titles tells a different story, and these chapter names preside over the vignettes like gauntlets thrown down at Gilroy's recollections in a play between story and structure. The chapters are named after mostly racist speech acts directed towards her or about her: Chapter Two, 'I Don't Mind Coloureds'; Chapter Six, 'Keep Your Hands Off Me'; Chapter Ten, 'She Ain't Got No Spear'; Chapter Twelve, 'Black, White, Paki, Half-Caste'. These titles give a sense of the limited discursive arsenal of British racism – a reminder of the dull repetitiveness of anti-Blackness – as well as the ubiquity of their sentiment. They do not tell a story of multicultural progress and they forestall the narrative of multicultural meritocracy that Gilroy otherwise seems to be telling: the reward of hard work for fighting the odds stacked against her. The chapter titles are the memoir's scaffolding, holding the narrative together, and this structural environment provides a sense of the ground on which Beryl is compelled to move while carrying out labour that exceeds the bounds of professional and personal spheres, however much she tries to keep them separate.

---

15 Beryl Gilroy, *Black Teacher* (1976; London, 2022), p. 42.
16 Gilroy, *Black Teacher*, p. xiii.

To produce good students, Beryl supplements gaps in state education and childcare. The first time she depicts her home is in the early 1960s, when she transforms it into an extracurricular reading club for children in her neighbourhood whose parents are out at work. Local children come to listen to literature, but also to play around and talk about themselves and their thoughts about their lives. Motherhood gives her another way to connect her professional life to her personal one: she starts a mother's club for discussing books, plays, local schools and food. Out of this, she suggests that 'school consciousness should start with maternity classes', making school a focal point in her own community. Rather than penalise or isolate 'problem' mothers, she is interested in giving mothers intellectual, personal and psychological support, taking on the soft work of meritocratic cohesion.

Gilroy is at her most political when teaching. The children in her schools are more creative with their resistance to instruction than those she taught in Guyana. She devises ways of engaging with her students that break from her own training there, and remembers that in Guyana,

> 'Play' never came into it. 'Play', as part of the preparation for life, never figured in the scale of values. Playing was just not accepted as a child's all-through-childhood right. Behind it all was a concept of worth through work – something that had its roots in the rigours of a slave society, and the greed and callousness of the slave owner.[17]

Now, working in the place responsible for cultivating this deficit, she finds the freedom to explore play as pedagogy. The memory of Guyana activates a game of freedom in the classroom. Later in the memoir, in the early 1970s, Black British-born children begin to appear in her classes. These children have no direct memory of the islands and arrive in the classroom ashamed of not being white. At this point, her references to Guyana and the Caribbean lose their sense of anachronism. She manages to stay one step ahead of complaints and attacks from her colleagues and her students' parents, which is less to do with how hard she works than it is about her ability to play the kinds of games produced through the organisation of the plantation. These are activated here through responses emerging in this environment where her life and work are consistently devalued.

Gilroy's memoir crosses three phases, and these plot Beryl's transformation from migrant worker to community organiser. First, she makes her way slowly into teaching against the impediments of gender, race and nationalism. Then, socialised by this effort, she notices 'the frenetic immi-

grant' of the 1960s, the 'noisy people' who arrive and begin immediately
to protest, ungratefully (it seems to her, at points) at the living conditions.
In her neighbourhood, the construction of a council home in the 1970s,
where new migrants are sent, prompts alarm from white locals ('a predict-
able howl'), although no one mentions race, 'only social attitudes, habits,
and classes'.[18] The native chorus in Gilroy's background is volatile and often
anonymous, one from which she finds herself estranged repeatedly. Unlike
Eliot's peripheral characters, this knowable community emerges in irritated
murmurs or shouts of disapproval and in acts of exclusion against which
Beryl must remain calm.

The third phase of Gilroy's memoir covers the period when she becomes
Headteacher at Beckford School in West Hampstead and encounters the
'disintegrated energy' of second-generation migrant children in the late
1960s. These are the children who, by the early 1980s, may have shared the
disaffection and distrust of Black and Asian communities in the apparatus
of welfare reaching their localities. In the last chapter of *Black Teacher*, she
arrives for the first time at the school where she has been made headteacher
and is horrified: 'my school seemed to me like some monstrous animal with
a cacophonous voice and syncopated pulse'.[19] She has taught in difficult
schools before, but this is something different: 'I doubted whether I'd ever
seen such disintegrated energy'.[20] The final chapter sees a sharp turn in her
perception of what is going on in her classrooms. The children have licence
to come to school, to sit in classrooms, to play outside, and to 'freely respond
and react at random, freely ignoring other people, freely rushing from happening to happening with whoops and yells and delirious abandon', but they
are 'never free in the true sense of the word'.[21]

Unlike her previous schools, where she taught children from predominantly low-income families, this new school has a 'very strong middle-class
element [...] due to the circumstances of the catchment area'.[22] This middle-
class influence produces an impossible aspiration among working-class Black
children: 'If a little black child has any particular aspiration, it's to be a middle-class white'.[23] The direction of mobility plays out in a knotty fulcrum
of race and class; the Black children wish to become wealthier and whiter:

---

18   Gilroy, *Black Teacher*, p. 157.
19   Gilroy, *Black Teacher*, p. 240.
20   Gilroy, *Black Teacher*, p. 240.
21   Gilroy, *Black Teacher*, p. 240.
22   Gilroy, *Black Teacher*, p. 242.
23   Gilroy, *Black Teacher*, p. 242.

'I was white once,' said Roger, who had been fostered by white middle-class parents in Brighton. 'I got black when I came home.'

Tunde, from Nigeria, kept referring to his father as 'The Man' or 'That Black Man'. He just couldn't relate to black people. He even disowned his own photograph. And when I persuaded him to paint his self-portrait and colour it, he wailed, 'Stop it! I don't want all that blackness on me.'

These lines draw out a difficult paradox: how to reconcile these children's receipt of benefits (state education and fostering) with their experiences of a racist national environment that negate their sense of being this system's desired subjects? In Roger's intuition, becoming Black means becoming aware of not being white. For Tunde, his own image becomes a source of shame, an imposition from the outside. In a dive up to the surface of the present tense, Gilroy comes out of her narration to say 'I can't help feeling a little sad that they give up their indigenous cultures in such a way'; her grammar indicates the continuity of this process.[24]

John McLeod offers a complementary configuration of this problem: how might literary works think through 'the enriching ways in which adoptive and biogenetic relations may be brought and thought together differently, beyond the good and evil of nature and nurture, as concomitant filaments or lifelines of polyvalent personhood open to all'.[25] McLeod offers a way to read Beryl's response to her students' apparent abandonment of heritage as a correction to her own ambivalence about her heritage years before, when she worked for Lady Anne. In this response, she goes beyond the state provision of education and shelter to resurrect an alternative mythic chorus, telling them about her childhood in a village in Guyana by the sea. She describes African Caribbean festivals, birthdays and weddings and teaches them songs and ring-games: 'When I danced with them, they tittered at first but then joined in'.[26] Beryl also tells them about Anansi, the Spider Man trickster. Anansi, of Akan origin and moving through the tribal worlds of central Ghana, is not a deity; there are no shrines to him, and no sacrifices made to him. Anansi is able to 'restructure both the divine and human worlds through his chaotic antics and cunning tricks', as Emily Zobel Marshall writes.[27] He breaks rules, and this made him a conduit 'through which colo-

---

[24]   Gilroy, *Black Teacher*, p. 242.
[25]   John McLeod, 'Against Biocentrism: Blood, Adoption, and Diasporic Writing', *Études Anglaises*, 70 (2017), pp. 28–44 (p. 42).
[26]   Gilroy, *Black Teacher*, p. 244.
[27]   Emily Zobel Marshall, 'Anansi, Eshu, and Legba: Slave Resistance and the West African Tricksters', *Bonded Labour in the Cultural Contact Zone: Transdisciplinary Perspectives on Slavery and its Discourses*, ed. R. Hoermann and G. Mackenthun

nial power could be both resisted and challenged'.[28] Anansi was, as Barry Chevannes puts it, 'the symbolic focus of the resistance in the minds of the Africans [and was] used to provide them with resilience and with modes of escape'.[29] Through this creolised intervention, the good immigrant plot gives way to symbolic resistance that arrives through a long history of anticolonial rebellion in the Caribbean, moving across generations, and generated as a tactic to teach the next generation how to play different kinds of games. This is not only a disruption of the status quo; it activates structural elements of folklore that expand the classroom from a space of pedagogical dependency on a remote Anglican code-system to the more proximate myths Gilroy has at hand.

The Problem Mother

If Gilroy finds a participatory, though resistant, role as a teacher within the postwar welfare state, Leila in *The Final Passage* occupies the passive position of welfare recipient. *The Final Passage* is a version of the Windrush story via an unstable family that breaks up quickly on arrival in London. Leila is the problem mother whose own mother uses up state resources, receiving end-of-life care in a state hospital. Her husband Michael is a counterpoint to this, socially mobile and on the lookout for an upward drift as he goes around London. The couple arrive in Britain with their son Calvin on the SS *Winston Churchill* from St Patrick. This story feels real enough, but this journey never happened: there was no SS *Winston Churchill*, and the island does not exist. Unlike Gilroy's narrative, which unfolds in chronological time, Phillips's novel is structured like an archipelago. It starts with the ship, then pulls back to an extended section on 'Home,' describing life on St Patrick, followed by a final part about Michael's and Leila's increasingly separate lives in London. The family is held in a fiction: the tiny island, the former site of an old plantation, named after a fifth-century Christian missionary, now a place where tourists drink and eat together at the top of the hill, and where inhabitants go round in circles underneath them on old motorbikes. On the island, time goes round, not forward.

Arriving in London, it seems at first that the circular movement of the island will be replaced by the forward motion of the metropolis. The family moves in straight lines, from ship to gate to train to road. It does not take

---

(Münster, 2010), pp. 177–92 (p. 178).
[28]   Marshall, 'Anansi, Eshu, and Legba', p. 177.
[29]   Cited in Marshall, 'Anansi, Eshu, and Legba', p. 181.

long for the cycle to catch up with them, as they pass from one housing scam to another. Leila goes straight to hospital where her mother is dying; that duty done, she retreats inward, into the house and into herself, barely speaking. Michael heads out into the city, makes friends, meets prospective business partners, and starts a relationship with a white woman. Leila stays at home, trying to make the small, damp flat they eventually find liveable, collecting things that will make it homely, and taking care of her son alone. Phillips plays Michael's *laissez-faire* individualist seeking entry into lucrative networks against Leila's deviant subject, a single mother who refuses to look for a job or join in the work of social cohesion.

The novel ends with Leila getting ready to depart after five months in London, after having been confined to one room in a cold, damp flat, 'not understanding this country in which a smile could mean six things at once, a nudge on a bus from a stranger either an accident or a prologue to a series of events that might actually lead to your destruction'.[30] Amidst these confusions, Leila's world has shrunk. While Michael's journeys outside show him hunting for a trajectory to jump-start his life in Britain, preferably one that will satisfy both erotic and economic cravings, Leila's London is one of obscure simultaneity: faces fixed in expressions that cannot be decoded, where – for her – the West Indian's fate is immobile. Unlike Michael, Leila is both unwilling and unable to give up her sense that time cannot move forward for people like them in England. Michael's aspiration takes him out of Leila's migrant plot of desperate squalor and into a network of immanent exchange, while Leila's return to the island foreshadows decolonial demands for independence and reparation over hand-outs and prolonged dependency.

What was life like before Leila and her family came to England? Michael wants to forget life on the island, the 'land of nothing', which makes him nothing.[31] His life circles a restricted constellation of women's dwellings: mother, wife, lover. He is scared of the sea and wants to be up the hill with the white tourists at the holiday resort, drinking and eating without having to think. He does not like being forced to remember the conditions that make this thoughtlessness possible. He marries Leila because she is closer to being white than he is, and because she might be useful to him. His grandmother tells him repeatedly, 'She can help you'.[32] Leila loves the sea, but her freedom to move around the island is restricted by the ambivalence of her class position and racial identification, attached on the one hand to a white father whom she has never met, and on the other to her mother's house, paid for

---

30 Caryl Phillips, *The Final Passage* (London, 2004), p. 198.
31 Phillips, *The Final Passage*, p. 80.
32 Phillips, *The Final Passage*, p. 11.

by her absent father. At school, she is the 'mulatto girl'; on the beach, among white people, she is an object of erotic fixation. She is bored by the man who wants to make a difference on the island and to develop its economy for the sake of national development and chooses Michael instead – aimless, restless, usually intoxicated in some way or another, always looking for trap doors or exit signs that will lead him away from the island. In England, these circular movements do not end and the cycle of dissonance and amnesia continues. The 'artificial cylinder' of state support might have sustained the fiction that they could survive together, because the promise of migration was also the promise of inclusion. Michael envisioned a world where he might have 'a car and a big house and a bit of power under my belt, like any man does want.'[33] The island's seasonal time of cane production followed by off-season indolence does not offer access to this future.

The delay between the novel's historical timeline and its publication date introduces a narrative time that layers later events over Leila's return to St Patrick. Writing in the 1980s, Phillips imagines Leila's departure in the 1960s from the far side of New Cross and Brixton, and their signification of a failed promise to postwar Caribbean migrants: death and exclusion over mobility and assimilation. On the closing pages, Leila visits a cemetery with Calvin, pregnant again:

> Leila left the cemetery the same way she had come in, through the tall iron gates. On her way home she did not stop to listen to the carols or to buy presents. She walked quickly through the back streets, wanting to keep off the main roads and away from people. Calvin was asleep in her arms and the baby she carried in her body felt heavy.[34]

Ending the novel in a cemetery in December has the feel of calculated melodrama, a place where ghosts of Christmas future might lurk beside gravestones inscribed with one's own name. Like *A Christmas Carol*'s Scrooge, Leila walks away from this future, but not towards the carol singers or to buy presents for the poor to make up for a parsimonious refusal to participate and make connections; the cemetery is the last stop on a route that takes her out of this national myth. The narrative is back to circular motion, rather than upward mobility. The suggestion is that Leila came to England to bury her mother, not to start a new life; the country's promise of inclusion slides off Leila, who is propelled instead to close off a cycle.

---

33   Phillips, *The Final Passage*, p. 103.
34   Phillips, *The Final Passage*, p. 204.

One way of reading the ending would be to say that the cemetery scene plays out Leila's alienation from a national narrative structure. This interpretation might foreclose her enjoyment of this space, an affect incompatible with migrant purpose in postwar British cities. Beryl takes pleasure in the incompatibility of enjoyment and purpose in London's interstitial wastelands. She recounts trips with students to the graveyards and bombsites of the city that are starting to produce signs of new plant life. She finds something calming about being in a cemetery. For her the cemetery is 'peaceful and expansive and, in its way, a marvellous leveller. Over it hung the comforting thought that all who went there were equal'.[35] Striking here is Gilroy's use of 'expansive,' a word charged in the imperial situation with territorial conquest. With quasi-supernatural irreverence, Gilroy reshapes this word in the cemetery, where national monuments are weathered by blasts and neglect, giving herself access to a word that has otherwise foreclosed her presence in this very English space, a burial ground from which her ancestors on Guyana's plantations were excluded. Reading Leila next to Beryl, something else might be at play in *The Final Passage*'s departure from the Gothic didacticism of Dickens's festive moral fable.

The Long Fire

A clue to this departure comes a few pages before, in a scene where Leila burns all the objects she has collected since coming to London. This burning happens in private – she stacks the grate of the flat's small fireplace – but the fire recalls a series of fires that came earlier and later in time. This antiphony of fires past and future allows a different reading of Leila's departure as neither defeat nor escape, but as the recursive plotting of a subterranean connection across the Atlantic, where the historical passages between two islands are remembered. In the cemetery, imagining her sons venturing out to England in later years and returning, she imagines that they will finally have 'something' to 'share'.[36] This anticipated intergenerational resolution may be a painful one, but it will give them something to work with. Having decided to leave England, Leila clears the grate, fills a pillowcase with Michael's clothes and her unanswered or half-written letters to him, and burns them:

> The room became warm and Leila began to laugh as she searched everywhere finding new things to drop in the now empty pillowcase. A bunch of plastic

---

35 Gilroy, *Black Teacher*, p. 83.
36 Phillips, *The Final Passage*, p. 204.

flowers, a shopping bag, a small vase, a set of ashtrays; and in the kitchen cups, food, anything. Things that would not burn like cutlery, pots, and pans she left, for she did not need to get rid of everything. What would not fit into her suitcase she would simply abandon. And what she would abandon she would not need. As she watched objects flare, then finally die, blacken, then flake, Leila fell asleep, sure that she could hear the sound of the sea.[37]

Leila's domestic fire is too private and practical to draw unwanted attention from outside the windows of the flat, but it also marks an interior return to a historical precedent: fires as a strategy of liberation. Freedom here is located in choosing what to give up, and for Leila, burning these objects is the way out of the city and back to the soundscape of the home island. This means refusing the dependency on which welfare consensus depends, keeping active the feeling that England is a space that has already been liberated, within and without its island borders. The death of the fire – the finality of this domestic arson – affords her a half-waking access to a passage back across the Atlantic at the edge of her dimming consciousness.

The fire links Leila to another form of diasporic care that would later come to occupy the streets she slips along as she tries to go unnoticed: the liberation theologies of Rastafarianism overlaying the dub rhythms of Brixton's Frontline at Railton Road in the 1970s and 80s, which connected Kingston-produced reggae to British soundscapes. The fire as a technology of judgement – clearing the ground for a new world – is central to Rastafari worldmaking. In the early months of 1981, the Kingston reggae artist Hugh Mundell was doing a world tour for his album *Jah Fire* (1980), playing shows in Birmingham and London in February and April. The London show at the Hammersmith Palais was four days before the Uprising. The subject of the song 'Jah Fire Will Be Burning' is the Day of Judgement, 'Jah Jah judgement', when a great fire will turn 'the sun into darkness' and bring about a levelling of power, when 'Vatican city will be falling'. The lyrics rehearse Rastafari critical eschatology, its 'semiotic promiscuity' and its distrust of governments, churches and law enforcement.[38] 'Jah Fire' is the least lively track of the album; what sticks out is the looping motif of the horns played in synchrony by Deadly Headly, Cedric Im Brooks and Bobby Ellis. On paper, the motif looks like a heartbeat on a monitor: a steady line that jumps up and descends, jumps up lower and descends again. The horns are the tonal counterpart to

---

[37] Phillips, *The Final Passage*, p. 201.
[38] Christopher Partridge, 'Babylon's Burning: Reggae, Rastafari and Millenarianism', *The End All Around Us: Apocalyptic Texts and Popular Culture*, eds. John Walliss and Kenneth G. C. Newport (London, 2014), pp. 43–70 (p. 54).

the lyrics, bringing in a wry liveliness alongside the prophetic weight of the singer, interrupting the words as much as they accompany them. The dub beats underneath these two lines are low and constant: they are not going anywhere, a grounding place for the other instruments to begin. This grounding might constitute a sonic alternative to the 'fiction discrepant with [the Caribbean migrant's] lived reality', to borrow from Sam Caleb's discussion of George Lamming's critique of mid-century cricket meritocracy: the fiction that through good play, Caribbean subjects might be able to scale up over the baseline of national aspiration, while in reality constituting a base-level wage labour which other citizens should strive to rise above.[39]

On 10 April 1981, Michael Bailey was stabbed on Atlantic Road, the road running through Brixton market underneath the railway arches to Railton Road. In the weeks prior, the Metropolitan Police had begun implementing Operation Swamp 81, an intense stop-and-search action carried out as part of its war on crime. Brixton's Black men were being stopped *en masse*: 943 in the five days before the Uprising. On Railton Road, a crowd gathered and demanded that Bailey be released from the car. The next day, two police officers stopped and searched a taxi driver and took him away. At this point, riots broke out and a crowd that represented Brixton's mixture of the diasporic and counter-cultural, across racial divisions, fought back.

While documentary and institutional accounts of the Brixton Uprising make Railton Road sound like a site of recreation (music, dancing and drugs), it was also a site of political organisation and housing activism. In 1972, Olive Morris and Liv Turnbull, members of the Brixton Black Panthers, occupied a flat at Number 121. The flat continued to be used for meetings and was a key location in the Brixton squatters' movement in Brixton from the 1950s to the 1990s, becoming an activity centre with a bookshop and café and a dancefloor in the cellar. This informal arrangement worked for Lambeth Council, because social housing was oversubscribed. It was in the Council's interests to allow these informal arrangements to continue – an unofficial supplement akin to the Saturday reading club described by Gilroy. In policy reports, Brixton was a space where the effects of unemployment and poverty were making themselves visible in higher crime rates. In these accounts, Brixton was a tinderbox ready to be set alight, a community pushed to the brink due to lack of social housing, over-policing and sixty-eight per cent unemployment among young Black men. In March, thousands marched between Deptford and Hyde Park during the Black People's Day of Action to mark deaths of the thirteen people who died in the New Cross Fire.

---

[39]   Sam Caleb, 'Athletic Figures: Games and the Postwar Avant-Garde Novel', Ph.D., University College London (ongoing), p. 45.

Railton Road had become the Frontline of Black British resistance against police violence and welfare exclusions.

Fire has played a large role in the aesthetic and political legacy of the Brixton Uprising, a compelling and fearsome image of the destructive power of Black resistance and an element that can be contained and put out. After Brixton, Black families became included in the 'problem family' category through the metaphor of doused flames. Kenneth Newman, who took over as the Commissioner of the Metropolitan Police in 1982, worked with other public departments (Health, Education, Environment and social services) to douse nascent flames in the months and years following the Uprising. These were 'quickly and effectively extinguished' by taking a developmental approach to dealing with unrest, as Paul Gilroy observed a few years later.[40] Newman's language repeatedly invokes 'the image of disorderly and criminally-inclined black youth', as Gilroy writes: 'The disparate activities of the various agencies involved are linked along a continuum of professionalism and can be synchronized by police leadership and common responsibility for the enhancement of social order'. The logic here is containment. A fire can be contained and hosed down. Tumultuous energies can likewise be doused and directed elsewhere, into worthy pursuits, perhaps even into aspirational trajectories.

Less easy to contain and redirect is the historical memory of the diaspora. In 1831, 150 years before Brixton, another fire caused millions of pounds' worth of damage to British property: the destruction of the Roehampton Estate during the Baptist War in Jamaica. While Britain abolished the slave trade in 1807, plantation slavery in the British Caribbean was not outlawed until 1833. In the build-up to the Baptist War, a group of Freemen who were members of the autonomous Ethiopian Baptist Church, founded by George Liele, had sought emancipation from King William through a missionary but were denied. In response, a nine-day rebellion began, joined by around sixty thousand enslaved people across the island. In Adolphe Duperly's 1833 lithograph 'The Destruction of the Roehampton Estate in the Parish of St James in January 1832', militant rebels stand on the upper ground of the drawing, raising scythes and machetes of the sugar cane fields as they look towards the great house at the centre, watching the building burn. The rebellion was suppressed violently by the full military force of the plantocracy and the British Army. The fatality ratio was seven whites for every two hundred and fifty Black people: fourteen white people in total and five hundred Black. The huge economic loss from property destruction – around £52 million today – contributed to the passing of the Slavery Abolition Act, which outlawed

---

[40]   Paul Gilroy, *There Ain't No Black in the Union Jack* (London, 1987), p. 137.

plantation slavery in the British Caribbean from 1834, and legal freedom was granted to all former slaves in 1838.

The fires of Brixton and the Roehampton Estate are both conjured in Leila's fire. Phillips looks back to the first wave of Caribbean migration in the 1950s to prefigure their children's resistance to the colonial legacy of the 1980s and invokes a history of collective destruction of plantation capital. Leila's burning of property is a spectacular way of separating herself from the circulation of Black labour into white capital. When Beryl conjures Anansi as a way of reminding the children in her class about their history, she brings the trickster into teaching as a detail that might reshape the worlds they live in, as an alternative to the welfare fictions of scholarship boys and the Angry Young Men. The ways that people keep tumbling into each other in Gilroy's and Phillips's works suggest not only that departure cannot stand as real escape, but also that making life work in post-imperial Britain requires more creativity than variations on fantasies of meritocratic advance.

At the end of his 1971 study of pre-abolition Jamaica, Kamau Brathwaite identified an unrealised social possibility: the 'little' traditions of former slaves might have been used as the basis for a 'creative reconstruction, the development of a new parochial wholeness, and a difficult but possible creole authenticity'.[41] This was an extraordinary claim to make about what Jamaica could have become after 1838, an audacious, counterfactual, even nostalgic speculation, sent across time and the sea from the frontline of the Caribbean Artists Movement. Responding to Steve McQueen's film *Grenfell* (2023), which begins with the camera moving over West London towards the burned tower in which seventy-two people died in 2017, Paul Gilroy decries the Grenfell fire's incorporation into the normal and the routine: 'We have been habituated to that blankness and encouraged to imagine that there can be no alternatives to this particular way of organising human life and calculating its minimal, transient value'.[42] This bracket of creative reconstruction and habituated blankness extends in both directions: it expands the space for diasporic speculations and insists on defending the 'destabilising, commemorative perception' of grotesque realities.[43] The versions of welfare Britain offered by Beryl Gilroy and Caryl Phillips draw this history away from the habituated and disposable fiction of the good immigrant and her deviant other. They draw out the shifting, routine grid on which their characters are

[41]   Edward Kamau Brathwaite, *The Development of Creole Society in Jamaica, 1770–1820* (London, 2005), p. 308

[42]   Paul Gilroy, 'Never Again Grenfell', Serpentine Gallery (London, 2023), p. 8. <https://www.serpentinegalleries.org/art-and-ideas/never-again-grenfell/>.

[43]   Gilroy, 'Never Again Grenfell', p. 13.

forced to move, exhausting the nostalgia of knowable communities. These lateral movements and their subcultural affordances expand the aesthetic spaces of English realism towards the 'exceptional fabulations' of the diaspora, reconstructing these spaces through a lattice of overlapping life worlds.

9

The Disciplines of English and the Ideals of Welfare in Ireland in the 1980s

NEIL VICKERS

Irish Social Corporatism

Can literary studies provide a form of intellectual welfare, or do they tempt students into an apolitical utopia? This chapter debates the issue by reflecting on my own experience as an undergraduate in Modern English and French at Trinity College, Dublin, in the early 1980s.

On enrolment, it was unclear what my teachers wanted from me, or I from them. It was unlikely to be a passport to a job, still less a career. Unemployment in Ireland at that time had reached twenty-two percent. Approximately 450,000 Irish people emigrated in the 1980s, more than ten percent of the population. It was the most skilled generation to leave Ireland.[1] Governments were scrappy and short-lived. Charles Haughey, by turns Taoiseach and leader of the opposition, waged a criminal and sometimes violent campaign against his opponents and presided over a tax fraud scheme based in the Cayman Islands which enabled him to be bribed on a lavish scale by some of the wealthiest people in the country (between 1979 and 1986 he took at least £7m in clandestine payments, a colossal sum back then).[2] Sexual politics were equally mired in controversy. In 1983, the Eighth Amendment to the Constitution of Ireland was passed by two thirds of the population in a referendum, scuppering any possibility of legal abortion. The wording of the amendment was so ambiguous that the High Court and the Supreme Court came to different judgments about its meaning; it was overturned only in 2018. The introduction of divorce was defeated in a referendum in 1986. A charismatic lecturer in Trinity's Department of

---

[1] On the social history cited in this paragraph, see Thomas Bartlett, *The Cambridge History of Ireland: Volume IV, 1880 to the Present* (Cambridge, 2018), pp. 379–552, 641–72.

[2] 'Report of the Tribunal of Inquiry into Payments to Politicians and Related Matters' (Dublin, 2006). <https://moriarty-tribunal.ie/wpcontent/uploads/2016/09/SITECONTENT_26.pdf>.

English, David Norris, engaged in lengthy legal action to repeal the law banning homosexual acts between men, which he eventually won at the European Court of Human Rights in 1988, though homosexual acts were legalised only in 1994. It was almost the only victory for progressive politics in that era in the Republic.

Tom Inglis, whose account of the rise and fall of Irish Catholicism is perhaps the most significant work of Irish sociology to date, observes that 'attainment of social acceptance and respect in Ireland [has typically involved] avoiding conflict, especially through argument, and surrendering individual interests by engaging in practices which help others'.[3] Twentieth-century Ireland was a state marked by such social corporatism, where important functions of the State were exercised through the Church. There were Catholic schools and Protestant schools, Catholic hospitals and Protestant hospitals. Social insurance was meagre because the Churches and the politicians favoured the traditional nuclear family as the primary source of social support. Welfare payments were made to men and were withheld from 'non-working' wives. Motherhood was encouraged.[4] The state provided those who could pay with an attenuated form of private health insurance, which bought nicer rooms and better food in Church-controlled and often Church-run hospitals. The twenty-two percent of the population who were unemployed included all farmers, entitled to unemployment benefits as an earnest of the State's commitment to Ireland's future as an agrarian society.

By the 1980s, there were signs of stress in this clerically-based corporatism. The power of the Catholic Church came into question when the State attempted to consolidate itself by appealing to rural Ireland, effectively forcing people to choose between Catholicism and other aspects of their social identity, in the referenda on the Eighth Amendment and divorce. After Vatican II, many Irish Catholics – clergy included – believed the Church was taking a more progressive direction, and expected this to have a benign effect

---

[3]   Tom Inglis, *Moral Monopoly: The Rise and Fall of the Catholic Church in Modern Ireland* (Dublin, 1998), p. 71.

[4]   Article 41.2 of the Constitution of Ireland (1937) states: '1. In particular, the State recognises that by her life within the home, woman gives to the State a support without which the common good cannot be achieved. 2. The State shall, therefore, endeavour to ensure that mothers shall not be obliged by economic necessity to engage in labour to the neglect of their duties in the home' (an amendment to remove this article was defeated in a March 2024 referendum). Moreover, maternity payments were made by the state; with so many restrictions on women working outside the home, children's allowances (paid by default to mothers not fathers) were an important source of income for women, Patricia Kennedy, *Motherhood in Ireland: Creation and Context* (Cork, 2004).

on all of the institutions under its supervision. The strong conservative wing of Irish society disagreed. This struggle was played out at an elite level in the pages of an academic journal innocently titled *Studies*, whose home page declared it to be 'published quarterly by the Irish Jesuits [...] *Studies* examines Irish social, political, cultural and economic issues in the light of Christian values and explores the Irish dimension in literature, history, philosophy and religion'.[5] *Studies* ran from 1912 to 1921; cabinet ministers, academics, civil servants and clergy queued up to write for it, their opinions published under Church auspices.

There were, however, few contributors to *Studies* from Trinity College. Trinity was nominally an Anglican foundation but was secular in ethos. Intellectually it was the university over which the Church exercised the least control, and for that reason it occupied an awkward place in the corporatist settlement. Today, the cultural Catholic elite send their children overwhelmingly to Trinity, but in the early 1980s the National University of Ireland, comprising University College Dublin (UCD), University College Cork, University College Galway and Maynooth University, was more important, and its colleges were all heavily accountable to the Church. Fintan O'Toole recalls studying English at UCD in the second half of the 1970s, a course dominated by 'the commanding Denis Donoghue and the intense, intellectually fiery poet Seamus Deane'. By contrast,

the philosophy department, where I was also a student, was like a thinly disguised seminary. My professor Desmond Connell, was a priest whose doctoral thesis had been on Malebranche and the thought processes of angels. His idea of fun was to write a mock treatise in Latin on why women should not be allowed to drive. He believed, and thought, that scholasticism, as practised by Thomas Aquinas, had the standing of science, and most of what came after was merely and obviously erroneous. Most of his lecturers were also priests, hired for their orthodoxy rather than their brilliance. And this clerical domination extended not just into logic and ethics as subjects but into departments like sociology and psychology. The institution was, in theory, secular, but in this respect, it was still obviously the successor to the Catholic University of Ireland, founded in 1854 by John Henry Newman.[6]

There was, I think, no one like Desmond Connell teaching at Trinity – and indeed, when the College invited him, as Catholic Archbishop of

---

5   'Studies: An Irish Quarterly Review', JSTOR. <https://www.jstor.org/journal/studiesirishrev>.
6   Fintan O'Toole, *We Don't Know Ourselves: A Personal History of Ireland Since 1958* (London, 2021), pp. 255–6.

Dublin, to attend a ceremony conferring an honorary doctorate on the
newly-ordained Church of Ireland Archbishop of Dublin, Donald Caird,
Connell told *The Irish Times* that the invitation was an insult to him, and
through him to the entire Catholic population of Dublin![7] Instead, Catholic
members of Trinity's Theology Department made it a centre of Liberation
Theology. A phenomenon that often escapes British students of Ireland is the
role of *ex*-clergy, who tended to be among the most radical and intellectually
curious people in the country, perhaps redirecting the energy of the Church.
The Trinity Socialist Society was run by former Jesuits who had become
Trotskyists (I spent years in Trotskyist groups as a result).

Ex-clergy were behind the principal answer to *Studies* in 1977, when
Richard Kearney (a philosophy lecturer at UCD), Mark Patrick Hederman
(a Benedictine priest) and Barre Fitzgerald (a former Benedictine) launched a
periodical called *The Crane Bag* to critique aspects of the culture of the Irish
State founded in 1922. The editors hoped, gingerly, that the journal 'would
help in a small but specific way to clarify the problems which have haunted
every Irish person over the last two decades'.[8] What were these problems? A
clue can be found in the titles of its themed issues. The first ten looked at,
respectively 'Art and Politics,' 'Nationalism,' 'The Other Ireland' (half of which
was about James Joyce and half about Irish mythology), 'Tradition,' 'Anglo-
Irish Literature,' 'Images of the Irish Woman,' 'Minorities in Ireland,' 'The
Northern Issue,' (appearing in the aftermath of the IRA Hunger Strikes of
1981), and 'The Irish Language and Culture.' The list for 'Minorities in Ireland'
comprised the following groups: The Poor, The Insane, Sexually-Enlightened
People, Travellers, Northern Irish Protestants, Homosexuals, Artists, Southern
Irish Protestants, culminating in a series of interviews and articles about the
peculiarities of Irish Catholicism. These minorities were a roll call of those who
stood outside the corporatist settlement. *The Crane Bag* was also outward-fac-
ing in a way that *Studies* was not, featuring interviews with Noam Chomsky,
Paul Ricoeur and Jean Vanier, and contributions from Jorge-Luis Borges and
Terry Eagleton. Moreover, the journal was taboo-breaking: Hederman inter-
viewed the chief-of-staff of the Irish Republican Army, Seamus Twomey.

The existence of *The Crane Bag* marked a hinge moment for its readers
because it called into question the entire social and cultural legacy of the
State. It heralded the critique of Irish nationalism carried out from within
its own ranks by the Field Day Theatre Company. The Troubles continued

---

[7]   Frank McNally, 'Cardinal Given A Doctorate', *Irish Times* (7 November 2001).
<https://www.irishtimes.com/news/cardinal-given-a-doctorate-1.335938>.
[8]   Mark Patrick Hederman, '"The Crane Bag" and the North of Ireland', *The
Crane Bag*, 4.2 (1980/81), pp. 94–103 (p. 94).

a mere seventy miles away from Trinity, and around a third of my peers at Trinity came from Northern Ireland. Students from the South didn't discuss the Troubles very much, but we occasionally liked to watch Northerners discuss them. We were interested in what Seamus Heaney, Derek Mahon and John Montague had to say about them, and we knew they were the implicit subject of popular plays like Brian Friel's *Translations* (1980) or Frank McGuinness's *Observe the Sons of Ulster Marching Towards the Somme* (1985). We read the Field Day pamphlets, written mostly by Northern Irish authors such as Tom Paulin, Seamus Heaney and Seamus Deane, as they began to appear. Dublin's thriving cultural scene also encouraged Trinity students to look outside traditional models of thought. There was a special abundance of experimental theatre: Samuel Beckett occasionally directed productions of his plays, rehearsing the actors in Paris, and sending them back to be performed at the Peacock Theatre. Dublin's one art house cinema, the Irish Film Theatre, had closed, but Trinity's film society screened more classics than anyone could watch. The College hosted many writers who came to give talks. In my first year, Léopold Sédar Senghor, one of the most significant writers from French-speaking Africa, spent a few weeks in the French department meeting undergraduates and giving classes on poetry. As a recent president of Senegal, he was accompanied everywhere by strikingly dressed Senegalese army bodyguards whose caps were set off with long red feathers. European embassies with cultural institutes also hosted such talks. I recall hearing Desmond O'Grady, a former monk who became Ezra Pound's secretary, at the Italian Cultural Institute, talking about his life with Pound in Italy, and reading his own poetry.

Challenges by Literary Studies of the 1980s

Exciting times in Dublin, but what of the degree course itself? The following account is offered as a case study of the utopian potential for studying literature, acting as an institution of welfare to open up perspectives, and particularly that of what was to become Irish post-colonialism. University courses of the 1980s focused on the notion of the verbal contraption and considered questions such as 'What is literature?', 'Who writes it?', 'Who is written for?' and 'What are its appropriate subjects and forms?' Literature as verbal art was conceived as a form of welfare in its own right. To take part in the collective process of understanding a work of literature was to belong to a community in which human experience would be valued according to the most searching criteria available. In his entry on 'Welfare' in *Keywords*, Raymond Williams maps the word's itinerary from 'happiness' and 'prosperity' in the fourteenth century to 'merrymaking' in the fifteenth and sixteenth – '"such ryot and welfare and ydleness" (1470)' to '"wine and such welfare" (1577)' – before settling in the early twentieth century on its current meaning: 'an object of organised care or provision'.[9] I certainly saw my degree as a source of organised care. Ireland in the 1980s was on the brink of bankruptcy. Living standards were plummeting and governments appeared unable to do anything about it.

My degree appeared to insulate me from these realities by opening up an alternative world to which I was more temperamentally suited. Literature became, for me, what John Steiner calls a 'psychic retreat', a bulwark against a world I did not wish to reckon with.[10] It was a transitional object for me, in the sense in which D. W. Winnicott first employed that term in 1953.[11] It enabled me to separate my own inner world from the world outside. It was a medium for the discovery of a personal identity with only attenuated connections to family life (a distinct advantage as I lived at home with my parents). And it promised, in Michael Warner's words, 'an open future of personal and collective liberation, of full citizenship and historical belonging'.[12] I had not had a Catholic upbringing or education, and had felt an outsider as a result.

And yet, at the same time, the 1980s Trinity degree course mirrored Alexander Hutton's model of the welfare achieved by English studies from the 1930s onward.[13] Like L. C. Knights, its teachers were openly and obviously interested in producing students 'equipped to be intelligent and responsible about the problems of contemporary civilization', who possessed a 'sensitive and flexible intelligence that can be brought to bear effectively upon the problems which concern the individual', as well as 'an ability to respond to what the past has to offer [...] that may be of value to the present'. In the spirit of Bonamy Dobrée, they were also concerned to make literary study 'relevant to the society of the present times, so that they can perpetuate

---

[9]   Raymond Williams, *Keywords: A Vocabulary of Culture and Society* (1976; London, 1983), p. 281.

[10] John Steiner, *Psychic Retreats* (London, 1995).

[11] D. W. Winnicott, 'Transitional Phenomena and Transitional Experience' (1953), *The Collected Works of D. W. Winnicott: Volume 4, 1952–1955*, ed. Lesley Caldwell and Helen Taylor Robinson (Oxford, 2016), pp. 159–74.

[12] Michael Warner, 'Uncritical Reading', *Polemic: Critical or Uncritical*, ed. Jane Gallop (London, 2014), pp. 13–38 (p. 14).

[13] Alexander Hutton, 'An English School for the Welfare State: Literature, Politics, and the University, 1932–1965', *English*, 65 (2016), pp. 3–34.

what is valuable in tradition, not so much to preserve it against attack as to re-create it in the context of to-day'.[14]

This potential was conveyed by way of a curriculum which framed the subject in three particular ways. First, the degree was largely if not exclusively canonical, in both literatures, and if that canon extended beyond the 1960s (still recent, then), I failed to take advantage of it. It was perhaps more open to contemporary poetry than to any other form of contemporary writing, because the kind of attention poetry required was the benchmark for understanding works in other genres. The English department urged us to read René Wellek and Austin Warren's *Theory of Literature* (1948), less as a form of what would today be called 'theory' than as a handy repository of *post-hoc* rationalisations for our own literary experience. This was not to say that the intellectual temper of the English department was anti-theory: when a well-known visiting speaker gave a series of lectures excoriating Derrida, the reception was frosty.

Most of the English teachers had been steeped in the culture of New Criticism, whose practice responded to the existence of a new kind of literature: High Modernism. T. S. Eliot was the key figure here. Nobody was in any doubt that he was a major poet; and so were W. B. Yeats, Ezra Pound, Wallace Stevens, William Carlos Williams, Marianne Moore and so on. The canon as we learned it was not a bulwark of reaction or a hideous 'Keep Out' sign, but a living thing, open to change. For me, it constituted an alternative society that existed speculatively in the realm of books. F. R. Leavis's *Revaluation: Tradition and Development in English Poetry* (1936) tied canonical status to rediscovery by successive generations of something of value in a precursor poet. Canonical status was partly a measure of a writer's importance *to other writers*. There was a nationalist agenda at work, too. More room was made in the undergraduate curriculum for Irish writing of all genres and from all periods. This enabled Trinity and UCD to build up the new sub-specialism of 'Anglo-Irish Literature', including offering taught Master's programmes which further varied the intellectual scene by attracting many American students. However, though the likes of Yeats, Joyce and Beckett were canonised, those of Elizabeth Bowen or Edna O'Brien were not. University English in Ireland was decolonised but not diverse, reflecting the country itself.

If a fully alternative culture existed anywhere, it was in France, which had immense intellectual and cultural prestige throughout the world at that time, and especially in Ireland. At Trinity, the French literature course rev-

---

[14]   Cited in Hutton, 'An English School for the Welfare State', pp. 10, 15.

elled in speculation: *Tel Quel*, Roland Barthes (who still shines brighter than almost any other critic for me) and Jean Starobinski were invoked on courses about the novel. Yet the core of the course was as canonical and as sexist as its English counterpart, ranging from Montaigne, Diderot and Rousseau to Baudelaire, Rimbaud and the *nouveau roman* of Alain Robbe-Grillet, Michel Butor, Nathalie Sarraute and Claude Simon to cater for the later period.

The second feature of the curriculum concerned the nature of the literary. It was taken as read that all literature worthy of the name was Modernist. Our task was to discover the Modernist poem that was hiding in plain sight between the covers of, say, *Sense and Sensibility*. Behind this assumption lay an axiom: true literary experience begins in bafflement. The student was to find the bafflement at the heart of every work, to advance formulae that would resonate with, and do justice to, that core. Criticism would be a series of adumbrations cast by the work itself. The circularity of the exercise did not preoccupy us, and it was only many years later, when I read Walter Benjamin, that I realised that such Modernism was, in fact, Romanticism:

> this is, in truth, not so much a standard of judgment as, first and foremost, the foundation of a completely different kind of criticism – one which is not concerned with judging, and whose center of gravity lies not in the evaluation of the single work but in demonstrating its relations to all other works and, ultimately, to the idea of art [...] Criticism of a work is, rather, its reflection, which can only, as is self-evident, unfold the germ of the reflection that is immanent to the work.[15]

The third feature was the pervasiveness of what I now think of as 'the Hegelian idea.' Hegel, as is well known, regarded all human activities as the workings of an absolute mind which thinks itself in us. Historical variants of the Hegelian Idea were explored in the teaching at Trinity, premising the notion that the absolute mind left a trace in language. As Williams's *Keywords* assumed, charting the changing meanings of words over time would allow a reader to understand the workings of this absolute mind, and perhaps even redirect it. Edward Said's *Orientalism* trilogy was far and away the most ambitious attempt to do this in the 1980s, and avidly read on the Trinity degree.[16] Said had uncovered an implicit partnership between novelists,

---

[15]   Walter Benjamin, 'The Concept of Criticism in German Romanticism', *Selected Writings, Volume 1: 1913–1926*, ed. M. Bullock and M. W. Jennings (London: 1996), pp. 116–201 (p. 159).
[16]   Edward W. Said, *Covering Islam: How the Media and the Experts Determine How We See the Rest of the World* (London, 1981); *Orientalism* (London, 1978); *The Question of Palestine* (London, 1979).

philological scholars and imperialists, who had collectively created something called the Orient: mysterious, irrational and ultimately inferior to the West. You could not understand a work like Flaubert's *Salammbô* (1862) without linking it to the endeavours of Renan and the French imperial expansion that took place contemporaneously with his work under Napoléon III in North Africa. And the same was true in reverse: you could not understand French imperial expansion in North Africa and give Flaubert a pass. What made Said so exciting was his insistence that this tying together of cultural activity meant literature had real-world effects on contemporary political life, both directly and indirectly, in the form of historical sedimentation. Western indifference to the plight of the Palestinians rested not only on guilt over the Shoah but on the historic residue of Orientalist attitudes which deprived the Palestinians of full human status.

At Trinity, we presumed no right to cast aspersions on the traditional canon of French literature, but the newly minted hybrid of Anglo-Irish literature was ours to dispose of as we pleased. The Hegelian approach upended our notions about the canon: was there an Irish literary tradition, and could a grand narrative be constructed about it? When Seamus Deane invoked the *Oxford English Dictionary* to explain that, etymologically, the word 'tradition' connoted both 'continuity' (passing something on) *and* 'surrender' or 'betrayal' (handing something over), we saw the beginnings of a role for our small island in the unfolding of the Idea. The British, said Deane, had the advantage of being able to convince themselves that they possessed a variety of 'unbroken' traditions (even though their strength lay precisely in their ability to break them), while the Irish tended to found theirs on the notion of betrayal. Thus, 'the central fact of Irish tradition' was that 'it was an attempt to describe what we have not yet built'.[17]

But could the Anglo-Irish canon perform the kind of demythologizing work that Said had executed in *Orientalism*? In *Celtic Revivals* (1985), Deane argued that underlying the Troubles was a set of beliefs, largely derived from Yeats, concerning Ireland and its relationship with Great Britain. Deane read Yeats as suggesting that a 'natural' cross-class alliance of the Anglo-Irish Ascendancy and the peasantry had been disturbed by alien – for which read 'British' – habits of mind. By means of this myth, Yeats hoped to 'obliterate or reduce the problems of class, economic development, bureaucratic organisation and the like, concentrating instead upon the essences of selfhood, community, nationhood, racial theory, Zeitgeist'.[18] By implication, the lit-

---

[17]   Seamus Deane, 'An Example of Tradition', *The Crane Bag*, 3.1 (1979), pp. 41–7 (p. 47).

[18]   Seamus Deane, *Celtic Revivals: Essays in Modern Irish Literature* (London,

erature of the Celtic Revival had actually set the terms of the Troubles, at
least for nationalists; so the canon of Anglo-Irish literature was an explosive
mythology, to be handled with care. Such an approach challenged the idea
that literature encourages readers to enter a private world, where the fictive
and the aesthetic have their own norms and logic, and are the true ultimate
object of English studies.

My contemporaries and I never felt we had to choose between these two
alternatives, in part, I suspect, because we understood them to be different
elaborations of the same skillset. Both saw the business of literary scholarship
as turning on *acts of attention*. Both were exquisitely attuned to the ways in
which imaginative worlds are constructed through voice, tone and psychology. Each was concerned with trying to understand the place of the text
within a universe of texts. They fostered wonder and awe, reflexive awareness, a flair for the counter-intuitive and tolerance of, or even pleasure in,
ambiguity.

In what sense, then, were English studies a form of welfare? They exposed
us to a variety of intellectual movements we would not have had access to,
or been able to engage with to the same extent, in any other way. This intellectual life was carried on in defiance of Irish public life at the time and was
sustained and paralleled by a rich programme of cultural events. The whole
evolving experience opened up what Ian Hacking called a new 'way of being
a person', which was enormously enabling.[19]

Coda: Literary Studies Now

English is in many respects a much saner discipline now than it was in the
1980s. It is far less grandiose: as Helen Small and Louis Menand point
out, few students today think the humanities have a monopoly on moral
insight.[20] Yet some still see the life of reading as part of an ongoing collective inquiry into the role of art in human life. John Guillory speaks of it as
one of the disciplines to have propelled 'a great shift in attitudes towards
minority groups in our society; they have encouraged universally, among the
college-educated, a desire to move beyond the injustices visited upon minor-

1985), p. 33.
[19]   Ian Hacking, 'Making Up People', *Reconstructing Individualism: Autonomy,
Individuality, and the Self in Western Thought*, ed. Thomas C. Heller, Morton Sosna
and David E. Wellbery (London, 1986), pp. 222–36.
[20]   Helen Small, *The Value of the Humanities* (Oxford, 2013); Louis Menand, *The
Marketplace of Ideas: Reform and Resistance in the American University* (New York,
2010).

ity populations'.[21] Formalism is no longer the core approach, students today tending to see literature as a report on experience, even as a special kind of social science data. Good writing is held to be that which is relevant and inclusive, both in content and style, and the Modernist assumption that literary experience begins in bafflement does not make sense anymore.

Yet the formal aspect of English has not been abandoned: it has migrated to creative writing courses, enabling students to experience the creativity of literature very concretely. Some of my colleagues teaching non-contemporary literature set exercises in imitation as a way of familiarising students with literary genres and conventions that have passed out of use, an antidote to 'reading for gist', the besetting sin of literary reading.

The ethical programme of English as it is taught in schools means many students are disposed to admire the contemporary period more than any other. This is partly, as Guillory says, because 'only contemporary literature has any chance of representing real-world diversity'.[22] But it is also because the subject has increasingly sought to legitimise itself by demonstrating its relevance to contemporary life in instrumental terms. I am myself guilty of this, through my work in the medical humanities, which has displaced my research as a Romanticist. Many of us want to demonstrate the value of reading practices to understanding illness experience. Contributions from English to the digital humanities and the environmental humanities also have the effect of pulling the subject towards the contemporary period.

It is easy to exaggerate the differences between these two visions of literary study: the formalist vision that dominated the 1980s and the vision of literature that prizes its real-world aspects above all else. This realisation has been especially helpful to me in relation to the teaching of theory. Although the psychoanalytic view of the mind is no longer particularly fashionable, I am strongly committed to psychoanalytic ways of reasoning, and teaching the subject enables me to tap into a form of psychological-mindedness that some students possess in abundance. I try to show them that literature and theory are addressing the same issues in different ways and that it is sometimes possible to use one species of writing to deepen our sense of the other. This almost always turns on finding moments in a literary work that cannot be explained in a straightforward way. Why does Emma Woodhouse devote her waking hours to pairing off people who are so manifestly unsuited to one another? Has it got anything to do with her father's detestation of marriage? Does the novel – distinct from its characters – mourn its many absent

---

[21]   John Guillory, *Professing Criticism: Essays on the Organization of Literary Study* (Chicago, 2022), p. 73.
[22]   Guillory, *Professing Criticism*, p. 229.

mothers? How should we think about Antonio's generosity to Bassanio in *The Merchant of Venice*? Is it connected at all with the misogyny of the final scene? I have a small qualm about approaching literature in this way, which is that it can sometimes seem as if the only way to internalise a literary work is by making it argue for something. But if it changes students' sense of the nature of human experience, then I am attending to their welfare and giving them something for life.

Index